MW00800215

Elastic Language in Persuasion and Comforting

Grace Zhang · Vahid Parvaresh

Elastic Language in Persuasion and Comforting

A Cross-Cultural Perspective

Grace Zhang
School of Education
Curtin University
Bentley, WA, Australia

Vahid Parvaresh
School of Humanities and Social Sciences
Anglia Ruskin University
Cambridge, UK

ISBN 978-3-030-28459-6   ISBN 978-3-030-28460-2   (eBook)
https://doi.org/10.1007/978-3-030-28460-2

This Palgrave Macmillan imprint is published by the registered company Springer Nature Switzerland AG
The registered company address is: Gewerbestrasse 11, 6330 Cham, Switzerland

Acknowledgements

We would like to express our sincere gratitude to the anonymous reviewers whose invaluable feedback has been incorporated into this book. We also owe a debt of gratitude to staff members at Palgrave Macmillan for their help and patience during the production of this book.

We are immensely grateful to Judith Heaney for proofreading the manuscript. We would also like to extend our thanks and appreciations to the producers of *The Voice*, both in China and the USA, without whom this book would not have been possible. In this respect, we are profoundly grateful to Talpa Media for granting us permission to transcribe and use the English data.

We acknowledge, with gratitude, the research grants AAPI and RISP provided by Curtin University in Australia.

Finally, we thank our parents and spouses for their selfless support and never-ending love.

Contents

About the Authors

Grace Zhang is Professor in the School of Education at Curtin University, Australia. She was awarded a Ph.D. in Linguistics by the University of Edinburgh. She has published extensively on elastic/vague language and pragmatics, the most recent and relevant publication being *Elastic Language: How and Why We Stretch Our Words*, by Cambridge University Press (2015).

Vahid Parvaresh is Senior Lecturer in the School of Humanities and Social Sciences at Anglia Ruskin University, UK. His areas of interest include vague/elastic language use, pragmatics theory and societal pragmatics. He has published in various leading journals in the field, including the *Journal of Pragmatics*, *Discourse Processes*, *International Review of Pragmatics* and *Corpus Pragmatics*.

List of Figures

List of Tables

1

Introduction

Man: Will you marry me?
Woman: *Maybe.*

The man is proposing to the woman and her response, *maybe*, has more than one potential meaning (Verschueren, 1999). The most likely meaning is that she is uncertain about whether to marry this man; another interpretation could be that she is playing hard to get. *Maybe* is a type of language which is termed 'elastic language' (EL) (Zhang, 2015). EL refers to utterances with fluidity, where language interpretations overlap. EL enables language stretching which refers to a phenomenon where unspecific utterances are modified to accommodate particular communicative needs.

This book is a pragmatic study, investigating EL in Chinese and English from a cross-cultural perspective. Cross-cultural pragmatics has been a growing research field over the past two decades (e.g. Wierzbicka, 2003), and is one which requires further exploration. This book provides an original contribution to this field of study by making a comparison between Chinese and English EL data. This is an important but somewhat neglected area of language use. Based on data derived from US and Chinese reality television shows, this study carries

© The Author(s) 2019   **1**
G. Zhang and V. Parvaresh, *Elastic Language in Persuasion and Comforting*,
https://doi.org/10.1007/978-3-030-28460-2_1

out a pragma-linguistic analysis to reveal shared and culturally specific linguistic features of language stretching. It exposes the illusion of precision and contributes to the field of pragmatics of language as a conceptual and empirical enrichment of the study of language stretching.

This study has benefitted from a mixed methods research design which utilises both quantitative and qualitative analyses. The data analysis consists of a multifaceted investigation which includes lexical patterns and pragmatic functions. Sociocultural factors that may trigger and influence language stretching were also investigated to provide a suitable analysis.

This particular chapter establishes the tone of the book and includes definitions of the terms that are used in this study. Research questions, the purpose of this study and the organisation of this book will also be discussed here.

1.1   Definitions

This section discusses four definitions: EL, elasticity, language stretching and vague language (VL). More detailed discussion on the terms can be seen in Chapter 2.

1.1.1   Elastic Language, Elasticity and Language Stretching

EL, according to Zhang (2015), refers to a language which is used like a piece of elastic: it can be stretched to suit various communicative goals. In this case, 'stretch' refers to "extending or modifying the scope or meaning of an expression, and is a technical term with no negative connotation" (p. 6). The main feature of EL is its fluidity, manifested as "unspecific and overlapping, context-dependent and socially variable" (p. 6). Elasticity is an inexplicit form of linguistic communication and can be stretched and negotiated to suit communicative purposes (Zhang, 2011, p. 573). Elasticity refers to "the tendency of utterances to be fluid, stretchable and strategic", and stretchability is manifested as "rubber-band-like and with multiple trajectories" (Zhang, 2015, p. 6). For example, *about*, when added to 20, stretches 20 to the left and right to form an interval of numbers which potentially belong to *about 20*. *Very* stretches *cold* upwards to a greater degree of coldness and, conversely, *a little* stretches *cold* downwards to a lesser degree of coldness. *About 20, very cold* and *a little cold* are all examples of elastic expressions.

Language stretching refers to the ways in which unspecific utterances are modified to accommodate particular communicative needs. This study investigates language stretching in US and Chinese reality television discourse and provides a comparative analysis between different cultures to advance our knowledge of cross-cultural communication. Language stretching is enabled by employing EL which carries "non-specific and stretchable meaning, in that the speaker either cannot be more specific or (more often) strategically makes it less specific" (Zhang, 2015, pp. 4–5). For example, in 'He has left Perth, I think', 'I think' is an elastic expression to mitigate the degree of certainty.

The deciding factor as to whether or not the elasticity of communication is ethical or effective rests on the interactants in question and their communicative goals, rather than on EL itself (Eisenberg, 1984; Glinert, 2010). Glinert (2010, p. 58) uses the concept of a rubber band to metaphorically describe how words are stretched to meet the needs of both sides in the interaction, for example, to serve the different face needs in a confrontational situation, or to resolve misunderstanding between people with different languages and different cultures.

Language stretching adheres to Grice's (1975) cooperative maxims (e.g. 'don't say more than you need to say'), and Sperber and Wilson's (1986/1995) relevance theory: effective communication enables interlocutors to obtain optimal cognitive effect with the least processing effort. While these two are relevant to this study in some respects, elasticity theory (Zhang, 2011, 2015) has been specifically developed to explain the phenomenon of EL, which will form the primary theoretical framework for this study. The theory proposes three interconnected principles of language, namely fluidity, stretchability and strategy, and four maxims, go approximate, go general, go scalar and go epistemic.

In particular, it explains how and why we stretch our words in response to the demands posed by the context.

This study fills the research gap by exploring the richness and diversity of EL, and offers a new perspective derived from reality television discourse. In particular, the cross-cultural aspects and comparisons between speakers of English and Chinese contribute to its overall significance.

1.1.2 Vague Language

The term 'EL' is developed from the term 'vague language' (VL). The two terms are essentially interchangeable, but EL is perceived as having more positive connotations than the latter (Zhang, 2011, 2015).

Traditional approaches which feature dichotomous (either/or) thinking do not work when faced with a world that is full of complementary, gradual and interdependent phenomena (Munné, 2013). A non-linear approach represents our actual use of language more realistically and appropriately.

Various definitions of VL exist which are based on different foci (Channell, 1994, p. 18; Cotterill, 2007, p. 98). Claiming that most things around us have precise definitions "is perhaps best seen as a useful fiction" (van Deemter, 2012, p. 69). Given that this study investigates VL from a pragmatic perspective, definitions with a pragmatic focus are most relevant here. VL is defined as a language which deliberately adopts an imprecise way of referring to people and things (Carter & McCarthy, 2006, p. 928), which is inherent and purposive (Powell, 1985, p. 31). VL has to be interpreted with the help of contextual indexing, namely it is context-dependable and context-irresolvable. Even with the help of context, VL would not be interpreted precisely (Cheng, 2007, p. 162).

There are purposive and non-purposive forms of VL: the former uses VL as a strategic move, while the latter uses VL when there is no other choice (e.g. there is no precise information available). The latter form is called 'forced vagueness' by Trappes-Lomax (2007, p. 122) or 'intrinsic vagueness' (e.g. the prediction of stock markets) by Channell (1994, p. 20). These two types of VL use are also termed 'want to' and 'have to' by Zhang (2015, p. 18). This study looks at both types of VL, purposive and non-purposive, because both occurred in the data and therefore need to be represented here.

In terms of the classification of VL, some researchers, such as Channell (1994) and Ruzaitė (2007), prefer a narrow categorisation: conventional types of vague quantity (e.g. *about 10, a lot*), vague category indicators (e.g. *or things like that*), and placeholders and totally vague words (e.g. *thingy*). Other researchers, such as Prince, Frader, and Bosk (1982), prefer a wider categorisation: epistemic markers (e.g. *perhaps, I guess*) in addition to conventional types, which forms the 'broadest definition' (Trappes-Lomax, 2007, p. 122). This study adopts the broader approach while also keeping VL within a close set of identifiable items (Cheng, 2007, p. 162), which ensures more manageable data analysis.

Representative studies have been undertaken in the field of VL. Channell (1994) and Wu (1999) were seminal works on VL in English and Chinese; Hyland (1998) explores the hedging phenomenon in academic settings (particularly with regards to scientific research articles), one of the earliest studies of the topic. Chen and Wu (2002) discuss the categorisation of the fuzziness of language by using a cognitive approach, a primarily theoretical piece of work. Parvaresh (2018) explores VL functions in political discourse. Cutting (2007) covers topics of vagueness and genre, the psychology of vagueness and cross-cultural vagueness. Ruzaitė (2007) focuses on the quantifiers and approximators of British and American English in educational settings. Kaltenböck, Mihatsch, and Schneider (2010) conduct a study of hedging, particularly the fine-tuning of existing hedging categories in real-life contexts. Sabet and Zhang (2015) examine the use of VL by Chinese-speaking and Persian-speaking learners of English, and compare their use of VL with that of L1 speakers of American English.

This study challenges the 'all-or-none' theories of linguistics and provides a refreshing insight into EL stretching in cross-cultural communication. It is one of the few attempts that have been made to explore how Chinese and English speakers use EL and how communication games are played out in different cultures. The evidence-based findings may help speakers from different cultural backgrounds to understand each other better and to interact more effectively, thereby reducing miscommunication.

1.2   The Purpose of the Study

The purpose of this book is to explore the use of EL through the lens of pragma-linguistics, by exploring its frequency, pragmatic functions and the interaction between language stretching and sociocultural factors.

The two key objectives are: (1) to find patterns of language stretching realised in Chinese and English; and (2) to investigate the impact of sociocultural factors on language stretching. The objectives can be achieved by addressing the following three research questions:

1. How and why is EL used in persuasion and comforting?
2. What are the similarities and differences between EL use in Chinese and English?
3. How do sociocultural factors impact on language stretching?

The first research question is pragma-linguistic in nature and lays the foundation for the following two questions. The second involves a comparison between the two languages, with the final question being socio-pragmatic in nature and which investigates the influence of sociocultural factors on language stretching. This study of Chinese and English highlights the importance of understanding cross-cultural communication. It provides a rigorous account of language stretching by revealing how EL functions in different cultures.

In this study, the terms VL and EL are primarily interchangeable for the convenience of literature reviews and discussions.

1.3   The Organisation of the Book

This book comprises eight chapters. This chapter is an introduction and sets the tone of the book. It specifies definitions, and details the purpose of the study. Chapter 2 is a literature review which provides a theoretical foundation. It discusses the issues of speech act theory, VL and related issues, positive and negative politeness/faces, EL, and the linguistic categories and pragmatic functions of EL. Chapter 3 is a discussion of methodology, and includes the rationale behind the research design (e.g. mixed methods, public and formal discourse, naturally occurring data and video data), the data collected, data analysis (lexical analysis, pragmatic function analysis and sociocultural analysis) and the limitations of the research.

Chapter 4 examines how and why EL was used for persuasion and comforting purposes in the Chinese corpus, primarily from the perspectives of lexical items and pragmatic functions. Chapter 5 details the same data analysis but, in this case, conducted on the English corpus. Chapter 6 is a comparison between Chinese and English contexts to uncover any similarities and differences in EL patterns. Chapter 7 investigates the possible impact of sociocultural factors, such as gender, age, culture, directness and indirectness, political correctness and discourse, and how they can influence the use of EL. Chapter 8, the final chapter, discusses the conclusions and implications of this study, and also details potential future research.

1.4   Concluding Remarks

The working definition of EL that is used in this study, adopted from Zhang (2015), is a language with fluidity. The term EL has only recently been proposed and, thus, the majority of the existing literature uses the term VL. Therefore, it is necessary to refer to VL when discussing earlier research. VL and EL are largely interchangeable in this study for convenience and the continuity of the discussion.

This research explores how elasticity functions in reality television discourse, particularly with regards to how Chinese and US participants stretch language. The study of contrasting cultures, based on reality television interaction data possessing salient elasticity characteristics, reveals the dynamic linguistic and sociocultural features of language stretching. This cross-cultural approach produces far-reaching insights into language manipulation. This study considers how speakers stretch words to resolve challenging and sensitive situations (cultural and social), to hedge criticisms, requests and suggestions, or to deflect slip-ups. Participants may also stretch language for 'political correctness', and suchlike.

This is one of the first books to examine the discourse of reality television and to study the popular talent show, *The Voice*, from a cross-cultural perspective. This study provides an account of how the judges/coaches interacted with the contestants on stage (public discourse). It investigates the variation in language between English and Chinese, two of the world's most commonly spoken languages. Its insights and resources are expected to advance knowledge in the fields of contrastive pragmatics and cross-cultural communication, and inform strategies for bridging different cultures, language teaching, professional training and policy-making. This study highlights the need to give the elastic use of language the attention it deserves, and implies that language is non-discrete and can be stretched strategically.

References

Carter, R., & McCarthy, M. (2006). *Cambridge grammar of English.* Cambridge: Cambridge University Press.

Channell, J. (1994). *Vague language.* Oxford: Oxford University Press.

Chen, W. Z., & Wu, S. X. (2002). *Fanchou yu Mohu Yuyi Yanjiu* (in Chinese) [A study on category and semantic fuzziness]. Fujian, China: Fujian People's Publishing House.

Cheng, W. (2007). The use of vague language across spoken genres in an intercultural Hong Kong corpus. In J. Cutting (Ed.), *Vague language explored* (pp. 161–181). Basingstoke: Palgrave Macmillan.

Cotterill, J. (2007). 'I think he was kind of shouting or something': Uses and abuses of vagueness in the British courtroom. In J. Cutting (Ed.), *Vague language explored* (pp. 97–114). Basingstoke: Palgrave Macmillan.

Cutting, J. (Ed.). (2007). *Vague language explored.* Basingstoke: Palgrave Macmillan.

Eisenberg, E. M. (1984). Ambiguity as strategy in organizational communication. *Communication Monographs, 51,* 227–242.

Glinert, L. (2010). Apologizing to China: Elastic apologies and the meta-discourse of American diplomats. *Intercultural Pragmatics, 7*(1), 47–74.

Grice, P. (1975). Logic and conversation. In P. Cole & J. Morgan (Eds.), *Syntax and semantics. Volume 3: Speech acts* (pp. 41–58). New York: Academic Press.

Hyland, K. (1998). *Hedging in scientific research articles*. Amsterdam: John Benjamins.

Kaltenböck, G., Mihatsch, W., & Schneider, S. (Eds.). (2010). *New approaches to hedging*. Bingley, UK: Emerald.

Munné, F. (2013). The fuzzy complexity of language. In A. Massip-Bonet & A. Bastardas-Boada (Eds.), *Complexity perspectives on language, communication and society* (pp. 175–196). Heidelberg: Springer.

Parvaresh, V. (2018). 'We are going to do a lot of things for college tuition': Vague language in the 2016 US presidential debates. *Corpus Pragmatics, 2*(2), 167–192.

Powell, M. (1985). Purposive vagueness: An evaluative dimension of vague quantifying expressions. *Journal of Linguistics, 21*, 31–50.

Prince, E. F., Frader, J., & Bosk, C. (1982). On hedging in physician-physician discourse. In R. J. Di Pietro (Ed.), *Linguistics and the professions* (pp. 83–97). Norwood, NJ: Ablex.

Ruzaitė, J. (2007). *Vague language in educational settings: Quantifiers and approximators in British and American English*. Frankfurt am Main: Peter Lang.

Sabet, P., & Zhang, G. (2015). *Communicating through vague language: A comparative study of L1 and L2 speakers*. London: Palgrave Macmillan.

Sperber, D., & Wilson, D. (1986/1995). *Relevance: Communication and cognition*. Oxford: Blackwell.

Trappes-Lomax, H. (2007). Vague language as a means of self-protective avoidance: Tension management in conference talks. In J. Cutting (Ed.), *Vague language explored* (pp. 117–137). Basingstoke: Palgrave Macmillan.

van Deemter, K. (2012). *Not exactly: In praise of vagueness*. Oxford, UK: Oxford University Press.

Verschueren, J. (1999). *Understanding pragmatics*. New York: Oxford University Press.

Wierzbicka, A. (2003). *Cross-cultural pragmatics: The semantics of interaction* (2nd ed.). Berlin: Mouton de Gruyte.

Wu, T. P. (1999). *Mohu Yuyanxue* (in Chinese) [Fuzzy linguistics]. Shanghai: Shanghai Foreign Language Education Press.

Zhang, G. (2011). Elasticity of vague language. *Intercultural Pragmatics, 8*, 571–599.

Zhang, G. (2015). *Elastic language: How and why we stretch our words*. Cambridge: Cambridge University Press.

2

Theoretical Foundations

This chapter provides a review of the existing literature in the field, with the aim of informing the theoretical framework behind this research and highlighting gaps in the literature, thereby revealing the significance of this study. Several topics will be reviewed, ranging from speech act theory to elasticity theory.

2.1 Speech Act Theory

It is now widely established that speech act theory was broached by one of the philosophers of ordinary language, John L. Austin (1911–1958), who did not agree with the idea of describing language through the rules of logic. He was of the opinion, as were other scholars, that there is more potential and value to be derived from investigating the language of ordinary people than that which some philosophers and logicians were comfortable with at that time. As summarised by Cohen (1997), Austin (1956, p. 185)

© The Author(s) 2019
G. Zhang and V. Parvaresh, *Elastic Language in Persuasion and Comforting*,
https://doi.org/10.1007/978-3-030-28460-2_2

recommended English-speaking philosophers to study the meanings and uses of English words on the grounds that the ordinary language of the English speech community embodies "the inherited experience and acumen of many generations of men". By finding out what distinctions are implicitly present in the English vocabulary of some nontechnical activity, such as that of making excuses, one is sure, he said, to discover something worth knowing, however much one may also need to study the relevant technical requirements of jurisprudence or psychology. (Cohen, 1997, pp. 35–36)

In actual fact, Austin (1962/1975) revolutionised some of the more traditional ways of looking at language and communication. He argued that the utterances we make are performative in the sense that they enable us to 'do things with words'. In this respect, Austin distinguished "the locutionary act of saying something (e.g., *It's cold*), the illocutionary act performed in saying it (e.g., requesting the hearer to close the window), and the perlocutionary act achieved by saying it (e.g., persuading the hearer to close the window)" (Cohen, 1997, p. 36).

Austin's work was further developed by other scholars in the field, most notably by Searle. In a seminal paper, Searle (1965) asks, "What is the difference between just uttering sounds or making marks and performing a speech act?" Searle believed that "one difference is that the sounds or marks one makes in the performance of a speech act are characteristically said to have meaning, and a second related difference is that one is characteristically said to mean something by those sounds or marks" (p. 6).

As Leech (1983) clarifies, the best way to analyse speech acts is "with the well-known distinction Austin makes between three kinds of speech act" (p. 199). These include:

a. Locutionary act: Performing an act *of* saying something;
b. Illocutionary act: Performing an act *in* saying something;
c. Perlocutionary act: Performing an act *by* saying something
   (Adapted from Leech, 1983, p. 199).

A description provided by Bach and Harnish (1979) further illustrates the different aspects of a speech act. Let us suppose that:

- S is the speaker, H the hearer, e an expression (typically a sentence) in language L and C the context of the utterance, the main constituents of S's speech act can be schematically represented as follows:

> Utterance Act: S utters e from L to H in C.
> Locutionary Act: S says to H in C that so-and-so.
> Illocutionary Act: S does such-and-such in C.
> Perlocutionary Act: S affects H in a certain way
> (Bach & Harnish, 1979, p. 3).

As Bach and Harnish clarify, the acts mentioned and delineated above "are intimately related" and that "the success of the perlocutionary act depends on H's identifying one of the other acts" (Bach & Harnish, 1979, p. 3).

Inspired by this line of research, many scholars and researchers of language and communication, as well as many language philosophers have, over the past few decades, set themselves the task of investigating the range, functions, characteristics and features of speech acts in different discourses, languages and situations. Despite differences in terminology, the following speech act categories capture the range of speech acts that one typically encounters in communication:

a. **Declarations**: serve to change the world via an utterance. Examples include sentencing, resigning and appointing.
b. **Assertives**: serve to state what the speaker believes, does not believe, to be the case. Examples include stating, claiming and reporting.
c. **Expressives**: serve to state what the speaker feels. Examples include thanking, blaming and praising.
d. **Directives**: serve to get a person to do something. Examples include commanding and requesting.
e. **Commissives**: serve to commit the speaker to some future action. Examples include vowing and promising (Adapted from Searle, 1975a, pp. 354–367).

Whereas the idea of a speech act offers fresh insight into language and communication, one should not lose sight of the fact that, in reality, speech acts are closely tied to social and situational considerations. Hence, as Leech (1983) suggests, illocutionary functions may be classified into the following:

a. **Competitive**: The illocutionary goal competes with the social goal, such as ordering, asking, demanding and begging.
b. **Convivial**: The illocutionary goal coincides with the social goal, such as offering, inviting, greeting, thanking and congratulating.
c. **Collaborative**: The illocutionary goal is indifferent to the social goal, such as asserting, reporting, announcing and instructing.
d. **Conflictive**: The illocutionary goal conflicts with the social goal, such as threatening, accusing, cursing and reprimanding (Adapted from Leech, 1983, p. 104).

Traditionally, speech acts have also been categorised as direct and indirect (Searle, 1975b). Indeed, the majority of the sentences we produce serve to indirectly convey meaning. For example, a sentence such as "Is Julia at home?" may be used "in its literal sense to ask a question, a direct speech act" (Clark, 1979, p. 430). On the other hand, when used on the telephone, "it can also be used as a request to call Julia to the phone, an indirect speech act" (Clark, 1979, p. 430). Another example of an indirect speech act is the sentence 'Can you pass the salt?', the understanding of which, conventionally speaking, needs

> a description that says that in using 'can you pass the salt' to make a request, one is using the sentence with its literal meaning, with the intention of conveying a request […] but that in doing so one is following a convention about language use; the convention being, roughly, to request someone to do such-and-such indirectly, say the sentence 'can you (do such-and-such)?' (Morgan, 1977, pp. 22–23)

As summarised by Terkourafi (2011), indirect speech has been a topic of great interest and controversy, "since at least the early days of Speech Act Theory half a century ago" (p. 2861). Traditionally, a view shared among many scholars is that, although speakers can in principle "communicate a message which is informative, truthful, relevant and succinct" (p. 2861), they might on occasion opt to communicate the same message in a more indirect way. While there certainly exist many possible reasons for such indirect messages, politeness seems to be a plausible factor.

> Since politeness, and its psycho-social motivation, face, are necessary ingredients of human communication (Allan, 1986, p. 10; Scollon & Scollon, 1995, p. 38, and many others), it makes sense that humans should like to get things done without putting their social relationships constantly on the line. Indirect speech offers a means of achieving precisely that; it hits two birds with one stone, so to speak. (Terkourafi, 2011, p. 2861)

Of course, it is crucially important for both researchers and those actually involved in communication to pay particular attention to the motivation underlying indirect speech acts. In the words of Asher and Lascarides (2001), "the relationship between the surface form of an utterance and its underlying purpose is by no means always straightforward" (p. 183). Drawing on Searle (1975b), Asher and Lascarides argue that a sentence such as *Can you pass the salt?* is an example of an interrogative and serves to express a question. In this respect, one could safely claim that in this sentence "the speaker's goal in asking a question is to get an answer" (p. 183). However, as they note, *Can you pass the salt?* does have a different purpose: "it's a request, where the speaker's goal is for the interpreter to pass the salt." *Can you pass the salt?* is therefore "an indirect speech act, which Searle defines to be an utterance in which one speech act is performed indirectly by performing another" (p. 183). Indeed, with *Can you pass the salt?* "requesting the hearer to pass the salt is performed indirectly by performing another communicative act – asking about the hearer's ability to pass the salt" (p. 183).

As the aforementioned argument makes absolutely clear, persuasion, which is one of the main foci of this study, is an example of a directive speech act in the sense that it either makes a person do something or feel a certain way. Comforting, on the other hand, which is another important focus of this study, belongs to the expressive speech act category because of its face-enhancing nature. Of course, the boundary between these two different speech acts is not particularly clear, and persuasion and comforting arguably touch upon assertive speech acts. Persuasion, as described by Lakoff, is the "attempt or intention of one party to change the behaviour, feelings, intentions, or viewpoint of another by communicative means" (Lakoff, 1982, p. 28). Persuasion can be achieved through the use of a variety of strategies and devices, including, among other things, "hedges, reporting verbs, that-constructions, questions, personal pronouns, and directives have been examined for the role they play in this persuasive endeavour" (Hyland, 2005a, p. 174). In this respect, persuasion can be viewed as a skill, or even an art. To be persuasive, both speakers and writers need to make use of different value systems, "making rhetorical choices which evaluate both their propositions and their audience" (Hyland, 2005a, p. 174).

Persuasion has consistently been a topic for extensive study, as many researchers have focused their attention on the examination of rhetoric and the rhetorical devices that make some messages or utterances become more effective. One direct outcome of this endeavour has been "a comprehensive list of the principles of propaganda, an enumeration of the persuasive methods used by these orators to win unsuspecting listeners over to their cause" (Sears & Kosterman, 1994, p. 253). One of the best examples of persuasive discourse takes place in news broadcasting, and newspaper discourse produces some of the best examples of persuasion (Connor, as cited in Dafouz-Milne, 2008; see also Bell, 1991; Reah, 1998; van Dijk, 1988).

Comforting, on the other hand, seems to be closely related to the notion and practice of empathy, which can be defined as one's ability to understand and share the feelings of others (cf. Bloom, 2017; Parvaresh, 2019). Comforting strategies are defined as those messages that have "the intended function of alleviating or lessening the emotional distress arising from a variety of everyday hurts and disappointments" (Burleson, 1985, p. 254). As conceptualised by Nicolls, empathy appears to be "more than being sympathetic. Being sympathetic is feeling others pain, but not necessarily giving comfort. Empathy is the ability to feel the distress of others and to give them comfort" (Nicolls, 2015, para. 1). Suzuki lists some of the characteristics of a comforting speech act:

- a face-enhancing act for the hearer;
- shows sympathy for and soothes the hearer's sad or hurt feelings, to encourage him/her;
- belongs to Searle's expressive and Leech's convivial acts because of its face-enhancing nature (Adapted from Suzuki, 2008, p. 2).

Suzuki (2008, p. 2) also notes that a comforting speech act comprises several different sub-speech acts such as 'showing sympathy', 'giving advice' and 'encouraging' – to 'comfort' the hearer. Due to the importance of VL in persuasion and comforting, a discussion will be provided in the next section detailing how VL can potentially be used to persuade a person to do something or to comfort people.

2.2   Vague Language

Although, as Williamson (1996) argues, some logicians tend to view language as being precise, it has long been argued that vagueness is an inseparable part of human language (Channell, 1994). Even if one tries to ignore the vagueness of language, one "cannot make it perfectly precise" (p. 1). Indeed, even if we try to do so by clarifying and elaborating on what words mean, "our stipulations will themselves be made in less than perfectly precise terms, and the reformed language will inherit some of that vagueness" (Williamson, 1996, p. 1; see also Peirce, 1902; Stubbs, 1986).

As a corollary of this tendency, over the last two decades as increasing attention has been paid to spoken modes of communication, researchers have begun to consider other important aspects of language and communication, in addition to traditional topics such as style, genre and register. In this respect, VL has attracted much research interest (see, for example, Channell, 1994; Cutting, 2007b, 2012, 2015; Drave, 2002; Fernández, 2015; Gassner, 2012; Li, 2017; Metsä-Ketelä, 2016;

Parvaresh, 2017; Parvaresh & Ahmadian, 2016; Parvaresh & Tayebi, 2014; Ruzaitė, 2007; Sabet & Zhang, 2015; Sobrino, 2015; Zhang, 2011, 2015). In an apt description of the phenomenon under investigation, Cutting (2007a) argues that VL is "a central feature of daily language in use, both spoken and written" (p. 3).

Peirce (1902) appears to have been the first person to introduce the notion of vagueness to linguistic studies, but it was not until the 1990s that researchers began to seriously study the topic (Cutting, 2007a). Considering VL as an integral part of communication, Channell (1994) defines VL as language which "can be contrasted with another word or expression which appears to render the same proposition" and which is also "purposely and unabashedly vague" (p. 20). While "the terms used to refer to VL are somewhat vague themselves" (Cotterill, 2007, p. 98), researchers have, over the years, tried to devise their own classifications of VL. Parvaresh (2018, p. 169) clarifies why vague expressions are so important and worthy of attention by researchers working in the field:

(i) In any form of human communication there are certainly contexts which call for a "purposely and unabashedly vague" (Channell, 1994, p. 20) use of language. An example would be the vague item *maybe* [...] which is often used in contexts in which speakers want to highlight their lack of commitment to the propositional content of an utterance.

(ii) Some of the utterances we make arise from "intrinsically uncertain" contexts (Channell, 1994, p. 20), which necessitate the use of vague expressions. An example is found in "I wanted to know about their culture, experience etc.", when the speaker does not seem to have any precise referent in mind (Cutting, 2012, p. 284).

Traditionally, it appears that the most widely quoted categorisation of VL belongs to Channell (1994) who classifies VL into three main groups:

a. Vague nouns, for example, *things, stuff*;
b. Vague category identifiers, for example, *and stuff (like that)*, or *something (like that)*;
c. Vague approximators, for example, *about, around, or so*.

Recently, however, VL has been viewed, researched and elaborated on as an increasingly pragmatic phenomenon (Cheng, 2007). In this respect, researchers have shifted their attention from a focus on certain lexical items to the process of vague-ing (Zhang, 2015) achieved in the moment-by-moment use of actual language (Parvaresh & Tayebi, 2014). Consequently, Zhang (2015) argues that while VL has a certain degree of unresolvability, in the sense that its meaning is stretchable in various directions (stretchability principle) and in different degrees (fluidity principle) during the course of the interaction, the process of vague-ing enables communication to be effective (strategy principle). This phenomenon can be graphically captured as follows (Fig. 2.1).

This novel conceptualisation of VL can be clarified by focusing on a simple example such as:

- Your boss is *probably* angry at you now.

In this example, the word *probably* appears to have been used to stretch the tone of the utterance downwards, thus lowering the degree of certainty of the utterance in an elastic way within the context at hand. Needless to say, with a different reading of the sentence and in a drastically different context, the word *probably* can, of course, be used in an ironic way, that is to stretch the tone of the utterance upwards and to warn the hearer. In either scenario, the process of stretching the utterance has made the actual meaning of the sentence rather unresolvable, but it is still heavily dependent on the developing context for its interpretation and function.

Nowadays, a common belief upheld by researchers is that vague expressions comprise a much wider spectrum of expressions than was originally thought. Carter and McCarthy (2006) propose that VL should be defined as any language "which deliberately refers to people and things in a non-specific, imprecise way" (p. 928). In the same way, Zhang (2013) views VL as any linguistic unit that has "an unspecified meaning boundary, so that its interpretation is elastic in the sense that it can be stretched or shrunk according to the strategic needs of communication" (p. 88; see also Jucker, Smith, & Ludge, 2003). It should also be noted that there is a stark contrast between vagueness, a form of truth-conditional semantics, and VL. This has been captured in Table 2.1.

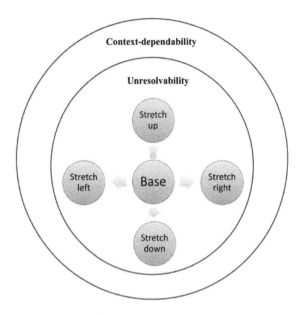

Fig. 2.1 Elasticity of vague language (Parvaresh, 2018, as motivated by and adapted from Zhang, 2015)

As Table 2.1 shows, while the concept of VL is commonly considered to be "a matter of pragmatics", the concept of vagueness appears to be "semantic-oriented" and focuses on "referential aspects of a concept without involving context" (Zhang, 2015, p. 19). As Parvaresh (2018) states, the sorites paradox is no doubt a classic example of vagueness:

If "the removal of one grain from a heap always leaves a heap, then the successive removal of every grain still leaves a heap" (Williamson, 1996, p. 4). Indeed, the word heap is vague because we cannot precisely explain where the boundary between a heap and a non-heap is to be found. (Parvaresh, 2018, p. 169, footnote)

In contrast to the literature on vagueness, research on VL, as stated above, is predominantly concerned with how the functions served by language are linked to specific contexts in the sense of being both purposive and intentional (Channell, 1994). As Ruzaitė (2007) notes,

Table 2.1 Differences between vagueness and vague language

Criteria	Vagueness	Vague language
Semantics or pragmatics	Semantics	Pragmatics
Conventional or conversational	Conventional	Conversational
Context-dependable or not	Non-context-dependable	Context-dependable
Literal or implicature	Literal	Implicature
Referential or inferential	Referential	Inferential

(Adapted from Zhang, 2015, p. 19)

VL is a "natural, usually purposive and multifunctional linguistic phenomenon that involves imprecision and is employed for certain communicative strategies" (p. 28). In keeping with this line of research, in this study we believe that VL is indeed a very desirable feature of language (Williamson, 1996), which no doubt plays a "huge role in human communication" (van Deemter, 2012, p. 93).

2.3 Vague Language in Different Languages and Settings

VL has been extensively explored from many perspectives, including cross-languages and cross-settings. These types of investigation reveal the multifaceted aspects of VL.

2.3.1 Vague Language in Different Languages

VL has been a topic of extensive research, not only in English but also in many other languages. The recent abundance of studies on VL in other languages highlights two things: (a) VL is an important feature of our communicative behaviour; and (b) VL appears to be a universal phenomenon, or rather a common feature of human languages. As Cutting (2015) notes, VL is no doubt "a feature of many languages, signalling a friendly attitude and modifying face threats" (p. 108).

In an earlier study devoted to the use of VL, Drave (2002) examines, by means of a corpus-informed methodology, not only the forms but also the functions of VL in intercultural conversation. Drawing on a rather large corpus of naturally occurring English conversations recorded between native speakers of English and native speakers of Cantonese, Drave's study sheds light on the main types of VL. The study reveals that, although native speakers of English tended to use more instances of VL than their Cantonese counterparts, similarities in the two groups were observed in terms of both the range of different types of VL and the major collocations.

Cheng and Warren (2001), in their corpus-based study which considered naturally occurring conversations collected between native and non-native English speakers in Hong Kong, shed further light on the use of vague expressions in such cross-cultural encounters. By providing a wide range of examples, Cheng and Warren's study reveals how both native and non-native speakers resort to VL to fulfil rather similar purposes. An important finding of their study is the fact that the use of VL rarely causes communication to break down, thus highlighting the ever-increasing importance of VL in real-life contexts.

Terraschke and Holmes (2007) is another noteworthy study of the topic. The authors investigate vagueness and general extenders both in German and New Zealand English. This study again draws on naturally occurring dyadic conversations by three groups of speakers, namely 'native speakers of New Zealand English', 'native speakers of German' and 'dyads comprising German non-native speakers of English with native speakers of New Zealand English'. After identifying a general pattern for the structure of general extenders in both languages, a list of the range of forms instantiating the pattern was provided (80,500 words) (p. 217). Their study reveals that "both the New Zealand students and the German students, whether speaking English and [*sic*] German, used general extenders to express a similar range of meanings, including both referential and interpersonal meanings" (pp. 217–218). They also reveal that German students in both languages and New Zealanders speaking English used general extenders "to express vagueness, and to hedge on the precision of lexical items and the validity of propositions" (pp. 218–219).

Studies in a variety of languages have been on the increase. In this respect, one could point to languages such as French in which Mihatsch (2010), for example, finds similarities between espèce de ('type of') and the English *sort of*. Lauwereyns (2002) investigated a similar phenomenon in Japanese. Andersen's (2010) study focuses on, among other things, vague nouns, confirming the long-held assumption that it is in informal settings that people tend to use more instances of VL.

In another study, Parvaresh and Tayebi (2014) focus on the use of vague expressions by native Persian speakers in informal contexts. The authors draw on a 15-hour corpus of colloquial Persian. The data included both telephone and face-to-face recordings. The study not only confirms the rather frequent use of vague expressions in Persian, but also attests to their versatility in actual and moment-by-moment communication. As Parvaresh and Tayebi's study reveals, in Persian, the most frequent category of VL is vague nouns. This tendency, as the authors note, is "in line with similar studies on the English language" (Parvaresh & Tayebi, 2014, p. 581).

Fernández's (2013) study is another noteworthy examination of the topic. Drawing on the Spanish Learner Language Oral Corpora, the author focuses on an important category of VL, namely general extenders, as used by undergraduate English L1 learners after a year spent abroad. Specifically, the author's analysis is based on the patterns that emerge from the concordance analysis of learner language production. Fernández's study again highlights the importance of vague expressions in everyday language use in a number of study-abroad situations.

Zhang (2011) studies the use of VL in the tension-prone environment of the Australian Customs in general, and, in particular, between Australian Customs officers and passengers. The study is indeed an example of intercultural encounters, as it involves a wide range of participants. While proposing a model for the analysis of VL, Zhang argues that although some people have a tendency to argue that vagueness has elements and features of being both contextually and culturally dependent, it is indeed a universal phenomenon in the sense that it enables interactants to achieve a wide range of functions by stretching their utterances.

Drawing on the semi-controlled spoken data of Australian English, Zhang (2013) investigates whether or not "the sensitivity of topics affects the use of VL, and if so, how the impact is manifested in terms of VL frequency at a macro level and VL form at a micro level" (p. 113). The study is unique in the sense that it offers empirical insight into how the sensitivity of a topic impacts on the use of VL. Zhang discovers that VL is used more frequently when speakers talk about sensitive topics. Zhang concludes that "the high level of subjectivity demands a high level of linguistic manipulation, so vagueness is often used" (p. 113).

Drawing on TV discussion data, Zhang (2016) examines the Chinese vague quantifier *yidian* (一点, a little). She shows how the vague item under investigation can fulfil a wide range of functions from mitigating to boosting functions. As she concludes, "while *yidian* indicates a small quantity and lesser degree, it can do 'big' things". Zhang discusses the expression's dynamic meanings which fulfil "competing as well as complementary pragmatic functions, deserving a rethink of its multidimensional uses" (p. 17). As the author argues, the elasticity of *yidian* is manifested in its fluidity, stretchability and strategy.

In another study concerning language comparisons, Overstreet (2005; see also Overstreet, 1999) uses data sets comprising both German and English telephone conversations, as well as face-to-face interactions in rather informal settings and including familiar speakers. Her study is predominantly concerned with the use of general extenders and she discovers that, in both German and English corpora, speakers used a wide range of general extenders and preferred disjunctive forms (*or something*) over adjunctive ones (*and stuff*).

The present study analyses two corpora in Chinese and American English. While the two languages are often explored in other areas of linguistics, they have not yet been subjected to a rigorous analysis in terms of EL and VL, particularly in the area of reality television discourse. It is anticipated that this study will offer new findings to the field.

2.3.2   Vague Language in Different Settings

Although, as noted by Cutting (2015), some people might "have a negative attitude" towards vagueness and have a tendency to express "a suspicion that VL makes addressors sound unreliable and causes comprehension problems" (p. 118), research shows that VL is a frequent and desirable trait of our communicative system (Parvaresh, 2018). Indeed, this has caused many researchers to investigate the use of vague expressions in different settings. As Jucker et al. (2003) note, these studies seem to have unanimously acknowledged that vagueness is "not only an inherent feature of natural language but also—and crucially—it is an interactional strategy" (p. 1739), the function of which should be investigated in context. This is indeed in line with Channell's (1994) proposal that one should not really care about whether the use of VL is good or bad, but rather whether it is appropriate.

Certainly, the appropriate use of VL is dependent on many factors, including language proficiency, familiarity with the situation and discourse types, and level of expectation of the audience. This is precisely the reason why no study of VL is complete without taking into account the contextual affordances of the situation and the context in which the data has been collected (Mey, 2001). With this in mind, researchers have, over the years, tried to study the semantic and pragmatic features of VL with reference to different contextual settings. This includes a wide range of fields and disciplines, including, but not limited to, poetry (Cook, 2007), advertising (Myers, 1994), courtroom discourse (Janney, 2002), medical discourse (Adolphs, Atkins, & Harvey, 2007), legal discourse (Li, 2017), business settings (Malyuga & McCarthy, 2018), classroom (Rowland, 2007) and TV discourse (Parvaresh & Zhang, 2019), and political debates (Parvaresh, 2018), to name but a few.

In one of the most revealing studies on the use of vagueness in literary texts, Cook (2007) argues that some of the greatest works of literature, texts that we have a great passion for, are those whose meaning is by no means straightforward. Indeed, as Cook argues, such vague meanings are appreciated by readers and, on occasion, they are part and parcel of a successful poem. Cook recommends that VL in each discourse type and setting "should be evaluated in quite a different way" (p. 36) and with reference to the characteristics of the audience and the general purpose of the communicative act.

In yet another study, this time devoted to advertising language, Myers (1994) sheds further light on the language used in advertisements, including its indeterminacy and vagueness. A useful lesson that can be derived from Myers' argument is that the patterns used by creators of advertisements, such as the level of indeterminacy, are crucially important in delivering a message.

Parvaresh and Zhang (2019) collate a number of studies which examine the discursive practices that can affect the number, type and function of the vague expression *sort of* in TV discussion discourse in a number of languages in the Asia and Oceania region. Contributing to a new cross-cultural understanding of the use of VL and opening new areas for future research, the studies reveal how the use of VL, in particular *sort of*, can contribute to the management of discourse even in a more formal setting such as TV discussions. These studies revealed multiple functions of VL and how a vague expression, such as *sort of*, performed important, fluid and stretchable functions during the negotiation of meaning between interactants.

The same patterns were reported in legal discourse. In a recent study, Li (2017) explores the role that VL plays in legislative texts. The author finds that "vague use is closely related to both the linguistic features and the communicative purposes of this variety of legal language" (p. 106). The author also identifies four semantic domains, namely, 'quantity', 'time', 'degree' and 'category' which, linguistically speaking, are associated with the use of VL. As reported in the study, "expressions associated with each domain exhibit shared usages in the context as well as unique features" (p. 106). Functionally, the author notes, "the analysis suggests that vague use may contribute to several communicative purposes of legislative texts, such as extending applicability of legal terms, providing flexibility for fulfilling an obligation or exercising power, maintaining a balance between precision and over-elaboration, and mitigating potential problems" (p. 106). Li recommends that VL use should "be considered as an important specialised communicative strategy in the drafting of legislative language" (p. 106).

Malyuga and McCarthy (2018) study the use of VL in spoken business and professional communication. They focus on two corpora: English business talk and Russian business/professional talk to compare the use of VL (e.g. *and things like that*) across the two data sets. The authors reveal that there is great similarity between the VL used in daily conversation and in business discourse. As the authors conclude, the functions of the vague expressions:

analysed from the Russian data largely correspond to those present in the English data, that is to say, the projection of non-lexicalised, fluid and instantial categories which both protect the speaker from over-explicit commitment and which tactically bond with the listener to create and maintain shared membership of individual enterprises, to create and consolidate business relationships and to project membership of the broad professional community. (p. 51)

Malyuga and McCarthy find that as markers of identity the vague items under examination point to "the nature of vague category marking as a co-constructed enterprise" (p. 51).

The general domain of business communication has also been a topic of great interest. In this respect, Zhao and Zhang (2012), for example, attempted to provide an answer to the important question of how and why VL (e.g. *many*, *a bit*) is used in Chinese business discourse. The authors draw on naturally occurring data which were analysed lexically, syntactically, sequentially and pragmatically. The authors also consider the relevant role that social and cultural factors play in this respect. The most important finding of their study, and a commonly held view in the field, is the idea that vague expressions are no less effective than exact, that is non-vague, expressions. Surprisingly, the authors claim that vague expressions may, on occasion, even prove to be effective in achieving communication goals, particularly in such an important and potentially tension-prone genre as business discourse. Zhao and Zhang's study reveals how in Chinese business discourse, unlike some other genres, vague expressions are first and foremost used for practical, rather than interpersonal, purposes in ways that are closely linked with such factors as age, distance and gender.

An earlier study by Koester (2007) also looked at the use of VL in workplace spoken interactions that unfolded in the offices of a number of organisations and companies in two geographical locations, namely North America and the UK. Koester's study sheds further light on the frequency of vague expressions "in genres like procedural discourse, briefing and service encounters can be linked to the speakers' focus on conveying information" (p. 52). In this respect, Koester provides further support in favour of the argument that "discourse which is more information-oriented is also likely to contain more vague language" (p. 53).

Importantly, as Koester's study reveals, when referring to facts and information, vague items are used for a number of reasons:

- They have a cohesive function, where the referent is specified in the context.
- The exact information may not be known.
- It is not necessary to be more explicit, because implicit reference conveys sufficient information, because of the knowledge shared by the discourse participants as members of the same professional discourse community (this is the most frequent use) (Koester, 2007, p. 53).

Adolphs et al. (2007) shed light on the use of VL in a medical setting. The authors study data obtained from two completely different contexts of health professional–patient interaction, which illustrates the range of VL items and their place in different healthcare contexts. The research focuses on the relationship "between the prominent uses of VL and the institutional requirements of the discourse" (p. 65). As the authors clarify,

> One set of data consists of the dialogue of NHS Direct phone-ins, where the institutional requirements from the health professionals are high in terms of the medical information they must obtain from the patient and the protocol they have to follow in the overall interaction. The other set of data consists of a series of conversations between patients and a hospital chaplain, where the requirements from the healthcare professional are to administer a spiritual and pastoral care rather than negotiate particular medical diagnoses and treatments. (p. 65)

Overall, Adolphs et al.'s (2007) study highlights some very important and usually neglected differences in the use of VL between the two settings under investigation. The study shows how the use of VL is directly linked to what institutional requirements are at work. The study attests to the important role that VL can and does in fact play in facilitating communication between people. Indeed, as the authors reveal, the use of VL in the chaplaincy data "is an important part of the chaplain's sensitive, informal management of the interaction, helping to facilitate the patient's conversational involvement, while mitigating the force of directives to such supply [*sic*] personal information" (p. 74). The nurse's use of VL in turn "adds a degree of tentativeness while still providing the patient with a clear idea of the serious nature of the topic she is attempting to broach. Given her intention to not alarm the patient, such tentativeness is understandable" (p. 74).

The use of VL in academic settings has also been of interest. In one of the most comprehensive studies on the topic, Ruzaitė (2007) investigates two categories of VL: quantifiers and approximators in British and American English educational settings. Ruzaitė finds that, although vague expressions are frequently found in educational settings, there are both quantitative and qualitative differences between the two types of English in terms of how approximators were used. Indeed, as the study shows, there were more instances of approximators in British data which, one could argue, demonstrate that VL could be influenced by different factors including cultural and institutional ones.

Another setting which has received a significant amount of attention regarding the use of VL is classroom discourse. For example, Walsh, O'Keeffe, and McCarthy (2008) conducted a cross-corpus comparative study between the following three corpora: Limerick-Belfast Corpus of Academic Spoken English, Corpus of Irish English, and Cambridge and Nottingham Corpus of Discourse in English. Walsh and his colleagues discovered that academic discourse does not feature as many instances of VL items as occurs in casual discourse, particularly vague category markers (e.g. *and that sort of thing*). Nonetheless, these expressions serve a number of important functions in such settings, which appear to be typical and characteristic of academic discourse. For example, as the authors clarify, these vague expressions can "help expedite the start-up phase of a lesson or activity since they can provide shortcuts that mark information or concepts that can be what is common ground and facilitate a speedy handing over to the task phase of the lesson" (Walsh et al., 2008, p. 26).

The use of VL has also been investigated in political discourse. For example, in a recent study, Parvaresh (2018) investigated the frequency and functions of the VL used in the 2016 US presidential debates by Hillary Clinton and Donald Trump. Parvaresh's study reveals how

Trump's speech included a greater number of vague expressions, despite it being less lexically varied than Clinton's speech. Parvaresh hypothesises that "the rather high number of vague expressions (e.g. 'things') in Trump's speech [...] might, to some extent, have resulted in his speech being less lexically varied" (p. 185). The study points to the importance of vague expressions in political communication and in accoutring the speakers with an unprecedented ability to respond to moment-by-moment communicative needs. The study further substantiated the argument that "regardless of whether or not VL is 'appropriate' within the context of political debates", and in other communicative settings, the candidates and other people tend "to resort to using vague expressions" (p. 185). Parvaresh argues that "the vagueness observed in political communication would be to attribute a politician's VL use to the situation he/she has found himself/herself in", hence, "the notion of 'appropriate' VL use has something to do with the range of strategic functions it serves in communication" (p. 185). As such, VL is frequently used in political language in general, and particularly in political debates in dynamic, elastic, stretchable and strategic ways.

Sabet (2013) investigated the use of VL by three groups of speakers/learners of English. The first group comprised L1 speakers (American English), the second group Chinese speaking learners of English and the third group Persian speaking learners of English, totalling a 150,000 word corpus. Performing a two level analysis (i.e. lexical and functional) analysis, Sabet's study shows that L2 speakers have a tendency to use more instances of VL, a tendency which the author attributed to, among other things, the versatility and usefulness of vague expressions in helping speakers get their messages across. In this respect, Sabet encourages "the explicit instruction on three important features on vague language; where, when, and how to use it. This can contribute to a more developed pragmatic competence by the learner of English" (p. 326). Sabet also recommends that VL "should be included in the curriculum and placed in language pedagogy" (p. 325).

VL researchers have also taken an interest in the written mode of communication. One particular study was conducted by Cutting (2012) who examined the abstracts that were submitted to conferences.

The author highlighted the use of vague universal general nouns (e.g. *people*) and vague research general nouns (e.g. *results*), with a view to defining the genre known as conference abstracts in terms of its VL features. The study points to the importance of VL as a feature of what is termed the conference abstract genre. Some of the most important findings of Cutting's study are as follows:

- general nouns were pervasive;
- the most frequent universal general nouns were *activity/ies, aspect/s, context, effect/s, factor/s, feature/s, implication/s, people, place/s, practice/s, resources* and *situation(s)*;
- universal general nouns had pre- and post-head modifiers that did not add much meaning, as in *a significant main effect* and *the issue of learner choice*;
- *people* was generally non-cohesive and non-modified, as in 'strategies people use';
- the most frequent research general nouns were *analysis, data, discussion/s, finding/s, investigation, method/ology, project, purpose/s, research, result/s, study/ies* and *work*;
- both types of general nouns fulfilled functions in addition to that of textual cohesion; they were used more as a matter of 'convenience' or 'anticipation', than of 'courtesy', 'caution' and 'self-defence' (Adapted from Cutting, 2012, p. 292).

VL appears to be an inseparable part of written discourse, particularly with regards to conference abstracts. This is why Cutting (2012) suggests that the English for Specific Purposes lecturers, especially those whose role is to provide support and guidance to less experienced academics, should familiarise themselves better with this important area of inquiry, that is VL use.

As the above-mentioned findings reveal, VL plays an important role in a wide range of settings and discourses. In this study, the setting of TV reality shows will be examined, an under-explored area in terms of VL use, with the aim of contributing to the field with new resources.

2.4   Vague Language in Persuasion and Comforting

Research studies on impoliteness have provided some convincing evidence regarding the effectiveness of VL in various communicative settings. In this respect, several studies have been conducted on the use of vague quantifiers in communication. One of the first scholars to investigate the importance of these vague expressions was Channell (1994), who highlighted their importance in general, and particularly the vague quantifiers that were used by interactants for persuasive effect. Similar evidence has also been provided by a number of other studies. Jucker et al.'s (2003) study is a case in point. The authors argue that, among other things, vague quantifiers can help the speaker achieve a certain purpose because they give "information in relation to a reference point" and are thus more "informative than an absolute number would be" (Jucker et al., 2003, p. 1751).

In this respect, Moxey and Sanford (as cited in Jucker et al., 2003, pp. 1751–1752) also argue that it would normally be more informative for the hearer to hear "Most of our students passed an advanced exam" than "Twenty-two of our students passed an advanced exam", particularly in those contexts in which the hearer may not know how many students were actually eligible to take that particular exam. Indeed, as Zhang (2015) notes, a vague quantifier, such as *most people*, seems to be "more impressive and persuasive than an exact number like 70%" (p. 30).

Similar observations have also been made by Pocheptsov (1992) who reveals how our minds can be more manipulated than is generally believed. As Pocheptsov clarifies, manipulators of, among other things, quantities "can be more powerful than we and they think", and also "because manipulators can exert influence in areas which we think are not accessible to them" (p. 404). Similar findings have also been reported in other studies, most notably in Ruzaitė (2007) who reveals how vague approximators and vague quantifiers can serve functions such as emphasising and mitigating that are closely related to the persuasive aspects of language. As demonstrated by Ruzaitė, the mitigating function of VL should be viewed as being part of the persuasive use of language. One example that was used by Ruzaitė, 'this may look *a little bit* confusing', shows that the vague expression *a little bit* appears to be used with a persuasive function in mind. Overstreet's (2005) study also reveals how, in both German and English, vague general extenders can be used to serve functions related to emphasis and persuasion.

Relevant findings have also been reported by Parvaresh, Tavangar, Rasekh, and Izadi (2012) who discuss how, even in non-native conversations, some vague expressions can be used as markers of emphasis and persuasion. One revealing excerpt is detailed below:

1. Parsa: He is a wet blanket!
2. Amirmasoud: Then talk to him. I am ready to come to your room and change my room with him?
3. Parsa: But he may be offended.
4. Amirmasoud: Then please don't nag anymore!
5. Parsa: I don't nag. It is difficult!
6. Amirmasoud: I don't know! Tomorrow will you talk to him **or what**?
7. Parsa: He will be offended, but I have to directly tell him
   (Adapted from Parvaresh et al., 2012, p. 274).

In this conversation, as discussed by Parvaresh et al. (2012), the general extender *or what* seems to have been used "as an intensifier to urge Parsa to finally say whether he is going to ask a third party (his roommate) to switch his room in the dormitory with Amirmasoud's" (p. 274).

Research shows that vague boosters can also be used for persuasive functions. The vague booster *very* constitutes a case in point as it enables the speaker to "enhance the strength of the utterance in an unspecific way" by conveying "a more assertively confident voice" (Parvaresh, 2018, p. 176).

Similar accounts of the persuasive use of vague boosters have also been provided by Bradac, Mulac, and Thompson (1995), Hyland (2000) and Zhang (2011). As Hyland (2005b) notes, some vague boosters help the speaker to (i) close down "possible alternatives", (ii) emphasise "certainty", and (iii) mark "involvement with the topic", thus taking "a joint position against other voices" (p. 53). Indeed, such reassured uses of VL are closely linked to the overall function of these expressions as markers of the speaker's attitudinal certainty (Hyland, 2005a, 2005b). Drawing on data pertaining to such tension-prone settings as customs cross-examination, Zhang (2011, p. 588) also reveals how airport officers use vague intensifiers to increase their force of persuasion to extract truthful answers from passengers.

The significant role that VL plays in alleviating emotional distress and comforting the speaker has also been highlighted and discussed in the literature. On a general level, it can safely be argued that, given its dependency on assumptions of shared knowledge and intersubjectivity between participants in any conversational exchange, VL is an attempt to emphasise "the collaborative nature" of communication (Evison, McCarthy, & O'Keeffe, 2007, p. 153), thus highlighting its significant role in mutual harmony and collaboration. This is, in itself, a rapport-management strategy which can in principle lessen any possible tension in conversation (Spencer-Oatey, 2004).

Indeed, research has shown how VL can create such an informal atmosphere that participants may even feel, however momentarily, that they are part of a socially coherent and supportive group (Evison et al., 2007). As Carter and McCarthy (2006) have noted, VL is often used to highlight, maintain or establish solidarity between interlocutors. That is why they suggest that VL can be viewed as being a marker of solidarity and rapport. This view has also been highlighted in other studies, most notably in Cutting (2007b).

Furthermore, in the words of Zhang (2011), "when the communicative goal is unclear, language is vaguer. Language needs to be adjusted constantly when working toward an agreeable solution" (p. 579). Obviously, the comforting function of VL is a discursively achieved endeavour and heavily dependent on contextual considerations. For example, in a recent study, it has been shown that, in the context of a person's death and his/her ongoing funeral, panegyrists tend to use vague expressions "in such a strategic way as to discursively console those who love the deceased, those who were close to the deceased, and those who must continue to live without the deceased" (Parvaresh, 2017, p. 79). Indeed, it has been demonstrated that panegyrists' use of vague intensifiers, such as truly, completely and really, at a funeral, can discursively serve to reinforce the good qualities of the deceased, thus providing solace and comfort to his/her family and friends (Parvaresh, 2017).

Terraschke and Holmes (2007) and Overstreet (1999, 2005) also provide convincing examples in support of the argument that one of the most important and pervasive functions of vague expressions in general, and in particular vague general extenders, lies in the fact that these expressions can and do significantly contribute, not only to the creation, but also to the discursive maintenance of solidarity or rapport. Indeed, given the importance of vague expressions in creating a sympathetic relationship and/or understanding, which is arguably achieved by the appeal of these expressions to shared experiences, Terraschke and Holmes (2007) and Overstreet (1999, 2005), as do many other researchers, consider the comforting and rapport-building functions of vague expressions to be of vital importance.

In summary, VL can serve persuasive as well as comforting purposes (Vallauri, 2016). These two aspects will form the focus of this study, which will be investigated through the use of two corpora of TV discussions in Chinese and English.

2.5   Positive/Negative Politeness/Face Theories

It is now widely established that one of the most influential theories of politeness is that proposed and discussed in Brown and Levinson's (1987) *Politeness: Some Universals in Language Usage*. The importance of Brown and Levinson's approach lies in the fact that they were able to support their analyses with real-life data (Eelen, 2001; Watts, 2003). According to Terkourafi (2001), Brown and Levinson's major contribution is "their (re)discovery of Goffman's notion of 'face'" (p. 8). Face had originally been defined by Goffman as:

> the positive social value a person effectively claims for himself by the line others assume he has taken during a particular contact. Face is an image of self-delineation in terms of approved social attributes. (Goffman, 1967, p. 5)

By envisaging a psychological motivation for politeness, Brown and Levinson argued that politeness "presupposes [a] potential for aggression as it seeks to disarm it, and makes possible communication between potentially aggressive parties" (Brown & Levinson, 1987, p. 1; see also Parvaresh & Tayebi, 2018). Based on this conceptualisation of face, Brown and Levinson "created the notion of a 'model person' who possesses two characteristics of 'rationality' and 'face'" (Tayebi, 2018, p. 26). Indeed, Brown and Levinson (1987) managed to combine "Goffman's notion of face with Paul Grice's framework, which was proposed for the analysis of conversations, and came up with their own model of politeness" (Parvaresh & Eslami Rasekh, 2009, p. 2). In this way, Brown and Levinson entertained the idea that "some basic aspects of politeness are universal; and, as a result, they contend that face is invested in the individual and can be lost and, therefore, it must be constantly attended to in the course of interaction" (Parvaresh & Eslami Rasekh, 2009, p. 2). This is exactly why some scholars term Brown and Levinson's approach 'face-based politeness'. Brown and Levinson (1987) define the two aspects of face as follows:

- Positive face: "The want of every member that his wants be desirable to at least some others", and
- Negative face: "The want of every competent adult member that his actions be unimpeded by others" (Brown & Levinson, 1987, p. 62).

Based on Brown and Levinson (1987), one could claim that people are generally inclined to avoid doing things that could potentially come across as face-threatening: "In general, people cooperate (and assume each other's cooperation) in maintaining face, such cooperation being based on mutual vulnerability of face" (p. 61). As Parvaresh and Eslami Rasekh (2009, p. 2) note, Brown and Levinson believe that each utterance might potentially impose a threat to the other interlocutor's face, hence the term 'face-threatening acts' (FTAs).

According to the face theory of politeness delineated above, the level of face threat posed by an act involves the following sociological variables:

- 'distance' (the perceived social distance between speaker and hearer);
- 'relative power' (the perceived power difference between them);
- 'absolute ranking' (the cultural ranking of a particular speech act) (Brown & Levinson, 1987, pp. 74–78).

Brown and Levinson argue that the seriousness of an FTA risks damaging not only the speaker's, but also the hearer's, face. According to the authors, the above-mentioned factors are not actual ratings of power, distance or ranking, but rather are the "actors' assumptions of such ratings, assumed to be mutually assumed, at least within certain limits" (Brown & Levinson, 1987, p. 76).

The importance of VL in the realisation of politeness has been underscored and discussed in various studies, particularly in those that have tasked themselves with investigating vague hedges (e.g. *may, might*). In this respect, studies conducted by Carter and McCarthy (2006), Hyland (1998a) and Koester (2010) are particularly relevant because they demonstrate how vague hedges can lessen the degree of face threat that an utterance can potentially cause, thus maintaining politeness considerations. Of course, this use of VL for politeness purposes has been reported in both formal and informal conversations and in a variety of contexts and interactional settings. For example, as Koester notes,

> This function of VL is most evident in service encounters, where vague tags were noticeably frequent, most occurring during a meeting between a supplier and customer. This is a situation in which the risk of face threats is very great: there is a discursive imbalance (in favour of the supplier), as well as a power imbalance (in favour of the customer), and the cost of performing a face-threatening act is extremely high – the supplier may lose the customer's business. (Koester, 2007, p. 53)

Indeed, VL has been found to be particularly useful when applied to contexts in which there is great potential for tension. This is arguably what some scholars, most notably Trappes-Lomax (2007), have referred to as a tension management device. As stated by Terraschke and Holmes (2007), vague expressions can be used to "express a range of affective meanings, including establishing rapport and reducing the degree of face threat of negatively affective discursive moves" (p. 213).

The use of EL for the purpose of politeness and face is relevant to this study, and two speech acts are expected to be dominant, namely persuasion and comforting. The role of EL in politeness/face-threatening contexts will be uncovered through an analysis of the two data sets collected for this study.

2.6   Elastic Language and Elasticity Theory

A slingshot, defined by the *Cambridge Online Dictionary* (2019), is "a Y-shaped stick or piece of metal with a piece of elastic [= material that stretches] attached to the top parts, used especially by children for shooting small stones". A slingshot is elastic in the sense that it can be adapted in different angles to accurately hit targets, and this is precisely why it has consistently been a popular gadget for both adults and children. It enables its users to make appropriate arrangements, not only in terms of the angle of their next shot, but also the strength and velocity of the stone being shot towards the target. Analogically speaking, human communication in general and the expressions that we refer to as vague expressions (e.g. *thing, stuff*) behave very similarly to the slingshot discussed above; they can be stretched in different directions "in response to the needs of communication" (Zhang, 2015, p. 54). In order to clarify this aspect of human language, let us consider this excerpt:

- *About* three hundred people have taken the General English course we are offering.

Indeed, in the above example, an expression such as *about* "shifts the number of people" (Parvaresh, 2017, p. 67) who attended the General English course in such a way as to provide the right amount of information for the hearer, in a context in which it would not be "possible" or "relevant" for the speaker to say exactly how many people took the course. As such, it appears that the word *about* has been used in an elastic way, thus stretching the utterance in which it is used 'sideways', that is horizontally, so that it can include a wider range of numbers. In other words, the elastic use of the word *about* in the above example can be taken to be evidence which suggests that linguistic expressions are, or rather can be, used in such "fluid and stretchable" ways (Zhang, 2015, p. 57). In this example, the manner in which the word *about* has been used indicates that its meaning boundary is unspecified, thus paving the way for the utterance to include numbers that are reasonably above and beyond 300.

In a series of seminal studies, Zhang (2011, 2013, 2015) defines EL as language whose "interpretation is elastic in the sense that it can be stretched or shrunk according to the strategic needs of communication" (Zhang, 2013, p. 88). As the example above demonstrates, the concept of elasticity is indeed a stretching strategy which is used "in the process of vague-ing to achieve communicative goals" (Zhang, 2011, p. 578). In other words, it appears that, in this typical example, elasticity is arguably nothing more than a manifestation of a potentially vague expression, such as *about*, in communication. As such, "the elastic nature of language and communication lays the foundation" for what can be called strategic elasticity. As conceptualised, developed and elaborated on by Zhang, the elasticity of language is a realisation of a main maxim and four specific maxims:

- Main maxim: Stretch language elastically in discursive negotiations to achieve communicative goals.
- Specific maxims:

  (1) Go just-right: provide the right amount of information (e.g. That tall woman is *very* kind).
  (2) Go general: speak in general terms (e.g. Do you have any convictions *or anything*?).
  (3) Go hypothetical: speak in hypothetical terms (e.g. It *could* be him).
  (4) Go subjective: speak in subjective terms (e.g. *I think* she is dishonest)
  (Adapted from Zhang, 2011, pp. 578–579).

In (1) the speaker uses the word *very* with a view to increasing the tone of the utterance and highlighting the kindness of the tall woman in question. Indeed, this is an example of the elastic use of language in the sense that the word *very* helps the speaker stretch the tone of the utterance upwards. The example in (2) is another manifestation of EL use. By using the expression *or anything* the speaker has stretched the utterance horizontally, thus creating an ad hoc category such as 'things and activities that are indicative of current or previous offences' without having to repeat a comprehensive list, an activity which might not be at all possible or feasible. Finally, in (3) and (4), the speakers have used the expressions *could* and *I think* to stretch the tone of the corresponding utterances downwards with a view to underscoring the hypotheticality of the situation, in (3), and the subjectivity of the situation, in (4), thus protecting the speaker "from the risk of being challenged and refuted" (Zhang & Sabet, 2016, p. 335).

As Zhang argues by drawing on empirical evidence, there are three main characteristics of VL elasticity:

a. Interconnected patterns of strategic elasticity: There are interconnections between the pragmatic functions of elasticity, their linguistic realisations and the four specific maxims. A particular linguistic category tends to serve particular pragmatic functions and to conform to certain appropriate maxims.
b. Determinant communicative purposes: Elasticityof VL is executed according to the moment-by-moment communicative purpose in a specific context. The direction and extent of VL stretching are underpinned by the needs of communication for that situated discourse.
c. Versatile pragmatic strategies: Elasticity consists of moving on a continuum of polarities, and is manifested through versatile pragmatic strategies. Elasticity of VL serves diverse and often contrastive pragmatic functions, including soft and tough, firm and flexible, cooperative and uncooperative moves (Adapted from Zhang, 2011, p. 579).

What such elastic uses of language have in common is the idea that they are of an interactive nature and are particularly useful in negotiating processes, where interactants are aware of the fact that the communicative goals "must be adjusted constantly when working towards an agreeable solution" (Zhang, 2015, p. 56). In this context, one could safely claim that there most definitely exists a relationship "between pragmatic functions, their linguistic realisations and the pragmatic maxims they conform to, with the communicative goal being the dominant factor which determines the language used" (Zhang, 2011, as discussed and interpreted by Mulder, Williams, & Moore, 2019, p. 14).

In light of the above, elasticity theory is an attempt to encapsulate how strategically various dimensions of language are used (Zhang, 2015). As argued by Zhang, the stretching of language is pretty much determined by the following principles:

- Fluidity Principle: Elasticity is a matter of degree.
- Stretchability Principle: Utterances can be stretched in different ways.
- Strategy Principle: Fluid utterances serve strategic purposes (Zhang, 2015, p. 57).

As Zhang confirms:

> the principles are interconnected and complementary. Fluidity indicates that language itself is rubber-band-like elastic. If language were not fluid, the other two principles would not exist. Stretchability enables speakers to realise their communicative goals: in other words, strategy is the purpose of stretchability. Without a purpose it would be pointless for speakers to stretch language, and indeed all speech has a purpose. In general fluidity is the basis, stretchability is the means, and strategy is the end. Combined, they make EL an indispensable part of effective communication. (Zhang, 2015, pp. 57–58)

The maxims proposed in Zhang (2013) aptly show how elasticisation works. However, in a more recent study, and in order to better reflect the dynamics of communication, Zhang (2015) combines 'go subjective' and 'go hypothetical' into a single maxim as "subjective and hypothetical maxims can be covered by a single epistemic maxim" (p. 63). In this new conceptualisation, 'go just-right' is split into two maxims, go approximate and go scalar, the purpose being exclusively for better clarification. This is reflected in the following manifestation of elasticity:

- Go approximate: elasticise in approximate form, e.g. *many, about 20, a few*
- Go general: elasticise in general form, e.g. *thing, stuff, and stuff like that*
- Go scalar: elasticise in scalar firm, e.g. *very, a bit, often*
- Go epistemic: elasticise in hypothetical and subjective form, e.g. *possible, could, might, I think*
(Zhang, 2015, p. 63).

The elasticity theory discussed above has proved to be particularly useful when analysing the pragmatic functions of expressions such as those found in the above table (see e.g. Parvaresh & Zhang, 2019). These expressions, which traditionally are referred to as 'vague language', have proved to be an inseparable part of human communication (Channell, 1994). As will be discussed below and throughout the book, the EL framework offers considerable possibilities for researchers to integrate detailed accounts of these expressions for cross-linguistic comparison, and to encourage in-depth studies of their pragmatic functions "in different types of discourse and cross-linguistically" (Mulder et al., 2019).

The justification for adopting the elasticity theory in this study is that it is the only theory that adequately explains EL. The classification that comes with this framework offers suitable and accurate devices for EL data analysis, in a systematic and effective way.

2.7   Linguistic Categories of Elastic (Vague) Language

Over the past few years, different categories of EL/VL have been proposed. However, defining what actually counts as VL has proved to be an increasingly nebulous task to undertake. In this respect, it has already been shown that, for VL, "a wide range of definitions exists", and that the "lexico-grammatical realisations and categories associated with VL vary considerably between researchers" (Adolphs et al., 2007, p. 62).

Despite terminological differences, VL can be conceptualised as those linguistic forms which can potentially be used by interactants in intentionally general, fuzzy and imprecise ways (Cutting, 2012). Similarly Trappes-Lomax (2007) defines VL as any "purposive choice of language designed to make the degree of accuracy, preciseness, certainty or clarity with which a referent or situation (event, state, process) is described less than it might have been" (p. 122). Following on from this, in this study we consider the following lexical categories to be examples of VL:

a. Vague quantifiers (e.g. *a few, many*): typically "occupy the determiner slot in a noun phrase" (Channell, 1994, p. 99; cf. Powell, 1985; Ruzaitė, 2007). However, in contrast to precise numbers, "they do not clearly specify the quantity involved" (Jucker et al., 2003, p. 1751).
b. Approximators (e.g. *about, around*): denote imprecision of quantity, they usually precede a numerical expression and qualify it (Jucker et al., 2003, p. 1758; cf. Mauranen, 2004).
c. Possibility indicators (e.g. *possibly, seem*): They help the speaker express what he/she views as the 'possibility' (or 'probability') of something. These expressions typically serve to indicate uncertainty on the part of the speaker, thus making speech less authoritative and less assertive (Carter, 2003, p. 11).
d. General extenders (e.g. *or something, and the like*): These expressions are not flexible in their syntactic distribution and are of crucial communicative significance to the extent that, as Stubbe and Holmes (1995) state, they are "oiling the wheels of verbal interaction" (p. 63; cf. Parvaresh et al., 2012; Tagliamonte & Denis, 2010). Typically, vague extenders "are multifunctional with the context, both linguistic and non-linguistic, helping to constrain the interpretation on particular occasions of use" (Cheshire, 2007, p. 157).
e. Boosters (e.g. *overly, extremely, very*): These expressions help the speaker maintain a persona of 'assertiveness' in contexts in which hearers would expect such assertiveness (Hyland, 1998a, 1998b, 2000; cf. Bradac et al., 1995; Holmes, 1990; Hu & Cao, 2011). In other words, by increasing the tone of speech, boosters allow speakers to convey a sense of conviction (Hyland, 2000).

f. De-intensifiers (e.g. *sort of, kind of*): They serve to decrease the tone of utterances (Berndt & Caramazza, 1978). As Zhang (2015) notes, vague de-intensifiers "express vaguely a low intensity degree, and decrease the tone of speech" (p. 90).

g. Vague nouns (e.g. *someone, thing*): These expressions are almost always one of the most common categories of VL as they enable the speaker to serve a wide range of communicative purposes (see Boakye, 2007; Koester, 2007). Most notably, vague nouns indicate "lack of precision" (Crystal & Davy, 1975, p. 112) and are typically used in contexts in which the required expressions are not known, cannot be retrieved (e.g. due to memory lapses) or cannot be mentioned (e.g. taboo words). By referring "to semantic categories in an open-ended way", vague nouns also "help the conversation go smoothly" (Shirato & Stapleton, 2007, p. 396).

h. Subjectivisers (e.g. *I believe, we think*): They help highlight the speaker's lower degree of commitment or certainty. Zhang (2013) argues that, due to "its manifestation of the speaker's veiled opinion", the category of *subjectiviser* is indeed "a salient indicator for possible differences of VL use" (p. 91). A subjectiviser such as *I think*, for example, signals "speaker commitment to an utterance" (Adolphs et al., 2007, p. 63). As Zhang and Sabet (2016) note, by using *I think*, "the speaker is not fully committing to the truth of his/her utterance". *I think*, the authors continue, "acts as a protector to shield the speaker from the risk of being challenged and refuted" (p. 335). Indeed, a vague subjectiviser counts as such because it fulfils its functions (e.g. avoiding commitment to the propositional content of the utterance) by being inherently vague and being purposefully used (Adapted from Parvaresh, 2018, pp. 170–172).

In fact, the view that VL informs the rather long list of lexical categories listed above originates from what can be termed the liberal approach towards the use of VL. Indeed, this is the view that we adopt in this study because we believe that VL is manifested in many aspects of communication, and that to be able to actually account for the dynamics of communication which involves VL, one should broaden the category and include all items to ensure that a more representative picture of VL use is painted. This view differs from more conventional approaches to VL (e.g. Channell, 1994) who considers categories such as vague quantifiers and vague extenders to comprise VL.

This study focuses on EL and, therefore, Zhang's (2015, p. 36) categorisation of the lexical items of EL is sufficiently appropriate and accurate to adopt for the coding of data; see Chapter 3 for details.

2.8 Pragmatic Functions of Elastic (Vague) Language

As was noted above, VL has proved to be a versatile feature of language in the sense that it enables speakers to achieve a wide range of communicative functions (Jucker et al., 2003; Ruzaitė, 2007). Due to this versatility, VL obviously is the mark of more skilled users of language (Carter & McCarthy, 2006; see also Mumford, 2009) whose use of VL points to the fact that VL "is neither all 'bad' nor all 'good'. What matters is that vague language is used appropriately" (Channell, 1994, p. 3). While the entire range of functions fulfilled by VL in moment-by-moment communicative interactions is currently impossible to review here, some of the most recurring functions of VL are delineated and discussed below.

2.8.1 Providing the Right Amount of Information

Vague expressions can provide information suitable for a given context (Channell, 1994). This can be done, amongst other things, through the use of vague nouns or vague quantifiers, "particularly on occasions when the speaker believes something is too complicated or does not need to be made precise" (Parvaresh & Tayebi, 2014, p. 584; cf. Parvaresh, 2015). In "I paid thirty pounds on notebooks, pencils and stuff like that", *and stuff like that* provides the right amount of information for the hearer, as it appears that the speaker feels that there is no need to detail all the individual items that he spent money on. Perhaps the listener does not care and can indeed infer, based on contextual clues and previous experience, that the items the speaker has in mind belong, in some form or other, to the general category known as stationery.

What is important in this respect is the established fact that providing the right amount of information through VL does not cause the smooth flow of conversation to be interrupted (Shirato & Stapleton, 2007). That the speaker does not feel the need to use more information appears to be consistent with what have been termed the Gricean maxims of quantity and quality:

Maxim of Quantity:

1. "Make your contribution as informative as required."
2. "Don't make your contribution more informative than is required."

Maxim of Quality:

1. "Don't say what you believe to be false."
2. "Don't say what you lack adequate evidence for"
   (Grice, 1975, pp. 45–47).

The use of VL as a strategy for providing the right amount of information satisfies both the Maxim of Quantity, in that the information provided is as informative as required, and the Maxim of Quality, in that the speaker, by not saying more than is required, is strategically avoiding saying something for which there is little or no evidence.

2.8.2 Mitigation

It goes without saying that there are occasions in speech in which interactants may, for various reasons, need to avoid being too direct or too imposing (Carter & McCarthy, 2006). In other words, there are situations in any communicative act that speakers may need to signal their "desire to reduce the face loss associated with the basic message" (Fraser, 1996, p. 183). Thaler (2012) notes that mitigation, as a pragmatic phenomenon, "is usually analyzed in terms of speech acts and, more particularly, by referring to illocution. Even when mitigation is said to focus on propositional content [...] or on perlocutionary effect [...] these categories still seem to be related to illocutionary force or at least to some of its components" (p. 908).

Zhang (2015) argues that mitigation is "perhaps the most natural and recognised function of VL, because of its nature and capacity" (p. 39). As Drave (2002) notes, the mitigating function of VL is found, among others, on occasions in which considerations of deference or politeness are high. In other words, one occasion in which the mitigating function of VL is most noticeable is "where potentially face-threatening advice is given" (Drave, 2002, p. 36). Hedges appear to be the most obvious category of VL and serve to mitigate the tone of speech. Indeed, research shows that the mitigating function of VL serves to soften the tone of speech for various reasons, including to convey politeness, to elicit rapport, to protect self or others, to withhold information or even to be evasive (e.g. Drave, 2002; Rowland, 2007; Ruzaitė, 2007; Trappes-Lomax, 2007; Zhang, 2015). VL items such as *sort of* serve to signal "imprecision", thus making statements "less assertive and less open to challenge or refutation" (Shirato & Stapleton, 2007, p. 396). The mitigating function of VL is particularly relevant to more formal and institutional discourse in which "the roles and responsibilities of the officers make them use VL as a tool, mitigating the imposition of requests and the laying down of rules" (Zhang, 2011, p. 593).

2.8.3 Politeness

It has now been widely established that the use of VL is predominantly a politeness strategy (Stubbs, 1986). If human communication has been shown to involve a certain degree of conflict (Leech, 1983), VL can potentially be used to avoid such conflict. Indeed, VL is a politeness strategy which saves one's *face*, that is their public self-image (Brown & Levinson, 1987) and therefore helps with maintaining interpersonal relationships (Ruzaitė, 2007). People have been found to use VL to avoid directly mentioning something for various reasons including, most importantly, maintaining privacy, or to save someone's *face* for politeness-related reasons (Zhang, 2011). The positive politeness dimension of VL has been summarised by Cutting (2015) in the following way:

> Vagueness can be employed in expressions of positive politeness that show solidarity towards an addressee (Brown & Levinson, 1987), signalling closeness and high involvement (Tannen, 1984) [...] Adjunctive general extenders such as 'and stuff' are markers of intimacy, exploiting the shared social space of a close relationship, which can be used to 'establish a social persona or a regional identity', stressing in-group membership, social similarity and positive politeness (Aijmer, 2013). (Cutting, 2015, p. 110)

According to Cutting, VL can also be used for negative politeness concerns, in which case it can help:

> the addressor to avoid imposing by mitigating the force of their utterances, softening complaints and criticisms (Jucker et al., 2003), avoiding appearing overly confident, authoritative, and direct, as in 'so you have to then try and go a bit further beyond the actual differences' (Ruzaitė, 2007, p. 168) or seeming offensive, derogatory and pretentious (Channell, 1994). (Cutting, 2015, p. 110)

Highlighting the importance of VL in maintaining politeness, Trappes-Lomax (2007) notes that VL can potentially be used to avoid and manage trouble pertaining to the interactional face needs of oneself or others.

2.8.4 Solidarity

Motivated by the considerations of positive politeness mentioned above, VL can create feelings of in-groupness, intimacy, rapport and solidarity. As Parvaresh and Tayebi (2014) note, "vague expressions can be used to create a friendly atmosphere by marking in-group knowledge, shared experiences, and common ground" (p. 589). Overstreet (1999) reveals how the vague expression *and stuff* fulfils what is referred to as "invited solidarity" (p. 99). To clarify, consider this excerpt:

Pam: Still having trouble with that equilibrium stuff?
Bob: Wh—yeah. It—well—just walking.
Pam: Mmhm.
Bob: Y' know uh if I pay attention I can do pretty good on flat surfaces but as soon as the surface gets uneven **an' stuff** um I—it—Yeah, it gets a little tricky.
Pam: Hmm. Bummer. (Adapted from Overstreet, 1999, p. 101)

As discussed by Overstreet, the topic of the above conversation is a camping trip that Bob and Pam have organised. As Bob has recently had brain surgery, instead of hiking to the site, he is considering taking a boat. In this exchange, "Bob describes his problem, and concludes with an appeal to solidarity *an' stuff*" (Overstreet, 1999, p. 101). As Overstreet notes, "Bob is concerned that his inability to hike the trail might disrupt the group's plans". By using the vague expression *an' stuff*, Bob therefore "appeals for understanding that hiking with poor equilibrium on an uneven trail can be tricky, and that his alternative plan is necessary" (Overstreet, 1999, p. 101).

The contribution of VL to the creation and maintenance of solidarity has led some researchers (e.g. Channell, 1994; Koester, 2007; Terraschke & Holmes, 2007; Zhang, 2015) to argue that the interpretation of VL as a solidarity marker rests heavily on assumptions of shared background knowledge.

2.8.5 Strengthening

VL can be used to increase the tone of utterances. Intensifiers are typically adverbs which are used to magnify a proposition. The most noticeable boosters seem to be words such as *absolutely, truly, really* and *undoubtedly*, which enable the speaker to "head off conflicting views and express their certainty in what they say" (Hyland, 2005b, p. 52). As Hyland (2005b) argues, "by closing down possible alternatives, boosters emphasize certainty and construct rapport by marking involvement with the topic and solidarity with an audience, taking a joint position against other voices" (p. 53), thus increasing the illocutionary force of utterances. Drawing on, for example, Hyland (2005b), Hu and Cao

(2011) note that "skilful manipulation of hedges and boosters" signals one's "epistemic stance towards propositional content", and marks him/her "as a competent member of the discourse community" (p. 2796). As Parvaresh and Tayebi (2014) note, however, a 'single, confident voice' expressed by boosters does not render these expressions any less vague (p. 576).

Indeed, the boosting function of VL is not only fulfilled by intensifiers (e.g. *very, extremely*). Quantifiers, such as *many* and *a lot of,* can also potentially serve as boosting strategies. In this respect, the use of boosting devices can, in turn, also serve persuasive functions (Channell, 1994). Regardless of the lexical items that are being used for boosting purposes, what is important regarding the strengthening function of VL is that the assertiveness associated with, and caused by, vague boosters is not necessarily a feature of vague boosters as lexical items, but rather is a dynamic product of the moment-by-moment interactional achievements in context.

2.8.6 Self-Protection

As was noted above, VL can be used for politeness purposes. This would, in principle, mean that VL can be thought of as a strategy for the protection of others. On a different level, however, VL can be used as a defensive device, protecting the speaker from being challenged and/or refuted (Jucker et al., 2003). As far as the strategic function of protecting the self through the use of VL is concerned, it could safely be claimed that vague expressions such as *sort of* and *I think* can convey "imprecision and make statements less assertive and less open to challenge or refutation" (Shirato & Stapleton, 2007, p. 396). Indeed, it appears that the self-protection function of VL is closely linked to its ability to distance the speaker from the propositional or attitudinal content of what is said (Ruzaitė, 2007).

Ruzaitė (2007) argues that expressions such as *could* and *probably* indicate "a lower degree of the speaker's commitment to the truth of the claim" and make "the claim less categorical" (p. 158). It therefore appears that the self-distancing function of VL is, in a way, similar to the concept of self-protection that was broached by Channell (1994).

As Bello and Edwards (2005) note, vague messages "are attempts by individuals to protect their own competence face and may be forms of self-approbation" (p. 163).

Self-protection should be seen as "a safeguard against later being exposed as wrong and is often used by people who are known to have the exact information" (Cheng & Warren, 2001, p. 98). In this respect, it has now been widely established that VL:

> is an often-used diplomatic strategy for leaving the course of future action unspecified while effectively sending a warning message to the other parties. It keeps the "opponent" guessing as to what will be done and keeps options open for a response to changing circumstances (Alston, 1964, p. 86). (Cheng & Warren, 2001, p. 98)

In light of the above, it would only be fitting to assume that VL is the same as the tentative language used when the speaker is less certain about what is being said (Tausczik & Pennebaker, 2010).

2.8.7 Withholding Information

As was noted by Channell (1994), VL "is part of our taken-for-granted world, and that normally we do not notice it unless it appears inappropriate—for example, when someone seems to be deliberately withholding information" (p. 4). The withholding function of VL shifts the focus of attention from vagueness as a cooperative strategy to one whose main goal is non-cooperation. This was further elaborated on by Zhang (2011):

> An uncooperative use of VL refers to negative and divergent language moves, and is rarely mentioned in the literature. This study investigates both cooperative and uncooperative use, by adding two categories as uncooperative strategies of VL: (1) Confronting: This VW [vague-work, noted by the author of this article] argues with a non accommodating tone, acting as a social divider, and (2) Evading: This VW deliberately avoids conveying correct/accurate information to manipulate the situation to the speaker's advantage. A negative attitude features in these two uncooperative moves. (Zhang, 2011, p. 577)

In light of the above, one could also claim that VL use is not intentional, but rather is "a means of self-protective avoidance" (Zhang, 2013, p. 111). From the perspective of the speaker, evasion might be a very desirable function of VL, but from the perspective of the hearer it might not be such a desirable feature of language. However, the degree and direction of the hearer's information interpretation is rather difficult to determine.

The above discussion of the pragmatic functions of EL is not exhaustive, other functions also exist. For example, EL can be an attitude marker, as in the following:

Mother: Where are you headed darling?
Son: *Out of town.*

Father: How was your meeting with your supervisor?
Daughter: *Usual.*

In both examples, the interlocutors use EL (*out of town, usual*) to show that they have an attitude. The son obviously does not want to let his mother know exactly where he is going, and a general word like *out of town* used in this situation passes on an 'It is none of your business' message to his mother. In the second example, the daughter chooses to answer *usual*, showing that she does not want to elaborate on the details, either because she cannot be bothered to do so, or she thinks her father would be able to infer what *usual* entails (they probably have had similar discussions before), or she senses that he is simply not interested in the details.

The review of the categorisation of lexical items and pragmatic functions in the literature informs the coding system that is adopted in this study, that is Zhang's (2015) framework (see Chapter 3 for details). The review of cross-cultural studies highlights areas requiring further work.

2.9   Concluding Remarks

While the investigation into how people make themselves understood has been a task that many researchers, particularly those in the field of linguistics, have set themselves, there are still many linguistic features which are worthy of further exploration. As an important feature of language, VL has proved to be of great significance in helping interactants achieve a number of pragmatic functions. Of particular interest in this study are the two speech acts of persuasion and comforting which, due to the delicate and high context-sensitivity of their nature, require a suitable knowledge of how language functions. To fill this gap, the specific contribution of this study is to demonstrate how and why EL is used in the discourse of reality television shows.

References

Adolphs, S., Atkins, S., & Harvey, K. (2007). Caught between professional requirements and interpersonal needs: Vague language in healthcare contexts. In J. Cutting (Ed.), *Vague language explored* (pp. 62–78). Basingstoke: Palgrave Macmillan.

Aijmer, K. (2013). *Understanding pragmatic markers*. Edinburgh, UK: Edinburgh University Press.

Allan, K. (1986). *Linguistic meaning* (Vols. 1 & 2). London: Routledge & Kegan Paul.

Alston, W. P. (1964). *Philosophy of language*. Englewood Cliffs, NJ: Prentice-Hall.

Andersen, G. (2010). A contrastive approach to vague nouns. In G. Kaltenboeck, W. Mihatsch, & S. Schneiders (Eds.), *New approaches to hedging* (pp. 35–49). London: Emerald.

Asher, N., & Lascarides, A. (2001). Indirect speech acts. *Synthese, 128*(1–2), 183–228.

Austin, J. L. (1956). A plea for excuses: The presidential address. *Proceedings of the Aristotelian Society, 57,* 1–30.

Austin, J. L. (1962/1975). *How to do things with words*. Cambridge, MA: Harvard University Press.

Bach, K., & Harnish, R. M. (1979). *Communication and speech acts*. Cambridge, MA: Harvard University Press.

Bell, A. (1991). *The language of news media: Language in society*. Oxford: Blackwell.

Bello, R., & Edwards, R. (2005). Interpretations of messages: The influence of various forms of equivocation, face concerns, and sex differences. *Journal of Language and Social Psychology, 24*(2), 160–181.

Berndt, R. S., & Caramazza, A. (1978). The development of vague modifiers in the language of pre-school children. *Journal of Child Language, 5*(2), 279–294.

Bloom, P. (2017). *Against empathy: The case for rational compassion*. London: Penguin Random House.

Boakye, N. G. (2007). *Aspects of vague language use: Formal and informal contexts*. Unpublished M.A. thesis, University of South Africa.

Bradac, J. J., Mulac, A., & Thompson, S. A. (1995). Men's and women's use of intensifiers and hedges in problem-solving interaction: Molar and molecular analyses. *Research on Language and Social Interaction, 28*(2), 93–116.

Brown, P., & Levinson, S. C. (1987). *Politeness: Some universals in language usage*. Cambridge: Cambridge University Press.

Burleson, B. R. (1985). The production of comforting messages: Social-cognitive foundations. *Journal of Language and Social Psychology, 4*(3–4), 253–273.

Cambridge Online Dictionary. (2019). Available at https://dictionary.cambridge.org/dictionary/english/slingshot. Last accessed 15 Apr 2019.

Carter, R. (2003). The grammar of talk: Spoken English, grammar and the classroom. In *New perspectives on English in the classroom* (pp. 5–13). London: Qualifications and Curriculum Authority.

Carter, R., & McCarthy, M. (2006). *Cambridge grammar of English*. Cambridge: Cambridge University Press.

Channell, J. (1994). *Vague language*. Oxford: Oxford University Press.

Cheng, W. (2007). The use of vague language across spoken genres in an intercultural Hong Kong corpus. In J. Cutting (Ed.), *Vague language explored* (pp. 161–181). Basingstoke: Palgrave Macmillan.

Cheng, W., & Warren, M. (2001). The use of vague language in intercultural conversations in Hong Kong. *English World-Wide, 22*(1), 81–104.

Cheshire, J. (2007). Discourse variation, grammaticalisation and stuff like that. *Journal of Sociolinguistics, 11*(2), 155–193.

Clark, H. H. (1979). Responding to indirect speech acts. *Cognitive Psychology, 11*(4), 430–477.

Cohen, L. J. (1997). Ordinary language philosophy. In P. V. Lamarque (Ed.), *Concise encyclopedia of philosophy of language* (pp. 35–37). Oxford: Elsevier.

Cook, G. (2007). 'This we have done': The vagueness of poetry and public relations. In J. Cutting (Ed.), *Vague language explored* (pp. 21–39). Basingstoke: Palgrave Macmillan.

Cotterill, J. (2007). 'I think he was kind of shouting or something': Uses and abuses of vagueness in the British courtroom. In J. Cutting (Ed.), *Vague language explored* (pp. 97–114). Basingstoke: Palgrave Macmillan.

Crystal, D., & Davy, D. (1975). *Advanced conversational English*. London: Longman Publishing Group.

Cutting, J. (2007a). Introduction to 'vague language explored'. In J. Cutting (Ed.), *Vague language explored* (pp. 3–20). Basingstoke: Palgrave Macmillan.

Cutting, J. (Ed.). (2007b). *Vague language explored*. Basingstoke: Palgrave Macmillan.

Cutting, J. (2012). Vague language in conference abstracts. *Journal of English for Academic Purposes, 11*(4), 283–293.

Cutting, J. (2015). *Dingsbums und so*: Beliefs about German vague language. *Journal of Pragmatics, 85*, 108–121.

Dafouz-Milne, E. (2008). The pragmatic role of textual and interpersonal metadiscourse markers in the construction and attainment of persuasion: A cross-linguistic study of newspaper discourse. *Journal of Pragmatics, 40*(1), 95–113.

Drave, N. (2002). Vaguely speaking: A corpus approach to vague language in intercultural conversations. In P. Peters, P. Collins, & A. Smith (Eds.), *Language and computers: New frontiers of corpus research*. Papers from the Twenty-First International Conference of English Language Research and Computerized Corpora (pp. 25–40). Amsterdam, the Netherlands: Rodopi.

Eelen, G. (2001). *A critique of politeness theory*. London: Routledge.

Evison, J., McCarthy, M., & O'Keeffe, A. (2007). 'Looking out for love and all the rest of it': Vague category markers as shared social space. In J. Cutting (Ed.), *Vague language explored* (pp. 138–157). Basingstoke: Palgrave Macmillan.

Fernández, J. (2013). A corpus-based study of vague language use by learners of Spanish in a study abroad context. *Social and Cultural Aspects of Language Learning in Study Abroad, 37*, 299.

Fernández, J. (2015). General extender use in spoken Peninsular Spanish: Metapragmatic awareness and pedagogical implications. *Journal of Spanish Language Teaching, 2*(1), 1–17.

Fraser, B. (1996). Pragmatic markers. *Pragmatics, 6*(2), 167–190.

Gassner, D. (2012). Vague language that is rarely vague?: A case study of "thing" in L1 and L2 discourse. *International Review of Pragmatics, 4*(1), 3–28.

Goffman, I. (1967). *Interaction ritual: Essays on face-to-face interaction*. Garden City, NY: Anchor Books.

Grice, P. (1975). Logic and conversation. In P. Cole & J. Morgan (Eds.), *Syntax and semantics. Volume 3: Speech acts* (pp. 41–58). New York: Academic Press.

Holmes, J. (1990). Hedges and boosters in women's and men's speech. *Language & Communication, 10*(3), 185–205.

Hu, G., & Cao, F. (2011). Hedging and boosting in abstracts of applied linguistics articles: A comparative study of English- and Chinese-medium journals. *Journal of Pragmatics, 43*, 2795–2809.

Hyland, K. (1998a). *Hedging in scientific research articles*. Amsterdam: John Benjamins.

Hyland, K. (1998b). Persuasion and context: The pragmatics of academic metadiscourse. *Journal of Pragmatics, 30*(4), 437–455.

Hyland, K. (2000). Hedges, boosters and lexical invisibility: Noticing modifiers in academic texts. *Language Awareness, 9*(4), 179–197.

Hyland, K. (2005a). Stance and engagement: A model of interaction in academic discourse. *Discourse Studies, 7*(2), 173–192.

Hyland, K. (2005b). *Metadiscourse: Exploring interaction in writing*. London: Continuum.

Janney, R. (2002). Cotext as context: Vague answers in court. *Language & Communication, 22*, 457–475.

Jucker, A. H., Smith, S. W., & Ludge, T. (2003). Interactive aspects of vagueness in conversation. *Journal of Pragmatics, 35*, 1737–1769.

Koester, A. (2007). "About twelve thousand or so": Vagueness in North American and UK offices. In J. Cutting (Ed.), *Vague language explored* (pp. 40–61). Basingstoke: Palgrave Macmillan.

Koester, A. (2010). *Workplace discourse*. London: A & C Black.

Lakoff, R. (1982). Persuasive discourse and ordinary conversation, with examples from advertising. In D. Tannen (Ed.), *Analyzing discourse: Text and talk* (pp. 25–42). Washington, DC: Georgetown University Press.

Lauwereyns, S. (2002). Hedges in Japanese conversation: The influence of age, sex, and formality. *Language Variation and Change, 14*, 239–259.

Leech, G. (1983). *Principles of pragmatics*. London: Longman.

Li, S. (2017). A corpus-based study of vague language in legislative texts: Strategic use of vague terms. *English for Specific Purposes, 45*, 98–109.

Malyuga, E., & McCarthy, M. (2018). English and Russian vague category markers in business discourse: Linguistic identity aspects. *Journal of Pragmatics, 135*, 39–52.

Mauranen, A. (2004). 'They're a little bit different': Observations on hedges in academic talk. In K. Aijmer & A. Stenström (Eds.), *Discourse patterns in spoken and written corpora* (pp. 173–198). Amsterdam: John Benjamins.

Metsä-Ketelä, M. (2016). Pragmatic vagueness: Exploring general extenders in English as a lingua franca. *Intercultural Pragmatics, 13*(3), 325–351.

Mey, J. L. (2001). *Pragmatics: An introduction*. London: Blackwell.

Mihatsch, W. (2010). The diachrony of rounders and adaptors: Approximation and unidirectional change. In G. Kaltenböck, W. Mihatsch, & S. Schneider (Eds.), *New approaches to hedging* (pp. 93–122). Bingley, UK: Emerald.

Morgan, J. L. (1977). *Two types of convention in indirect speech acts* (Center for the Study of Reading Technical Report 52). University of Illinois.

Mulder, J., Williams, C. P., & Moore, E. (2019). Sort of in Australian English: The elasticity of a pragmatic marker [Special issue]. *Journal of Asian Pacific Communication, 29*(1), 9–32.

Mumford, S. (2009). An analysis of spoken grammar: The case for production. *ELT Journal, 63*(2), 137–144.

Myers, G. (1994). *Words in ads*. London: Edward Arnold.

Nicolls, M. (2015). *Empathy: Giving comfort*. Retrieved from https://www.wellbeing.com.au/mind-spirit/mind/empathy-giving-comfort.html.

Overstreet, M. (1999). *Whales, candlelight, and stuff like that: General extenders in English discourse*. Oxford: Oxford University Press.

Overstreet, M. (2005). And stuff und so: Investigating pragmatic expressions in English and German. *Journal of Pragmatics, 37*(11), 1845–1864.

Parvaresh, V. (2015). Vague language that is vague^p in both L1 and L2: A comment on Gassner (2012). *International Review of Pragmatics, 7*(1), 129–143.

Parvaresh, V. (2017). Panegyrists, vagueness and the pragmeme. In V. Parvaresh & A. Capone (Eds.), *The pragmeme of accommodation: The case of interaction around the event of death* (pp. 61–81). Cham, Switzerland: Springer.

Parvaresh, V. (2018). 'We are going to do a lot of things for college tuition': Vague language in the 2016 US presidential debates. *Corpus Pragmatics, 2*(2), 167–192.

Parvaresh, V. (2019). Moral impoliteness. *Journal of Language Aggression and Conflict, 7*(1), 77–102.

Parvaresh, V., & Ahmadian, M. J. (2016). The impact of task structure on the use of vague expressions by EFL learners. *The Language Learning Journal, 44*(4), 436–450.

Parvaresh, V., & Eslami Rasekh, A. (2009). Speech act disagreement among young women in Iran. *CLCWeb: Comparative Literature and Culture, 11*(4), 11.

Parvaresh, V., Tavangar, M., Rasekh, A. E., & Izadi, D. (2012). About his friend, how good she is, and this and that: General extenders in native Persian and non-native English discourse. *Journal of Pragmatics, 44*(3), 261–279.

Parvaresh, V., & Tayebi, T. (2014). Vaguely speaking in Persian. *Discourse Processes, 51*(7), 565–600.

Parvaresh, V., & Tayebi, T. (2018). Impoliteness, aggression and the moral order. *Journal of Pragmatics, 132,* 91–107.

Parvaresh, V., & Zhang, G. (Eds.). (2019). Vagueness and elasticity of 'sort of' in TV discussion discourse in the Asian Pacific [Special issue]. *Journal of Asian Pacific Communication, 29*(1), 1–132.

Peirce, C. S. (1902). Vagueness. In M. Baldwin (Ed.), *Dictionary of philosophy and psychology II* (p. 748). London: Macmillan.

Pocheptsov, O. G. (1992). Mind your mind: Or some ways of distorting facts while telling the truth. *ETC: A Review of General Semantics, 49*(4), 398–404.

Powell, M. (1985). Purposive vagueness: An evaluative dimension of vague quantifying expressions. *Journal of Linguistics, 21,* 31–50.

Reah, D. (1998). *The language of newspapers.* London: Routledge.

Rowland, T. (2007). 'Well maybe not exactly, but it's around fifty basically?': Vague language in mathematics classrooms. In J. Cutting (Ed.), *Vague language explored* (pp. 79–96). Basingstoke: Palgrave Macmillan.

Ruzaitė, J. (2007). *Vague language in educational settings: Quantifiers and approximators in British and American English.* Frankfurt am Main: Peter Lang.

Sabet, P. G. (2013). *Interaction through vague language: L1 and L2 perspectives.* Unpublished Doctoral dissertation, Curtin University.

Sabet, P., & Zhang, G. (2015). *Communicating through vague language: A comparative study of L1 and L2 speakers.* London: Palgrave Macmillan.

Scollon, R., & Scollon, S. W. (1995). *Intercultural communication.* Oxford: Blackwell.

Searle, J. R. (1965). What is a speech act? In M. Black (Ed.), *Philosophy in America* (pp. 1–16). London: Allen & Unwin.

Searle, J. R. (1975a). *A taxonomy of illocutionary acts.* Minneapolis: University of Minnesota Press.

Searle, J. R. (1975b). Indirect speech acts. In P. Cole & J. L. Morgan (Eds.), *Syntax and semantics. Volume 3: Speech acts* (pp. 59–82). Cambridge, MA: Academic Press.

Sears, D. O., & Kosterman, R. (1994). Mass media and political persuasion. In S. Shavitt & T. Brock (Eds.), *Persuasion: Psychological insights and perspectives* (pp. 251–278). Boston: Allyn and Bacon.

Shirato, J., & Stapleton, P. (2007). Comparing English vocabulary in a spoken learner corpus with a native speaker corpus: Pedagogical implications arising from an empirical study in Japan. *Language Teaching Research, 11*(4), 393–412.

Sobrino, A. (2015). Inquiry about the origin and abundance of vague language: An issue for the future. In R. Seising, E. Trillas, & J. Kacprzyk (Eds.), *Towards the future of fuzzy logic* (pp. 117–136). Cham, Switzerland: Springer.

Spencer-Oatey, H. (Ed.). (2004). *Culturally speaking: Managing rapport through talk across cultures.* London: A&C Black.

Stubbe, M., & Holmes, J. (1995). You know, eh and other 'exasperating expressions': An analysis of social and stylistic variation in the use of pragmatic devices in a sample of New Zealand English. *Language and Communication, 15*(1), 63–88.

Stubbs, M. (1986). A matter of prolonged field work: Notes towards a modal grammar of English. *Applied Linguistics, 7,* 1–25.

Suzuki, T. (2008). *A corpus-based study of the speech act of "comforting": Naturalness and appropriateness for English language teaching.* Paper presented at the 13th PAAL Conference, University of Hawaii, Manoa, USA.

Tagliamonte, S. A., & Denis, D. (2010). The stuff of change: General extenders in Toronto, Canada. *Journal of English Linguistics, 38*(4), 335–368.

Tannen, D. (1984). *Conversational style: Analyzing talk among friends.* Norwood, NJ: Ablex.

Tausczik, Y. R., & Pennebaker, J. W. (2010). The psychological meaning of words: LIWC and computerized text analysis methods. *Journal of Language and Social Psychology, 29*(1), 24–54.

Tayebi, T. (2018). *Impoliteness in Persian: A cultural linguistics perspective.* Unpublished Ph.D. thesis, Monash University, Australia.

Terkourafi, M. (2001). *Politeness in Cypriot Greek: A frame-based approach.* Unpublished Ph.D. thesis, University of Cambridge, UK.

Terkourafi, M. (2011). The puzzle of indirect speech. *Journal of Pragmatics, 43*(11), 2861–2865.

Terraschke, A., & Holmes, J. (2007). 'Und Tralala': Vagueness and general extenders in German and New Zealand English. In J. Cutting (Ed.), *Vague language explored* (pp. 198–220). Basingstoke: Palgrave Macmillan.

Thaler, V. (2012). Mitigation as modification of illocutionary force. *Journal of Pragmatics, 44*(6–7), 907–919.

Trappes-Lomax, H. (2007). Vague language as a means of self-protective avoidance: Tension management in conference talks. In J. Cutting (Ed.), *Vague language explored* (pp. 117–137). Basingstoke: Palgrave Macmillan.

Vallauri Lombardi, E. (2016). Implicits as evolved persuaders. In K. Allan, A. Capone, & I. Kecskes (Eds.), *Pragmemes and theories of language use* (pp. 724–748). Cham, Switzerland: Springer.

van Deemter, K. (2012). *Not exactly: In praise of vagueness*. Oxford, UK: Oxford University Press.

van Dijk, T. (1988). *News as discourse*. Hillsdale, NJ: Lawrence Erlbaum.

Walsh, S., O'Keeffe, A., & McCarthy, M. (2008). '…post-colonialism, multilingualism, structuralism, feminism, post-modernism and so on and so forth': A comparative analysis of vague category markers in academic discourse. In A. Adel & R. Reppen (Eds.), *Corpora and discourse: The challenges of different settings* (pp. 9–29). Amsterdam: John Benjamins.

Watts, R. J. (2003). *Politeness*. Cambridge: Cambridge University Press.

Williamson, T. (1996). *Vagueness*. London: Routledge.

Zhang, G. (2011). Elasticity of vague language. *Intercultural Pragmatics, 8*, 571–599.

Zhang, G. (2013). The impact of touchy topics on vague language use. *Journal of Asian Pacific Communication, 23*, 87–118.

Zhang, G. (2015). *Elastic language: How and why we stretch our words*. Cambridge: Cambridge University Press.

Zhang, G. (2016). How elastic *a little* can be and how much *a little* can do in Chinese. *Chinese Language and Discourse, 7*(1), 1–22.

Zhang, G., & Sabet, P. G. (2016). Elastic 'I think': Stretching over L1 and L2. *Applied Linguistics, 37*(3), 334–353.

Zhao, X., & Zhang, G. (2012). *Negotiating with vague language: A Chinese perspective*. Beijing: China Social Sciences Press.

3

Methodology

This study is exploratory and empirical in nature, and is based on two corpora of the reality television show *The Voice*, one in Chinese and the other in English. The corpus is spoken and naturally occurring because VL/EL is particularly prevalent in spoken language (Biber, Johansson, Leech, Conrad, & Finegan, 2010; Carter & McCarthy, 1997; Channell, 1994, p. 197) and natural language is typically representative of EL patterns (Zhang, 2015). The analysis focuses on how and why elasticity is manifested, to reveal how interlocutors use EL and how utterances are stretched to effectively deal with situations.

Two main discourse types are investigated in this study: persuasion and comforting. These two forms of discourse are commonly found in everyday life, on an almost daily basis. The findings should be relevant for understanding the role that EL plays in these two contexts, and also useful for communicational education and training in general.

The data are naturally occurring, institutional and video recorded, which is most suitable for the objectives of this study. The specific methods employed in this study are designed to explore the research questions (stated in Sect. 1.2) by examining the interconnected aspects of EL word clusters, pragmatic functions, social factors and the impact

© The Author(s) 2019
G. Zhang and V. Parvaresh, *Elastic Language in Persuasion and Comforting*,
https://doi.org/10.1007/978-3-030-28460-2_3

of speech elements. Such a multi-faceted analysis aims to provide a robust account of EL, which is important to ensure the validity of the claims that are being made in this study.

3.1   The Rationale Behind the Research Design

This study uses a mixed methods research design, employing both qualitative (primary) and quantitative approaches. The data analysis is conducted at lexical, pragmatic function and sociocultural levels. At the lexical level, types and clusters of elastic terms are discussed to demonstrate how EL is realised. The contextualised analysis focuses primarily on verbal activities, strengthened by anecdotal non-verbal activities. Zhang (2015) finds that non-verbal activities can reveal or confirm the implicature interpretation and the speaker's intended meaning.

3.1.1 Mixed Methods Design

While this study is a combination of the quantitative (frequency) and qualitative (pragmatic functions, sociocultural factors), the latter is the main focus. The mixed methods research design maximises the strength of data triangulation, and takes advantage of the best parts of both quantitative and qualitative approaches (Jick, 1979; Schönefeld, 2011; Stubbs, 1986). Triangulation refers to employing a combination of the various types of data of the same phenomenon (Creswell, 2008, p. 553). In this study, frequency data provide a general picture of EL use, while pragmatic function and sociocultural factors data offer a contextual and in-depth explanation of the use of EL.

A frequency analysis provides the macro-patterns of EL use, with the remainder of the qualitative study painting, in detail, a micro-picture of EL use. Each, on their own, would not be ideal in terms of providing credible empirical evidence for the claims being made in this study, because the former lacks contextual information and the latter lacks important generalisation (Creswell & Plano Clark, 2007). These two methods complement each other, but they should not simply be put together: the results derived from them need to be integrated, compared and fully explained (Creswell, 2009). A mixed methods research design is justified in this study because it can provide a rich account of EL frequency, function and underpinning factors.

In this study, both types of data (qualitative and quantitative) are collected and calculated, but are not given equal weight. The focus is on qualitative data, as the pragmatic functions of EL and the underpinning sociocultural factors are the primary aims of this study. Thus, this study adopts a primarily qualitative approach, as it examines the comprehensive process of interaction and negotiation between participants, and presents a detailed analysis of the data with the help of the contextual information in question.

A discussion regarding function frequency is also provided to give an overall picture of how the pragmatic functions are distributed among the six categories. Based on these frequencies, we will also examine the relationship between the pragmatic functions and the speech acts of persuasion and comforting, for example, whether or not the comforting speech act would generate more mitigating moves.

The main qualitative and supplementary quantitative approaches are presented primarily in the two data analysis chapters, Chapters 4 and 5. Together they present general EL patterns, as well as contextualised explanations for these frequency patterns.

3.1.2 Public and Formal Discourse

EL, such as *sort of*, is found less frequently in TV socio-political interviews than in conversations (Parvaresh & Zhang, 2019). This is perhaps because EL tends to be used in informal rather than in formal situations (Aijmer, 1984), although it is also frequently found in formal situations such as academic and public discussions (Lin, 2010). The setting for this study is public and formal, rather than private and informal, which might influence how language is used. Cotterill (2007) states that a courtroom discourse differs from conversation discourse, because conversational concessions are not available to the defendant and lawyer in a courtroom. Similarly, in TV shows, participants are aware that this is a public arena, and something that they may say in private would not be suitable for airing on TV.

Cheng (2007) compares four types of spoken discourse: academic (e.g. lectures, telephone interviews), business (e.g. meetings, informal office talks), conversation (e.g. chats in pubs and homes) and public (e.g. public speeches, forum discussions). She finds that the type of discourse appears to be the main factor in terms of the frequency and form of VL used in the data: conversation and business discourses attracted more VL use, whereas formal academic and public discourses influenced VL use to a lesser degree. Cheng attributes this to differences in the communicative purposes and formality of the discourse types. She also raised an important point: "There remains the possibility that VL may be achieved with other, less frequent forms in more formal discourse events, such as academic and public discourse, rather than that they are less vague" (p. 178). This aspect was explored in this study, where some less frequent forms did occur, as illustrated in the data discussions of Chapters 4–6.

3.1.3 Naturally Occurring Data

This type of data is naturally occurring, which provides the necessary contextual cues for the pragmatic analysis of EL, and is the most appropriate for this study. For example, invented language examples can be misleading (Sinclair, 1991), because although they might be grammatical, they are not appropriate in real-life communication (Channell, 1994, p. 38). According to Channell, linguists' intuitions may not be empirically valid, and using real-life is much more superior than using invented data. Discourse completion tests and role-play data are somewhat decontextualised examples and are collected in a non-natural setting and, therefore, "they are at best indicative of the understandings which may arise in natural settings" (Channell, 1994, p. 76).

As argued by Zhang (2011, 2015), while public TV shows differ from private conversations to some extent, according to research data collection ethical protocols, they are similar because participants are aware that they will be recorded, whether in a private or public setting.

Therefore, in this sense, none of our collected data is completely natural, as commented on by Labov (1972, on the observer's paradox), Speer (2002) and Gassner (2012). Naturally occurring data best represent our actual language use, and are certainly better than other methods in terms of getting close to real-world communication.

A wide range of language discourse occurs in the real world and, therefore, our research needs to be representative of the types of discourse that exist. Media discourse, including TV reality shows, is an integral part of our daily life, and studies of media discourse should be just as relevant as those of non-media discourse. It might be a little premature to think that all research should be based on day-to-day conversations, with any other types being less representative of language use. Media communication is increasingly becoming more important in our digital world and, therefore, this study on TV reality shows is justified for being current and useful in the promotion of well-informed and evidence-based research on media communication.

In a way, media communication is just as naturally based as day-to-day conversation, because the former occurs every day and we cannot live without it. While some evidence of edited dialogues was detected in the data, they were limited in number. However, the focus of this study is on the pragmatic functions of language use, rather than in speaking turns themselves, and so the impact of some limited editing would be minimal.

3.1.4 Video Data

The data for this study are in the form of video recordings, a much superior format compared to audio only recordings. Video data provide both sound and image, and it is possible to replay and review the fine details of both verbal and non-verbal activities (Psathas, 1995). The greater accuracy and reliability provided by the data analysis, particularly with regards to contextual clues such as facial features, eye movements and body language, will develop a deeper and better understanding of language use. Where appropriate, this study will utilise this additional non-verbal information in the data analysis in conjunction with verbal information. Although the non-verbal aspects are not the focus of this study, an ad hoc analysis can and does still produce some useful contextual clues in determining the speaker's intentions, the implicature of the language used and so on. The tabulation approach enhances the credibility of the data analysis.

The demographic information of the participants in video data is another advantage, and is particularly useful for a qualitative study like the current one (Zhang, 2015). As she highlights, demographic information is useful in examining the possible influences of both cultural and social factors (e.g. age, status) which will be analysed in this study.

All the above information cannot be captured by audio recordings alone (Dörnyei, 2007). Video data allow information to be recalled for clarification purposes, where needed. By using this type of data, the researcher may be able "to gain access to the thoughts, feelings, concerns, interpretations, reactions, etc." of the participants (Pomerantz, 2005, p. 96).

Video data are commonly used for its versatility, richness, flexibility and dynamics (Zhang, 2015, p. 71). While it is more problematic to obtain video data and more time consuming to analyse it (Dörnyei, 2007, p. 139), the benefits of using it may still warrant choosing it for the visual information about contexts and participants that it provides to the data analysis (Zhang, 2015, p. 71).

3.2   Data

The documentary television genre has been preferred for its authenticity and sociality (Thornborrow & Morris, 2004; Tolson, 2006). The corpora in this study are taken from the reality TV show *The Voice*. Few studies have investigated the genre of reality TV shows (Lorenzo-Dus & Blitvich, 2013), and this study aims to contribute new resources to this field.

Video recordings of the series were obtained online, mainly from YouTube. It is an international, reality, television singing competition franchise, originally created by the Dutch television producer John de Mol. *The Voice* is a popular programme; other countries have adapted the format and aired their own versions since 2011. The show features five stages of competition: producers' auditions (not televised), blind auditions, battle rounds, knockouts and live performance shows. The second stage, the blind auditions, is the focus of this study.

A blind audition involves interactions between four coaches, who tend to be renowned music experts, and the contestants themselves. The contestants sing, with the coaches then deciding whether he/she wants that singer on his/her team. The coaches sit in chairs which face away from the stage to avoid seeing the contestants. If a coach likes what they are hearing, they press a button to rotate their chair to signify that they are interested in working with that contestant. If two or more coaches want the same singer, then the tables are turned and the singer has the choice of which coach they want to collaborate with. The blind auditions end when each coach has decided upon a set number of contestants to work with. Coaches will then oversee the training of each chosen team member and prepare them for the next stages, including the battle rounds (the vocal face-off) and live performance shows, to decide the final winner of the show, who will be named 'The Voice' and receive the grand prize of a recording contract.

The Chinese version of *The Voice* has two names: (1) *Zhongguo Hao Shengyin* (中国好声音, *The Good Voice of China*) screened between 2012 and 2015 and (2) *Zhongguo Xin Shengyin* (中国新歌声, *The New Voice of China/Sing! China*) screened since 2016 in a new format. The producer of both is Zhejian Satellite Television. For this study, the data were collected from all the seasons screened between 2012 and 2017 (six seasons in total), with each season having five episodes. Each episode lasted approximately 90 minutes and each contestant performed for approximately 8.5 minutes, giving a total of 45 hours of recordings. Each episode had ten contestants on average, resulting in a total of 316 contestants in the Chinese corpus.

The American version of *The Voice* was first broadcasted on NBC in 2011 and is based on *The Voice Holland* (*The Voice*, US TV series), and has already aired for 15 complete seasons. Each season of *The Voice* begins with 'blind auditions', during which four coaches do all in their power to form their own team of artists by convincing the best contestants to join them. The coaches then continue mentoring their team members throughout the entire season.

The American version is similar in basic structure to the Chinese version: the coaches' chairs are faced towards the audience during each contestant's performance; "those interested in an artist press their button, which turns their chair towards the artist and illuminates the bottom of the chair to read 'I want you'" (*The Voice*, US TV series). When the performance concludes, "an artist either defaults to the only coach who turned around, or selects his or her coach if more than one coach expresses interest" (*The Voice*, US TV series). Since the 14th season, a new twist called the "Block" has been introduced, "which allows one coach to block another coach from getting a contestant" (*The Voice*, US TV series).

The selection of *The Voice* data is in keeping with the purpose of this study. The data can provide situations of persuasion and comforting, enabling the investigation of how EL is used in TV reality shows to proceed. Participants employ strategies to persuade or comfort, and EL is expected to play an important role in these situations. *The Voice* was selected for this study because it provided data rich with persuasion or comforting interactions, which can be hard to find elsewhere. Excerpts exhibiting EL use were selected and discussed. This study concentrates on the 'blind auditions' section of the programme, as they provide more EL and interactions among the participants for analysis. Specifically, the auditions produce two main situations: a contestant is either chosen by one or more coaches, or is not chosen at all. In the former case, if more than one coach wants to collaborate with the contestant, they need to persuade the contestant to join his/her team, so often an act of persuasion is required. In the latter case, coaches may need to comfort those contestants who fail to be selected, and thus a comforting act is needed. This study investigates the use of EL in persuasion and comforting, and the blind audition data serve this aim well.

The blind auctions involve the singing performance itself (no interactions) and interactions among participants (the data for this study). The data are sufficiently substantial to ensure the empirical credibility of this study. In the case of the Chinese data, the corpus consists of 30 episodes (five episodes per season) across all six seasons from 2012 to 2017 (one season per year). For the English data, as the number of episodes per season tended to vary, and due to issues around availability and access, a total of 34 episodes from seasons 8 (2015) to 16 (2019) were chosen. The approach of selecting all data from a time range is more random than a pick and choose approach from different seasons and episodes. The criterion used in the selection of the English data episodes was the availability of video recordings.

The transcription of data was completed by the two authors and their research assistants. Only relevant excerpts were transcribed for data analysis. To ensure agreement between the different transcribers, a transcription guideline was developed which each transcriber had to adhere to. Transcripts were double-checked for accuracy, with some minor changes being made during the second round of checking. The transcription process used conventional orthography, which adequately served the purpose of the analysis. It included actual speech and basic non-verbal activities, such as pausing and salient body language. Non-verbal activities were used in the analysis to help with interpreting the intentions of participants.

The data are mostly comprised of non-confrontational interactions between coaches and contestants, and among the coaches. Occasionally a coach talks directly and briefly to the camera to communicate with the TV audience. The dynamics of the televisual show included both the participants on TV and off TV, where they are ratified participants or 'encircling hearers', covertly in the background of 'display' talk (Cotterill, 2007, p. 100; Goffman, 1981, p. 137).

3.3   Data Analysis

The data analysis in this study adopts Zhang's (2015) coding system. This study adopts the position that EL is manifested through a closed set of identifiable items, which need to be interpreted in the relevant context (Cheng, 2007, p. 162). EL signals that the utterance is to be interpreted vaguely, as a result of the negotiation between the speaker and the hearer (Cheng & Warren, 2001, p. 82).

This study examines the elasticity in language use, "manifested particularly by the frequency, form and functions of the language, which will vary between different groups of speakers, among other variables"

(Zhang, 2015, p. 6). The current analysis is performed at three levels, and these are integrated and appropriate for addressing the research questions that are listed in Chapter 1, namely the lexical, pragmatic function and sociocultural levels. Where appropriate, frequency analysis was conducted, for example, when examining the relationship between the number of chair turns and the use of the six lexical categories, the frequencies of the two items were compared.

Only interactions (e.g. dialogues) were analysed in this study, monologues (e.g. the introduction of contestants, voice-overs) were not, the reason for this being that the interactions which reveal the negotiation process among the participants and the role that EL plays are shown through the interplay between speaker and listener. The dynamics of dialogues is essential for presenting a collaborative account of EL use, which is lacking in monologues.

3.3.1 Lexical Analysis

A lexical analysis includes a discussion about words and word clustering, as the likely collocation of such items reflects the importance of the genre (Cheng, 2007, p. 171) and provides evidence of EL formations and the lexical-pragmatic choices of the speaker (Zhang, 2015, p. 73). For example, in the cluster of *sort of expensive*, *sort of* is the stretcher and *expensive* is a clustering element. The analysis also looked at the padding words that occur with them, including discourse markers and fillers: *I don't know, well, you know, erm* and others. The lexical categorisation used in this study is adopted from Zhang (2015), whose system consists of the following four types:

a. Approximate stretcher: two subtypes (approximators and quantifiers), exemplified by *about, many*.
b. General stretcher: three subtypes (general terms, placeholders and category makers), exemplified by *something, thingy, or things like that*.
c. Scalar stretcher: two subtypes (intensifiers and softeners), exemplified by *very, a bit*.

d. Epistemic stretcher: namely epistemic stance markers, exemplified by
possibly, *I think*.
(Zhang, 2015, p. 36)

The above four categories make up a closed set of EL items, and supports Cheng's (2007) concept. Dealing with a closed set of language entities should make the research range more tangible and easier to verify.

In Table 3.1, some words can be placed into more than one category, and the contextual information in question may help to make that decision. For example, *dagai* (大概, about, perhaps) can be both an AQ and an EP. When it is used in conjunction with a number, it is more likely to form an AQ as an approximator, e.g. Ta **dagai** shisui (他大概十岁, he is about ten years old). Here *about*+number = an AQ (making an approximation). However, when used in conjunction with a verb, it is more likely to form an EP as an epistemic stretcher, e.g. Ta **dagai** zou le (他大概走了, perhaps he's left). In this case, *perhaps*+verb = an EP (highlighting the speaker's opinion).

Table 3.2 lists the elastic items that were typically found in the English data of this study. The following is an example of how EL is used in English:

> Wife: You *seem* to be talking to Mary *a lot* recently.
> Husband: I talk to *everyone*.

The wife uses *seem* to tone down her accusation, and *a lot* to tone up the frequency of talking. In his answer, the husband uses *everyone* to head off his suspicious wife. In the category of general stretcher (e.g. *things*), this study will also include words like *everyone*, *everything* and *everywhere*, as they perform an intriguing function as shown in the above example. The *everyone* form of usage has been omitted from the literature, and this study explores its unique features which were revealed in the data.

Four maxims of language stretching are proposed in Zhang (2015), namely 'go approximate', 'go general', 'go scalar' and 'go epistemic'.

Table 3.1 Chinese EL lexical items in the data

Items	Examples
Approximate stretcher (AQ)	yue, dayue, dagai, shaoliang, shaoshu, daduoshu, jishaoshu, jiangjin, jin, xuduo, yidian, dian, yidiandian, xie, yixie, youdian, chaoguo, gaoyu, zhishao, diyu, shaoyu, duoyu, dabufen, daban, duoban, yishang, yixia, jihu, xiexu, zuoyou, shaoxu, shaowei, jinhu, rutong, jihu, man, shaoxu, daduo, jihu, dajiliang, zhuduo, daliang, ji, liang, sannian, chabuduo, wushu, (chang) liangju, shangbai, baishilaige, kuai (sannian)
	约，大约，大概，少量，少数，大多数，极少数，将近，近，许多，一点，点，一点点，些，一些，有点，超过，高于，至少，低于，少于，多于，大部分，大半，多半，以上，以下，几乎，些许，左右，稍许，稍微，近乎，如同，几乎，满，少许，大多，几乎，大剂量，诸多，大量，几，两、三(年)，差不多，无数，(唱) 两句，上百，百十来个，快 (三年)
	about, around, more or less, small amount, minority, most, very few, near, close to, many, a little, a bit, a little bit, some, a little, somewhat, over, higher than, at least, lower than, less than, more than, majority, most, majority, over, below, almost, some, about, a little, a little bit, almost, similar to, almost, very, little, most, almost, large amount, many, large amount, several, two or three (years), almost, countless, (sing) a couple of sentences, about 100, over 100, close to (three years)
General stretcher (GE)	dongxi, deng. dengdeng, mouwu, moushi, mouren, moushi, zheyang nayang de, youshi, youxie, youde, youdian, mouxie, zhexie, youren, huoduohuoshao, duoduoshaoshao, duo shao, qiyu, budeng, bufen, yixie, shengyu, dadaxiaoxiao, daxiao, zhongzhong, ge zhong, gezhonggeyang, yiduan, xie, canyu, bushi, geshigeyang, youshime (xiang shuo?), (chang ge ge) shimede, (chang ge) shenme (qing ge a), xiang ni zheyang yilei xue yuan, (buguan shi xiege, hai shi zuoren yehao) huozhe shi zenmeyang, (jiu shi ta shuo de) na zhong /na xie, (mei you tamen geli xiede) naxie shenme (haoche a, meinü a) zhexie dongxi
	东西，等，等等，某物，某事，某人，某时，这样那样的，有时，有些，有的，有点，某些，这些，有人，或多或少，多多少少，多少，其余，不等，部分，一些，剩余，大大小小，大小，种种，各种，各种各样，一段，些，残余，不时，各式各样，有什么(想说?)，(唱个歌)什么的，(唱个)什么(情歌啊)，像你这样一类学员，(不管是写歌，还是做人也好)或者是怎么样，(就是他说的)那种/那些，(没有他们歌里写的)那些什么(豪车啊，美女啊)这些东西
	things, etc., etc. etc., something, something, someone, sometime, and that kind of, sometimes, some, some of, a little, some, these, someone, more or less, more or less, more or less, the rest, and things like that, a part of, some, the remaining, a variety of, more or less, all kinds, a range of, all kinds, a period, some, the remaining, from time to time, all kinds, what (to say?), sing a song or something, (sing a love song) or something, students like you, (whether it's write a song and be a person) or something like that, (that's what he says) that kind or those kinds, (nothing like written in their songs) those things (e.g. luxury cars, pretty women) these things

(continued)

Table 3.1 (continued)

Items	Examples
Scalar stretcher (SC)	tongchang, qingwei, ou, ou'er, ji, chang, changchang, duo, xiangdang, shifen, shao, hen, tebie, daduo, shaozhiyoushao, po, jingchang, jiaoduo, wangwang, guofen, tai, jin, zhi, guodu, yuan, dafu, bushi, jiduan, shichang, xuduo, zheme, name, jidu, yuanyuan, gaodu, lüe, dada, youdian, dongbudong, hao (duo), man (duo), geng, ting (hao), chao (duo), butai (shihe), zhende (henhao), zhen (bang), (deng) yixia, dabu (miao), ruci (dongting), haohao (xiangxiang), verb + verb (e.g. shishi), verb yi verb (e.g. shiyishi)
	通常，轻微，偶，偶而，极，常，常常，多，相当，十分，少，很，特别，大多，少之又少，颇，经常，较多，往往，过分，太，仅，只，过度，远，大幅，不时，极端，时常，许多，这么，那么，极度，远远，高度，略，大大，有点，动不动，好（多），蛮（多），更，挺（好），超（多），不太（适合），真的（很好），真（棒），（等）一下，大不（妙），如此（动听），好好（想想），verb + verb (e.g. 试试), verb 一 verb (e.g. 试一试)
	usually, slightly, occasionally, occasionally, extremely, often, often, more, quite, very, little, very, specially, most, very few, quite a few, often, quite a few, often, overly, too, only, only, excessive, far, large scale, frequently, extreme, often, much, so, such, extreme, far, highly, a little, very much, a bit, quite often, much (more), quite (a lot), even, quite (good), really (good), not very (suitable), really (nice), so (good), (wait) for a second, very much not (good), such (pleasant to hear), (think) very carefully, verb + verb (e.g. try a bit), verb yi verb (e.g. just try it)
Epistemic stretcher (EP)	kenen, yexu, huoxu, kansi, xiangsi, xiangxin, sihu, fangfu, haoxiang, juede, buyiding, shuobu ding, guji, ba*
	可能，也许，或许，看似，像似，相信，似乎，彷彿，好像，觉得，不一定，说不定，估计，吧
	possible, perhaps, perhaps, appears, seemingly, believe, looks like, as if, seems, feel, unsure, uncertain, estimated, ba

Note *ba: this expresses the speaker's uncertainty (Zhang, 2016). For example, Ni shi Lao Wang de erzi ba? (你是老王的儿子吧? You are Lao Wang's son, aren't you?). In this case, the speaker is not 100% sure, and is just asking for confirmation

These maxims tally with the four lexical categories which are discussed in the data analysis of this study, most notably in Chapters 4 and 5.

While the four categories stated in Tables 3.1 and 3.2 are the focus of this chapter, discourse particles such as *well, you know, erm,* also need to be analysed, as they might indicate that the speaker needs to buy time to perform a word search or conduct self-repair. Similarly, non-verbal activities (e.g. facial expressions, pauses) may help in the classification of the pragmatic functions of EL.

Table 3.2 English lexical items

Terms	Examples
Approximate stretcher (AQ)	about, at least, a couple, a couple of, a few, a little, a little bit more, a little bit of, a lot, a lot more, a lot of (noun), a million, a nudge, a while, as much as, couple of, enough, less, lesser, lots of, one, one or two, many, more, most, much, plenty of, some (of), thousands, tons of, years
General stretcher (GE)	all kinds of, all that, all this, and all that, and everything, and like that, and stuff and stuff like that, any, anybody, anyone, anything, anytime, certain point, every, everybody, everyone, everything, no one, nobody, nothing, nowhere or something, other, parts, some, somebody, someone, something, somewhere stuff, thing(s), this thing, those, whatever, wherever, whoever
Scalar stretcher (SC)	almost, apparently, a bit, a lot, absolutely, at all, amazingly, as much, all about as much as, badly, clearly, completely, definitely, desperately, extremely, far beyond, far and beyond, fully, incredibly, kind of, most, more, much, much more, not too much, over-, pretty, really, seriously, so, such, such a, super, tremendously, the most, too, totally, truly, very, very much, way, whole lot
Epistemic stretcher (EP)	appear, as if, believe, could (not), feel, feel like, may, maybe, might, most likely, I think, in my opinion, possible, possibly, probably, seem(s), like, sounds like, to be honest with you, would

3.3.2 Pragmatic Function Analysis

This level of discourse analysis examines the discursive moves that manifest how EL is used to serve the speaker's communicative goals, in particular how the coaches persuade the chosen contestants to join their teams and also, when needed, how they comfort the disappointed contestants who failed selection.

For classifying the pragmatic functions of EL, this study adopts the six categories provided by Zhang (2015, p. 44):

a. Just-right elastic: when precise information is lacking or unnecessary, an unspecific but right amount of information may be provided, e.g. there were *a couple of thousand* people in the square.

b. Rapport elastic: form a close relationship among the interactants, e.g. Do you want a drink *or something*?
c. Mitigating elastic: tone down the utterance for politeness, face wants, etc., e.g. I *sort of* don't want to go.
d. Intensifying elastic: tone up the utterance to strengthen the claim, e.g. This is *very* important, you have to attend.
e. Self-protection elastic: qualify the commitment to shield the speaker from the risk of making mistakes or being wronged, e.g. She *might* like you, but I'm not sure.
f. Evasive elastic: withhold information inappropriately, sometimes bordering on deception, e.g. *I think* I have not seen her before. (Note: it is not true, though.)

The pragmatic functions of this study have been analysed according to the above six categories. For example, self-protection is a strategy to minimise and protect against communicative risk, and is used to achieve indirectness and avoidance of commitment but not to deliberately confuse or deceive. The distribution of the above six categories may vary between discourses. For example, in this study where persuasion and comforting are the focus, intensifying elastic and mitigating elastic would be more applicable than evasive elastic.

While we are able to fairly clearly distinguish between the data using the above classification, there will evidently be some cases of overlapping, as noted by Zhang (2015). The cases can be explained by considering the concept that one particular EL utterance may serve more than one function (e.g. Cheshire, 2007; Zhang, 2016). The above six categories are conceptually formulated to aid the discussion of the pragmatic functions of EL. However, in reality, there is fluidity between the categories, and thus, where relevant, the issue of the multifunctionality of EL is discussed in this study.

All available contextual clues were utilised to help with the coding of the pragmatic functions. For example, gesture is considered to be an integral part of manipulating language; as with verbal language, gesture can also perform descriptive, indicative and pragmatic functions (Kendon, 2004). In this study, gestures and other non-verbal activities are considered to be ad hoc evidence when coding EL.

3.3.3 Impact Factor Analysis

Exploration of the factors that impact on the elasticity of EL was conducted to better understand the linguistic behaviour of EL. For example, factors of age, gender, culture and political correctness were investigated in this study. Another issue investigated by the study was the indirect and direct approaches that were adopted by the participants. For example, in China, it is traditional to perform the 'refusal dance' (e.g. A offers B a drink, A should insist at least two or three times, and B should not accept the first time). Is this kind of tradition an underpinning factor in shaping stretching behaviours in the data? The manner in which culture, socio-interpersonal relationships and linguistic features are interrelated may shed some light on the study of language stretching.

Excerpts from the data were selected to illustrate both how EL was used and the stretch work unfolded. They demonstrated the ways in which the elasticity of language helped speakers to achieve their goals. Each individual excerpt analysis is prefaced by some brief background information to place it in context. Participants had their names provided by the shows. To avoid the common mistake of overlooking responses from the hearer, the discourse level analysis focuses on the speaker–hearer interaction, which helps to reveal the illocutionary force of the speaker.

The different levels of analysis are expected to produce rather intricate results. One challenge lies in ensuring the accuracy of the analysis. The two authors are linguistically trained to perform data analysis: one author coded the Chinese corpus and the other coded the English corpus. Some borderline cases were discussed to reach an agreement.

3.4 Limitations of the Research

This study has some potential weaknesses and, where possible, their impact will be minimised to enhance the validity of the findings.

TV documentaries and traditional linguistic data differ in that the former may be an edited version of lengthy footage (editing is performed prior to the programme being aired), but the latter is often verbatim data which has not undergone editing (Zhang, 2015). This difference could influence how EL behaviours are represented, but the impact "should be in limited capacity" (Zhang, 2011, p. 584). While TV show data may be edited before being aired, editing should be limited and, therefore, there is no reason to doubt the validity of such data (Zhang, 2011, 2015).

This study draws on data obtained from TV shows, a form of public discourse. Conclusions that are derived from public discourse are likely to differ from those obtained from private discourse. The impact of these different forms of discourse should not be overlooked. For example, institutional talks display adaptations and variations to ordinary conversations (Atkinson & Heritage, 1984; Drew & Heritage, 1992). The key is to avoid over-generalisation, and the conclusions observed in this study are based on "specific contexts of interaction", they are not "laws and general principles", but "clues and guidelines" (Cheng & Tsui, 2009, p. 2367). Therefore, this study does not intend to claim more than is supported by the data, and it is hoped that the findings will be applicable to other forms of discourse or, at the very least, have some implications for other areas of linguistics.

Very often, researchers are faced with the dilemma of coding linguistic data confidently and categorically, particularly when the pragmatics of language use is involved (Cheng & Tsui, 2009; Zhang, 2011, 2014). The classification of the pragmatic functions of EL tends to be problematic because "pragmatic inferences are not always clear" (Shuy, 2014, p. 22). The classification can only be performed with the assistance of contextual cues and, as no one can be absolutely sure what the speaker had in mind, we need to be cautious when using the classification of VL categories (Cotterill, 2007). In this study, coaches and contestants cannot be contacted to clarify why and what they said. However, this situation was improved by the researchers coding the data on the basis of contextual cues (verbal and non-verbal), and their expert judgement (Holmes, 1995, p. 40).

In particular, although we cannot be certain whether EL was used to save time and energy (O'Keeffe, 2003, p. 9) or to be deliberately vague (Powell, 1985, p. 31), participants are able to infer the reasons why a particular utterance was said (Levinson, 1983, p. 53). This ability to infer together with the careful coding conducted by the researchers have enabled the speaker's intention to be closely estimated, regardless of the fact that we can never be absolutely certain when coding the pragmatic functions of EL (Zhang, 2015, p. 74). Zhang also states that contextual triggers can also indicate the implicature of EL, including the immediate co-text that can determine the function of EL, as well as a wider context. Another approach that could be taken in this study is to explore the interaction between the speaker and hearer, though the latter should not be overlooked as "they are more open to empirical observation than information about speakers' intentions" (Channell, 1994, p. 26). It is hoped that a combination of researcher expertise and all the above-mentioned contextual clues may enhance accuracy when coding the pragmatic functions of EL.

Given that pragmatic function can never be a clear-cut issue, a different but important approach was employed to deal with the multifunctionality of EL. In this way, problems associated with the traditional practice of single function coding could be resolved. The elasticity approach is the only sensible way to minimise the impact of the unachievable, precise coding of EL. See Chapters 4 and 5 for further details.

3.5   Concluding Remarks

This chapter has discussed the methods that are employed in this study to answer the research questions listed in Chapter 1. This study is primarily qualitative in nature, coupled with an ad hoc frequency discussion where appropriate. This qualitative approach includes an exploration of a combination of EL forms, clustering, pragmatic functions and sociocultural factors.

The corpora consist of naturally occurring spoken data from *The Voice* in Chinese and English, enabling a comparative study to be made between the two languages. The reality TV programme, which was screened in the USA and China, involves expert coaches selecting and mentoring talented contestants with the aim of winning a recording contract. The data comprise 45 hours of Chinese and 43 hours of English recordings, a total of 88 hours, which is more than sufficient to ensure the empirical credibility of this study. The shows are rich in persuasion and comforting interactions, and language stretching is clearly evident. The two sets of English and Chinese data are comparable, and follow a similar format and speech setting.

The chosen corpora contain numerous persuasion and comforting situations, which are ideally suited to the objectives of this study. On-screen data provide both audio and video information, ensuring that every fine detail of each interaction is available for analysis; other data-gathering methods are unable to provide this level of information. The opportunity to recheck information, both verbal and non-verbal, helps to ensure the findings are accurate, which is particularly important for the qualitative analysis in terms of the detailed discourse features.

The use of real-life data is also promoted for highlighting the dynamic situations that contribute to language use, particularly when a qualitative study of language use is the focus of investigation. The data analysis is conducted: at a lexical level (types and clusters of elastic items) to show how EL is realised; at a discourse level (pragmatic functions) to show why EL is used; and at a sociocultural level to underscore the factors behind the use of EL. The data enable the linguistic realisation of EL to be investigated, and the correlation between EL forms, pragmatic functions and underpinning sociocultural factors to be determined. It was also shown that participants made strategic moves through their use of EL to achieve their communicative goals.

The data analysis of this study adopts primarily the EL classification proposed in Zhang (2015), which is more streamlined and is specifically devised for the coding of EL. Lexical items are classified into four categories: approximate stretchers, general stretchers, scalar stretchers and epistemic stretchers. Pragmatic functions are classified into six categories: just-right elastic, rapport elastic, mitigating elastic, intensifying elastic, self-protection elastic and evasive elastic.

This study reveals a few potential limitations. One is the possibility that the TV show data were edited before being aired, and thus the corpora are not truly 'naturally occurring data'. However, data editing was limited to only a few cases, reducing the likelihood that the credibility of the data will be compromised. Another limitation is the possibility of fluidity in the data coding, where an utterance could be classified in more than one category. To resolve this problem, unlike the traditional approach in which one utterance is assigned only one function, this study adopts the concept of multifunctionality for EL use, that is when coding EL, more than one function can be assigned to any given utterance. Given the above-mentioned limitations, we must be mindful not to overclaim when drawing conclusions from this research.

References

Aijmer, K. (1984). 'Sort of' and 'kind of' in English conversation. *Studia Linguistica, 38,* 118–128.

Atkinson, J. M., & Heritage, J. (Eds.). (1984). *Structures of social action: Studies in conversation analysis.* Cambridge: Cambridge University Press.

Biber, D., Johansson, S., Leech, G., Conrad, S., & Finegan, E. (2010). *Longman grammar of spoken and written English* (8th ed.). London: Longman.

Carter, R., & McCarthy, M. (1997). *Exploring spoken English.* Cambridge: Cambridge University Press.

Channell, J. (1994). *Vague language.* Oxford: Oxford University Press.

Cheng, W. (2007). The use of vague language across spoken genres in an intercultural Hong Kong corpus. In J. Cutting (Ed.), *Vague language explored* (pp. 161–181). Basingstoke: Palgrave Macmillan.

Cheng, W., & Tsui, A. B. M. (2009). 'Ahh ((laugh)) well there is no comparison between the two I think': How do Hong Kong Chinese and native speakers of English disagree with each other? *Journal of Pragmatics, 41*(11), 2365–2380.

Cheng, W., & Warren, M. (2001). The use of vague language in intercultural conversations in Hong Kong. *English World-Wide, 22*(1), 81–104.

Cheshire, J. (2007). Discourse variation, grammaticalisation and stuff like that. *Journal of Sociolinguistics, 11*(2), 155–193.

Cotterill, J. (2007). 'I think he was kind of shouting or something': Uses and abuses of vagueness in the British courtroom. In J. Cutting (Ed.), *Vague language explored* (pp. 97–114). Basingstoke: Palgrave Macmillan.

Creswell, J. W. (2008). *Educational research: Planning, conducting, and evaluating quantitative and qualitative research* (3rd ed.). Upper Saddle River, NJ: Prentice Hall.

Creswell, J. W. (2009). *Research design: Qualitative, quantitative, and mixed methods approaches* (3rd ed.). Los Angeles: Sage.

Creswell, J. W., & Plano Clark, V. L. (2007). *Designing and conducting mixed methods research.* Thousand Oaks: Sage.

Dörnyei, Z. (2007). *Research methods in applied linguistics.* Oxford: Oxford University Press.

Drew, P., & Heritage, J. (1992). Analyzing talk at work: An introduction. In P. Drew & J. Heritage (Eds.), *Talk at work* (pp. 3–65). Cambridge: Cambridge University Press.

Gassner, D. (2012). Vague language that is rarely vague[p]: A case study of "thing" in L1 and L2 discourse. *International Review of Pragmatics, 4*(1), 3–28.

Goffman, E. (1981). *Forms of talk.* Philadelphia: University of Philadelphia Press.

Holmes, J. (1995). *Women, men and politeness.* London: Longman.

Jick, T. D. (1979). Mixing qualitative and quantitative methods: Triangulation in action. *Administrative Science Quarterly, 24,* 602–611.

Kendon, A. (2004). *Gesture: Visible action as utterance.* Cambridge: Cambridge University Press.

Labov, W. (1972). *Sociolinguistic patterns.* Philadelphia, PA: University of Pennsylvania Press.

Levinson, S. C. (1983). *Pragmatics.* Cambridge: Cambridge University Press.

Lin, C. L. (2010). Discourse analysis and the teaching of translation. In V. Pellatt, K. Griffiths, & S. Wu (Eds.), *Teaching and testing interpreting and translating* (pp. 27–49). Bern: Peter Lang AG.

Lorenzo-Dus, N., & Blitvich, Pilar. (2013). *Real talk: Reality television and discourse analysis in action.* London: Palgrave Macmillan.

O'Keeffe, A. (2003). 'Like the wise virgins and all that jazz': Using a corpus to examine vague language and shared knowledge. In U. Connor & T. Upton (Eds.), *Applied corpus linguistics: A multidimensional perspective* (pp. 1–20). Amsterdam: Rodopi.

Parvaresh, V., & Zhang, G. (Eds.). (2019). Vagueness and elasticity of 'sort of' in TV discussion discourse in the Asian Pacific [Special issue]. *Journal of Asian Pacific Communication, 29*(1), 1–132.

Pomerantz, A. (2005). Using participants' video stimulated comments to complement analyses of interactional practices. In H. T. Molder & J. Potter (Eds.), *Conversation and cognition* (pp. 93–113). Cambridge: Cambridge University Press.

Powell, M. (1985). Purposive vagueness: An evaluative dimension of vague quantifying expressions. *Journal of Linguistics, 21,* 31–50.

Psathas, G. (1995). *Conversation analysis: The study of talk in interaction.* Thousand Oaks, CA: Sage.

Schönefeld, D. (Ed.). (2011). *Converging evidence: Methodological and theoretical issues for linguistic research.* Amsterdam: John Benjamins.

Shuy, R. W. (2014). *The language of murder cases.* Oxford: Oxford University Press.

Sinclair, J. M. (1991). *Corpus concordance collocation.* Oxford: Oxford University Press.

Speer, S. A. (2002). 'Natural' and 'contrived' data: A sustainable distinction? *Discourse Studies, 4,* 511–525.

Stubbs, M. (1986). A matter of prolonged field work: Notes towards a modal grammar of English. *Applied Linguistics, 7,* 1–25.

Thornborrow, J., & Morris, D. (2004). Gossip as strategy: The management of talk about others on reality TV show 'Big Brother'. *Journal of Sociolinguistics, 8*(2), 246–271.

Tolson, A. (2006). *Media talk: Spoken discourse on TV and radio.* Edinburgh: Edinburgh University Press.

Zhang, G. (2011). Elasticity of vague language. *Intercultural Pragmatics, 8,* 571–599.

Zhang, G. (2014). The elasticity of I think: Stretching its pragmatic functions. *Intercultural Pragmatics, 11*(2), 225–257.

Zhang, G. (2015). *Elastic language: How and why we stretch our words.* Cambridge: Cambridge University Press.

Zhang, G. (2016). How elastic *a little* can be and how much *a little* can do in Chinese. *Chinese Language and Discourse, 7*(1), 1–22.

4

Elastic Language in the Chinese Data

This chapter examines the linguistic behaviour of EL in Chinese. The data were obtained from blind auditions. The specific process for a blind audition is as follows: a contestant sings a song, and the coaches turn their chairs around if they like the performance. After that, the contestant is in the position to choose one coach and join their team for the competition. The excerpts selected below are the interactions that were conducted after each contestant was told whether they had been successfully selected. When none of the coaches turned around, the contestant generally needed to be comforted. When only one coach chose the contestant, normally very little persuasion was needed for the contestant to join their team, as the coach was not in competition with the other coaches. Persuasion tended to intensify when all four coaches turned their chairs around and were competing for the contestant. Often, as more coaches turned their chairs around, the competition between them intensified. In other words, if one coach turned around, there was the least competition; if two coaches turned around, the competition was more than with one coach; if three coaches turned around, the competition was more than with two coaches; and if all four coaches turned around, the competition was the most intense.

© The Author(s) 2019   **83**
G. Zhang and V. Parvaresh, *Elastic Language in Persuasion and Comforting*,
https://doi.org/10.1007/978-3-030-28460-2_4

As the competition heated up, the degree of persuasion also intensified, which provided rigorous interactional data for analysis.

The contestant usually chose the coach who was the most persuasive, and this provides us with the opportunity to investigate how the coach won over the contestant. This chapter looks at the role that EL plays in persuasion. The Chinese data were analysed on two levels, lexical and pragmatic, and the categorisation of these levels follows that previously discussed in Chapter 3.

4.1   Lexical Items

Four lexical categories are to be analysed here: approximate stretcher, general stretcher, scalar stretcher and epistemic stretcher (Zhang, 2015). This study adopts these four categories, and also adds additional, specific Chinese forms which are drawn from the Chinese corpus under investigation. For example, the Chinese final article *ba* indicates possibility and can be categorised as an epistemic stretcher. The reduplication of verbs and adjectives in Chinese expresses a strengthened or mitigated claim, which can be classified as a scalar stretcher, depending on the context in question.

4.1.1   Approximate Stretcher

According to Zhang (2015), approximate stretchers typically include two types: approximator + number (e.g. *about 20*) and vague quantifier (e.g. *many*). They are illustrated below.

Excerpt 1 (5/4/7*): Three speakers over three speaking turns. The contestant, Yang, sings well, so coach Zhou and coach Na want Yang in their team. [* denotes Season 5, Episode 4, Contestant 7, and so on.]

> T1** Na: Canting zai na tiao jie? (餐厅在哪条街? Which street is the restaurant in?)
> T2 Yang: Wusheng Donglu. (武圣东路。 Wusheng Road.)

T3 Yu: Li Na Ying jia hao jin, **dagai chabuduo** liangge xiaoshi **ba**. (离那英家好近, **大概差不多**两个小时**吧**. Very close to Na Ying's house, should be **about** two hours, **isn't it**?) [laughs]
[**T1 indicates 'speaking turn 1', and so on.]

Coach Na has been competing with Zhou to win over contestant Yang. Yang mentions that he is a small restaurant owner in Beijing. Towards the end of the conversation, it is time for Yang to select his coach. Just before Yang calls out the name of the coach, Na strategically stops him and asks where Yang's restaurant is in Beijing. Upon hearing the street name, coach Yu (who is not competing for this contestant) says, 'Oh it is very close to Na's house, would be **about two hours** away'. In T3, Yu uses three elastic expressions in a row, *dagai* ('about'), *chabuduo* ('around') and *ba* (final particle—tag, 'isn't it'). The first two are approximate stretchers, making the original precise number imprecise (Channell, 1994). In this case, *two hours* is a precise number, but *about two hours* is not. The final particle *ba* functions here as a discourse marker (Zhang, 2016) and brings in uncertainty: the speaker is not very sure about the statement, and adds *ba* to seek confirmation.

Yu appears to be joking here. While we don't know for sure whether or not coach Na's house is in the vicinity of Yang's restaurant, the fact is that Yu uses two contradictory expressions *haojin* ('very close') and *dagai chabuduo liangge xiaoshi* ('about two hours'). If it is 'about two hours' away, then it would not be 'very close' (although it might just be the case due to the sheer size and population of Beijing). Thus, this contradiction probably suggests that Yu is making fun of Na who appears to be slightly desperate. Yang's wife senses the funny side of this, and begins yelling out in the viewing room (family members were in a separate room where they can watch the contestant on a TV screen), 'We have take-away, take away'. By this time, coach Wang steps in and asks everyone to settle down to allow the contestant to have peace to think. In the end, Yang picked Na, perhaps because Na appeared so keen, and it would seem that Na's final 'desperate' bid has been rewarded.

Excerpt 2 (3/2/5): Two speakers over six speaking turns. The contestant, Zhang, sings very well (she turns out to be that season's winner), so the competition between the four coaches is intense.

T1 Qi: Ni jinnian ershiwu sui, dui ba? (你今年二十五岁, 对吧? You are twenty-five years old, right?)

T2 Zhang: Dui. (对。 Yes.)

T3 Qi: Fumuqin jinnian...? (父母亲今年...? Father and mother this year...?)

T4 Zhang: Baba shi shu niu de, mama shi shu hu de. (爸爸是属牛的, 妈妈是属虎的。 Daddy's animal year is a cow, and mum is a tiger.)

T5 Qi: Na du bi wo **dagai xiao ge liangsansui zuoyou**. Bama yinggai chang gen ni tiqi wo ba? (那都比我**大概**小个**两、三岁左右**。 爸妈 应该常跟你提起我吧? That's **about two or three** years younger than me. Do mum and dad often mention me to you?)

T6 Zhang: Dui. (对。 Yes.)

[all laugh]

All four coaches are fighting over the contestant. Previously, the other coaches have tried various things to persuade the contestant to join their teams. Coach Qi now tries a 'new trick': getting close to her parents. In T1, Qi begins by asking the contestant's age with the aim of establishing her parents' age group. It would appear that Qi knows contestant Zhang's age, but uses the sentential particle *ba* to show politeness (Zhang, 2016). Qi then moves on to ask about her parents' age and, upon hearing Zhang's answer, guesses their age by using elastic words in T4. The three approximate stretchers are: *dagai* ('about'), *liangsansui* ('2 or 3') and *zouyou* ('more or less'). Qi says that Zhang's parents are 'about 2 or 3 years' younger than him, as the two parents are not the same age. The elastic expression is a convenient way of conveying fluid information. It appears that no one is asking for an exact number in this case, so approximation does the trick.

In T4, Qi uses the parents' age as bait, the real intention is to have the opportunity to say that 'your parents should have mentioned my name very often, haven't they?'. Zhang confirms that this is the case, even if it is not, to save Qi's face. Despite Qi trying hard to force Zhang to join his team, unfortunately Qi's tactic did not work this time. Instead, Zhang chose another coach in the end.

Excerpt 3 (1/2/5): Three speakers over four speaking turns. The contestant, Dong, has not been selected, and when the coaches try to comfort and encourage her they discover the issue of online bullying.

T1 Liu: Dui. Guniang jintian ni zhai bu zhai xia zhege maozi du buyao-
jin. You yidian wo keyi zai zheli feichang chongfen di guli ni. Changge
yu zhangxiang mei name da guanxi. Wo Liu Huan changcheng zheyangzi [took off his hat and stood up, people are cheering him on].
(对。姑娘今天你摘不摘下这个帽子都不要紧。有一点我可以在
这里非常充分地鼓励你。唱歌与长相没那么大关系。我刘欢长
成这样子。Yes. It doesn't matter if you don't take off this hat today.
One thing that I can promise you here: singing does not have much to
do with appearance. Look at me, Liu Huan, I am very plain looking.)

T2 Yu: Hao! Hahaha! (好! 哈哈哈! Great! Hahaha!)

T3 Liu: Wo Liu Huan changcheng zheyang zai Zhongguo getan shang,
wo chang le **kuai** sanshi nian. Ye you **henduo** ren jiang buyao kandao
wo de changxiang. Danshi meiyou guanxi, wo jintian hai zhanzai
Zhongguo de liuxing yuetan shang. (我刘欢长成这样, 在中国歌坛
上我唱了**快**三十年。   也有**很多**人讲不要看到我的长相,   但是
没有关系, 我今天还站在中国的流行乐坛上。I, Liu Huan, don't
have a good look, but I've been a singer in China for **nearly** thirty
years. **Many** people say that they don't want to see my look, but it
doesn't matter, I'm still a pop singer in China today.)

T4 Na: Zenmeyang? (怎么样? What do you think?) [talking to the contestant and encouraging her to remove her face cover]

The contestant, Dong, wears something to cover her face because of
online bullying. She is a leading singer for online computer games, and
some bullies have attacked her appearance which forces her to cover
herself up. All the coaches condemn online bullying, stating that successful singers do not have to have good looks. Dong is encouraged to
show her face, but she is not ready to do so. At this point, Coach Liu
states, in T1, that it does not matter if she does not want to remove
the cover, but she needs to know that there is no connection between
singing and appearance as he, for one, is not at all handsome (yet Liu
is a very famous Chinese singer). Liu's comments are cheered by coach
Yu in T2.

In T3, Liu continues his argument that appearance has not impacted
negatively on his long and successful singing career. During his *kuai
sanshi nian* ('close to 30 years') singing career, *henduo* ('many') people have said that they did not want to see his face. The use of 'close

to 30 years' highlights the rounded number 30, ensuring that his career sounds longer than an exact number, for example 29, would sound. This would have been the case if Liu had known the exact number of years. However, there is another scenario: Liu does not remember the exact number and, in this case, the approximation also serves this purpose, with no one apparently having any problem when Liu uses the approximation. Similarly, Liu may be unable to provide a precise number for exactly how many people do not want to see his face, and 'many people' is probably used here to emphasise 'a significant number' (Moxey & Sanford, 1993), with a precise number not being relevant here.

In the end, Liu's persuasion is successful. After encouragement from all the coaches, the contestant took off her face cover, and the audience cheered her and gave her a big round of applause.

Excerpt 4 (1/1/4): Two speakers over four speaking turns. The contestant sang very well, with all four coaches turning their chairs around, so the competition is intense in this case.

> T1 Na: Shouxian, ni yao changde geng xini, wo lai bang ni, changde zai xini xie. (首先，你要唱得更细腻，我来帮你，唱得再细腻些。 First of all, you need to sing more refined. I'll help you to do that.)
> T2 Yang: Ta yijing hen xini le. (他已经很细腻了。He is already very refined.)
> T3 Na: Gangcai ni mei tingdao, you **jige** difang, you **jige** difang, changde … (刚才你没听到，有**几个**地方，有**几个**地方,唱得 … Just now, didn't you hear, there are **several** places, **several** places, sang …)
> T4 Yang: Wo juede feichang wanmei, perfect. (我觉得非常完美, perfect。 I think it's perfect, perfect.) [laughs from the others]

The coaches are strategic in persuasion. In this case, Coach Na tries to win the contestant over by highlighting where he can improve, hoping that he might value the opportunity to learn from a coach. In T1, Na tells the contestant that she can teach him to sing delicately and exquisitely. Coach Yang, a competitor to Na, disagrees with Na's comments, making this clear in T2. Then in T3, Na tries to substantiate her points, but Yang is having none of it and insists, in T4, that the contestant is perfect and has no need to learn from Na. In T3, Na uses an elastic expression *jige* 'several' twice, which is a quantifier with an underspecified meaning. Yang interrupts Na, and so we do not get to hear what Na says about these 'several places'. She might either go on to elaborate on what exactly these several places are, or she might choose not to do so, feeling that there is no need for elaboration.

Excerpt 5 (3/2/2): Two speakers over two speaking turns. The contestant, Zhou, sang well, with three of the four coaches turning their chairs around.

> T1 Qi: Zenme xuande zhe shou ge? (怎么选的这首歌? Why did you choose this song?)
>
> T2 Zhou: Yinwei wo feichang xihuan ting laoge, ranhou yinwei henduo laoge, you **yixie** shi fei chang de youmei, ye you **yi xie** shao dai **yi xie** kuse. Ranhou wo juede zhiyou laoge cai you zheyang de yunwei. (因为我非常喜欢听老歌, 然后因为很多老歌, 有**一些**是非常地优美, 也有**一些**稍带**一些**苦涩。 然后我觉得只有老歌才有这样的韵味。Because I like to listen to old songs very much, and many old songs, **some** are very beautiful, **some** have **some** bitterness. I think that only the old song has such a charm.)

Contestant Zhou has chosen a song which was originally sung by coach Qi's sister. Qi appears to want to seize the opportunity to get close to Zhou by asking why he has chosen that particular song, in T1. Qi might hope that Zhou would mention his sister when answering the question, thus giving Qi an edge. In response to Qi's question, Zhou explains that he has chosen the old song for its gracefulness as well as bitterness. Zhou uses 'some' three times in this excerpt. The first two occasions refer to 'some old songs', because the speaker may be unable to pinpoint the exact names of these old songs. On the third occasion, 'some' is an uncounted quantifier, 'some bitterness', and indicates a small amount of bitterness. Both countable and uncountable quantities are underspecified, they are approximate stretchers and serve various communicative functions which will be discussed in detail in Sect. 4.2 below.

4.1.2 General Stretcher

General stretchers (Zhang, 2015) include general terms, placeholders (Channell, 1994) and category markers: e.g. *thing, somebody, or something like that.*

Excerpt 6 (6/5/1): Three speakers over five speaking turns. No coach has turned around in this case, so the coaches are trying to comfort and encourage the group of disappointed contestants.

> T1 Qi [one of the three contestants who performed in this case] Danshi wo juede women congxiao de shenghuo beijing, meiyou tamen geli xiede **naxie shenme** haoche a, meinü a, **zhexie dongxi**. Suoyi wo juede yong zhezhong fangshi ba women ziji de **dongxi** dairu jinlai, wo juede zhe ge shi women zuo zhege yinye de zui da de yiyi suozai. (但是我觉得我们从小的生活背景，没有他们歌里写的**那些什么**豪车啊，美女啊**这些东西**。所以我觉得用这种方式把我们自己的**东西**带入进来，我觉得这个是我们作这个音乐的最大的意义所在。But I think when we were young we didn't have those luxury cars and beautiful women **and things like that**, as written in their songs. So I think in this way to bring our own **stuff** into our music, which I think is most important.)
> T2 Liu: Gangcai zhege dongxi zuode ye hen you yisi … (刚才这个东西做得也很有意思 … just now this thing is also made in a very interesting way.) [then Liu goes on to explain that the reason he didn't turn is that he is not specialised in hip hop music, so he feels that he has little to contribute]
> T3 Contestants: Xiexie! Xiexie! (谢谢! 谢谢! Thank you! Thank you!)
> T4 Chen: Rang wo da kai yanjie. (让我大开眼界。Open my eyes!)
> T5 Contestants: Xiexie! (谢谢! Thank you!)

After the usual polite chitchat, the contestants are asked why they chose this song based on a hip hop format. The song appears to have been written by the group. In T1, contestant Qi explains that he feels that their music aims to convey their own humble background and experience, rather than luxury cars and pretty women. He uses two general expressions: 'those luxury cars and pretty women and things like that' and 'our own things'. These expressions cover a wide range of things and have a general meaning. This kind of general term works well here because the speaker does not need to list all the things being referred to, and it may not even be possible to provide a complete list. In T2, coach Liu praises the contestants for their interesting musical compilation, and explains why he did not turn his chair around for them. Similarly, in T4, coach Chen also compliments the group. All these statements should make the contestants feel more appreciated, hopefully minimising their disappointment.

Excerpt 7 (2/1/2): Two speakers over two speaking turns. All the coaches have turned around for the contestant, Li, who is now in much demand.

> T1 Li: Qishi dangshi wo juede zai women xuexiao li, zai women ban litou, wo meiyou youshi. Danshi you **yige** pengyou gen wo jiang, ta shuo, Li Qi, ni zhidao ma? Ni zai changge de shi hou ni hui faguang. (其实当时我觉得在我们学校里，在我们班里头，我没有优势。但是有**一个**朋友跟我讲, 他说, 李琦, 你知道吗? 你在唱歌的时候你会发光。 Actually, at that time, I felt that in my school, in my class, I had no advantage. But **a** friend told me, he said, Li Qi, do you know? You shine whenever you sing.)
> T2 Yu: Tebie shuai! (特别帅! Fabulous!)

All the coaches are being generous in complimenting contestant Li. They try various ways to attract him, for example, coach Wang adopts a different tactic by suggesting how he can technically improve Li's performance. Coach Na disputes Wang's claim, by saying that Li does not need to consider technicality at that moment. Upon hearing the coaches' compliments, Li mentions that he does not believe that he is particularly good, but that one of his friends told him that he shone whenever he sang. Li uses *yige* ('a (friend)'), which is a general term and unspecific. It is likely that he knows the name of his friend but, for some reason, he chooses not to reveal it. In this case, using the general term serves Li's purpose rather well, whatever that may be.

Excerpt 8 (3/2/5): Two speakers over two speaking turns. All the coaches have turned their chairs around for the contestant, Zhang, who is a very promising singer.

T1 Yang: Na meihao de shiwu dajia du bixu **nage shenme** ma. [all laugh]
Wo zhuyi de bu guang shi tade waibiao, dangran xianzai zanshi meiyou
banfa zoudao tade neixin. Danshi ne, wo juede dui zheme yige cong
Hanguo xueye huilai de nühai, zhanzai zhege wutai shang, buguan jintian zenmeyang, qishi ni jiaxiang de gemi gei ni reqing shi zui relie de.
Ni yao ren shi dao zhe yidian. (那美好的事物大家都必须**那个什
么**嘛。我注意的不光是她的外表, 当然现在暂时没有办法走到她
的内心。 但是呢, 我觉得对这么一个从韩国学业回来的女孩, 站
在这个舞台上, 不管今天怎么样, 其实你家乡的歌迷给你热情是
最热烈的。你要认识到这一点。Naturally we all are **thingummy-
jig** to beautiful things, something like that. What is important to me is
not only good looks, of course (in such a short time) at this moment of
time I am unable to know her at a much deeper level. But, I think the
girl who came back from South Korea after studying there, the most
enthusiastic fans would be your fellow countrymen when you sing on
the stage, regardless of the competition outcomes today. You need to
realise this.)
T2 Na: Mei cuo. (没错。That's right.) [applause]

Zhang is a pretty girl, and coach Yang is a bachelor and is accused of
paying particular attention to beautiful girls. In T1, Yang defends himself by claiming that everyone loves beautiful things. He uses an analogy
here, with *things* referring to *beautiful girls*. Yang does not clearly specify
how people tend to react when they see beautiful things, but instead
he uses a placeholder word (Channell, 1994), *nage shenme* ('thingummyjig'), so that listeners can infer that 'thingummyjig' means 'love or
fancy'. Perhaps he uses the placeholder because it is inappropriate for
him to utter 'love/fancy' directly, and he is unsure whether the audience would approve of his behaviour. He hopes that the audience would
infer his meaning without him having to utter the word. It appears
that the audience has understood his hint, because people laugh after
his comments. A placeholder is part of the general stretcher category. In
T1, Yang also tell Zhang that her fellow countrymen are her most genuine fans, and not people from other countries. However, Zhang perhaps
did not fully appreciate what Yang said to her because she chose another
coach in the end.

Excerpt 9 (3/2/3): Three speakers over four speaking turns. Two of the four coaches have turned around for the contestant, Zheng, who is a 16 year-old high school student from Taiwan.

T1 Qi: Qishi wo tingdao de shi yizhong feichang qingchun … (其实我听到的是一种非常清纯 … In fact, what I hear is a very pure and innocent…)

T2 Na: Tianshi ban de. (天使般的。Angelic.)

T3 Qi: Ranhou meiyou teshu de zhuanyin, shi yao biaoda **shenme**, qu kongzhi ta. Keneng nian shao bu zhi chou ziwei, danshi hen qingsong hen fangsong de ba ta changwan. Wo juede fei chang hao, zheshi xiyin wo zui da de defang. (然后没有特殊的转音, 是要表达**什么**, 去控制它。可能年少不知愁滋味, 但是很轻松很放松的把它唱完。我觉得非常好, 这是吸引我最大的地方。And there is no special sound turns, but still express **something** and be in control. Maybe young men do not know the taste of sorrow, so he was able to finish the song in a relaxed way. I think it was very good, which is the biggest attraction for me.)

T4 Zheng: Xiexie laoshi. (谢谢老师。Thank you, teacher.)

Two coaches compete for contestant Zheng, with Qi being one of them. He praises Zheng on her pure singing. Qi particularly likes her style which, without much singing technique, is still very expressive. In T3, the general term *shenme* 'something' is used by Qi, because he does not need to specify what these things are, and 'something' is good enough to serve the purpose here (Jucker, Smith, & Ludge, 2003). In the end, Zheng chose Qi without much suspense. This was to be expected because the contestant actually sang a song originally sung by Qi.

Excerpt 10 (1/1/7): Four speakers over four speaking turns. Coach Yang and coach Yu compete for the contestant, Li.

T1 Yang: Suiran shi Yunnan ren, dan du shi hao ji bei yiqian de shier. (虽然是云南人, 但都是好几辈以前的事儿。Although all are from Yunnan, it is irrelevant today, as that was several generations ago.)

T2 Yu: Qie [a sound indicating a dismissive or unimpressed attitude], wo ba jiu shi Yunnan ren. (Qie, 我爸就是云南人。Qie, my dad is from Yunnan.)

T3 Li: Zhende, zhege jueze zhende hen jiannan, yinwei wo cong zhaizi limian dao qiu xue dao xianzai, yizhi du xihuan yinyue. Danshi yiqian canjia de **yixie** (jiemu), dajia du hui yi shanglai kan, hai mei deng wo chang, jiu bu gei wo zhege chang de jihui. Ranhou jiushi **youxie shihou** hui zhende bu zhidao ziji yao zenme zou xiaqu. Danshi zheme zhongyao de **ji wei** laoshi du renke wo, buguan zenmeyang, yihou wo hui yonggan di chang xiaqu. (真的，这个抉择真的很艰难，因为我从寨子里面到求学到现在，一直都喜欢音乐。但是以前参加的**一些** (节目)，大家都会一上来看，还没等我唱，就不给我这个唱的机会。然后就是**有些时候**会真的不知道自己要怎么走下去。但是这么重要的**几位**老师都认可我，不管怎么样，以后我会勇敢地唱下去。Really this choice is very difficult for me [crying], because I have always loved music, from my remote village to where I studied, to now. However **some** of the singing competitions I took part in in the past, people would not even give me a chance to sing, once they saw me (not handsome enough). Then, **sometimes** I really don't know how I want to go on. But today **several** renowned musicians here have recognised me. Anyway, I will keep singing with a brave heart.)

T4 Na & Yu: Yeah!

The contestant, Li, is 22 years old and is actually a real-life prince of the Hani ethnic group living in the Yunnan province of China. He was the centre of the universe in his village, but experienced a large fall in status when he moved away from his isolated village. Singing has given him confidence and makes him feel better.

Li is from Yunnan, and thus, in T1 and T2, coaches Yang and Yu claim, in turn, that they have family connections in that area, in an attempt to get close to Li. In T3, the contestant says that he has gone through rough patches and *youxie shihou* 'sometimes' he does not know how to keep going. The general word, 'sometimes', is used here because Li is perhaps unable to specify exactly when these rough patches have been, and a general statement seems to be more suitable here. Two further elastic items are used in T3: *yixie* 'some' (TV shows), which is used to avoid publicly naming those TV shows which selected singers on the basis of their appearance, and *jiwei* 'several', which possibly serves to save Li's own face. He knows perfectly well that two of the four coaches turned around for him, but yet he still chooses to use the vague quantifier 'several', perhaps because it sounds more than two.

4.1.3 Scalar Stretcher

Scalar stretchers include words whose job is to either strengthen or weaken the degree of a claim (Zhang, 2015). These stretchers act as modifiers to adjust words on a continuum. For example, intensifiers, such as 'very', can push the degree of coldness upwards as in 'very cold'. On the other hand, softeners, such as 'a bit', can pull it downwards, as in 'a bit cold'.

Excerpt 11 (3/2/9): Five speakers over six speaking turns. The contestant, Zhang, is a restaurant singer. Three of the four coaches have turned around for Zhang.

T1 Wang: … Wo bi ni **gengjia** de zhidao nage ziwei, yinwei wo ziji zhengshi zai zhuozi bian shang zhan zhe de… (我比你**更加**地知道那个滋味，　因为我自己正是在桌子边上站着的。I　know **even more** about that than you, because I myself have sung by the table (for diners).)

T2 Na: Zhende, na **ting** you yisi de. (真的，那**挺**有意思的。Really, that's **quite** interesting.) [the audience applauds]

T3 Qi: Na ni kan Kunr na ge biaoqing. Ta kending shi … (那你看坤儿那个表情。他肯定是… Look at Kun's expression. He must be…

T4 Yang: Wo gaosu ni wo shi zai niupaidian chang le shi'ernian de ge. Wo jiu xiang wen **yixia**, qishi women de jingli he zaoyu du shi bijiao xiangtong de … wo juede ni shuo de **tebie** dui. Qiaqia shi ni zai canting gongzuo le **name** chang shijian, leiji le **tai** duo **tai** hao de jingyan, dui ni yihou de zhege changge de chengzhang shi **feichang** you bangzhu de, zhende. (我告诉你我是在牛排店唱了十二年的歌。我就想问**一下**，　其实我们的经历和遭遇都是比较相同的…我觉得你说的**特别**对。　　恰恰是你在餐厅工作了**那么**长时间，累积了**太**多**太**好的经验, 对你以后的这个唱歌的成长是**非常**有帮助的, 真的。I told you that I sang in the steak restaurant for twelve years. I **just** want to ask, in fact our experiences and encounters are similar. I think you're **absolutely** correct. It's definitely the case that your **very** long time of restaurant work allows you to accumulate **extremely** rich and **extremely** valuable experience, which is **very** helpful for the development of your future singing, absolutely.)

T5 Zhang: Xiexie, laoshi. (谢谢老师。Thank you, teacher.)

... ... [Some text was omitted here, as it is not relevant to the subsequent data analysis]

T6 Qi: Ni zhidao tamen weishime jiao wo xiaoge ma? Yinwei wo chang de niantou bi tamen **duo de duode duo**. Ruguo ni dao wode duiwu dang zhong lai, wo xiang wo yiding hui yongjin wo de quanli lai chengquan ni. (你知道他们为什么叫我小哥吗?因为我唱的年头比他们**多得多得多**。如果你到我的队伍当中来, 我想我一定会用尽我的全力来成全你。Do you know why they call me brother? This is because I have sung **a lot more** years than they have. If you come to my team, I think I will try my best to help you.)

Zhang previously discussed his unpleasant experience of singing in restaurants, how he felt disgusted that he could smell steaks while singing. In T1, coach Wang uses the scalar stretcher *gengjia* ('even more') to say that he is even more aware than Zhang of that type of dreadful feeling because, being a violinist, Wang had to play next to the dining tables in close proximity with the diners. However, as a singer, Zhang would actually be performing at a distance removed from the diners. In T2, coach Na uses *ting* 'quite' to qualify the degree of *yisi* ('interesting'). In T4, coach Yang employs several scalar stretchers: *tebie* ('especially' correct), *name* ('so' long), *tai ... tai* ('extremely' rich, 'extremely' valuable) and *feichang* ('extraordinarily').

There is another scalar stretcher in T4, *yixia* ('a little bit'), which tends to follow a verb to mitigate the force of the request being put forward. For example, *wen yixia* ('ask about it') comes across as a polite request, but if *yixia* is omitted then the tone is less gentle. In T6, coach Qi uses a reduplication, *duode duode duo* (ABABA), which means 'lots lots of'. In this excerpt, the coaches use strengthening scalar words mainly to enhance the force of their persuasion, while some weakening scalar words (e.g. 'a little bit', 'quite') are used to convey a decreased degree or politeness.

Excerpt 12 (1/2/10): Three speakers over three speaking turns. The contestant, Ping, sang a popular Chinese song.

T1 Yu: Ta **tai** lihai le. (他**太**厉害了。He's **extremely** good.)

T2 Yang: Wo juede wo xuan ba, yinwei ta xuande zhege ge you shi yige **hen** zheng de yige ge, haoxiang hai tingdao le yidian yaogun de weidao. (我觉得我选吧，因为他选的这个歌又是一个**很**正的一个歌，好像还听到了一点摇滚的味道。I think I'll choose it, because the song he chose was a **very** positive song, sounds with a bit of rock and roll taste.)

… …

[Ping is asked why he prefers singing old songs; he says that his parents love to hear them.]

T3 Ping: Yinyue neng gei tamen dailai **feichang feichang** da de yixie guwu. (音乐能给他们带来**非常非常**大的一些鼓舞。Music can bring **a lot of** huge encouragement to them.)

The contestant, Ping, has a very good voice and tends to sing old songs. Coaches Yu and Yang adore him. They choose the following scalar stretchers to express their approval of Ping: *tai* ('extremely') in T1, *hen* ('very') in T2, to increase the strength of their approval. In T3, a reduplication of a scalar word is used, *feichang feichang* ('very' 'very' big), to indicate the extreme force with which he is strengthening the degree of the claim.

Excerpt 13 (1/2/8): Three speakers over three speaking turns. All four coaches have turned around for the contestant, Wang, who is a very strong contender.

T1 Na: Wang tongxue, nide shengyin zhendao wo le. Wo hai renshi henduo geshou, hai renshi henduo de zhizuoren. Wulun shi xuange fangmian, renhe yige fangmian, gei ni **geng**da de bangzhu, ni kan ni **haohao xiangxiang**. Zhe limian jiu wo yiwei nü laoshi. (王同学，你的声音震到我了。我还认识很多歌手，还认识很多的制作人。无论是选歌方面，任何一个方面，给你**更**大的帮助，你看你**好好想想**。这里面就我一位女老师。Classmate Wang, your voice struck me. I know many singers and a lot of producers. So whether it's choosing songs or anything else, we can offer you **much** better help, please do give **a lot of** thought to this. Among all coaches, I am the only female coach here.)

T2 Yu: Wenqing a, zou wenqing gongshi. Wo xiang qing wen **yixia**, ni shibushi diyin bi gao yin hao? (温情啊，走温情攻势。我想请

问**一下**, 你是不是低音比高音好? Soft power, go for softie strategy. I would like to **just** ask, are you better at bass than tenor?)

T3 Wang: Wo qishi ye **butai** qingchu. (我其实也**不太**清楚。Actually, I'm **not really** clear about it.)

In Excerpt 13, each coach tries everything to win over this excellent contestant. The female coach Na stresses her extensive networks and tender female touch, hoping that these would appeal to Wang. In T1, Na uses the scalar stretcher *geng* ('even more') when asking Wang to consider choosing her to be his coach, to enhance the degree of helpfulness. *Haohao* is a scalar expression indicating 'to a greater extent'. *Xiang* means 'think', and by using *xiangxiang* here, a tone of politeness and gentleness is brought into the conversation to mitigate Na's request that Wang should consider choosing her to be his coach.

In T2, not to be outdone, coach Yu changes the topic to singing techniques, which Yu hopes would interest Wang. Yu puts *yixia* ('just') after the request, softening the tone of speech. In T3, Wang admits that he is unsure whether he is a bass or tenor, where *butai* ('not really') is a softener.

Excerpt 14 (1/2/2): Five speakers over nine speaking turns. The contestant, Wang, is a good singer and all four coaches have turned around for her.

T1 Wang: Xianzai shi rang wo xuanze shi ba? (现在是让我选择是吧? Now let me choose it, right?)

T2 Yang/Liu: Dui. (对。Yes.)

T3 Wang: **Zheme** kuai? (**这么**快? **So** fast?)

T4 Yu: A? (啊? Ah?)

T5 Liu: Na xiageyue juede ye xing. (那下个月觉得也行。Okay let's leave it to next month.) [laughs]

T6 Wang: Qishi wo **zhenshi** mei xiangdao, qishi wo jintian xinli shi you yige da fangxiang de. Yang Kun laoshi, wo yizhi du **tebie** xihuan ni. (其实我**真是**没想到，其实我今天心里是有一个大方向的。杨坤老师，我一直都**特别**喜欢你。Actually I **really** didn't expect that, to be honest I have someone in mind today. Teacher Yang Kun, I have been **especially** fond of you.)

T7 Yang: Bie shuo naxie gongweihua. (别说那些恭维话。Don't be smooth talking.)

T8 Wang: Danshi wo kandao Najie, wo shizai shi **youdian** renbuzhu. Najie, wo **hao** xihuan ni. (但是我看到那姐，我实在是**有点**忍不住。那姐，我**好**喜欢你。But when I see sister Na, honestly I am **a bit** beside myself. Sister Na, I love you **so much**.)

T9 Na: Xiexie! (谢谢! Thank you!)

The contestant on stage, Wang, has shaved her head, and she appears to be an open minded and confident girl. When the final moment arrives and she needs to reveal who she will choose as a coach, she jokes about it light-heartedly. In T3, she uses *zheme* ('so' fast) to indicate that she has not quite made up her mind. Coach Liu also jokes around in T5, saying that maybe next month (instead of now) would also be fine for Wang to make a decision. In T6, Wang addresses coach Yang and shows her admiration by resorting to two scalar stretchers: *zhenshi* ('really') and *tebie* ('especially'). In T7, Yang is not impressed by Wang's smooth talking, which makes Wang then turn to coach Na. In T8, Wang uses *youdian* ('a bit') and *hao* ('very') to flatter Na. However, in the end, she chose Yu to be her coach instead.

Excerpt 15 (1/2/9): Three speakers over five speaking turns. The contestant, Dai, is a homemaker with a young daughter. Unfortunately, no one has turned around for Dai, and so the coaches are comforting her.

T1 Yang: Wo shi xiang wen **yixia**, women sige meiyou zhuanshen de guo-lai yihou, jintian wan shang nide zhege mengxiang wanzhuan di shuo meiyou shixian, ni xin limian shi zenme qu xiang de? (我是想问**一下**, 我们四个没有转身的过来以后, 今天晚上你的这个梦想婉转地说没有实现, 你心里面是怎么去想的? Can I please **just** ask, after four of us have not turned, this evening your dream, tactfully putting it, that did not come true, how do you feel?)

T2 Dai: Ruguo jintian wanshang you yiwei laoshi nenggou wei wo zhu-anshen de hua, wo shi dangran kending **hen** gaoxing. Danshi qishi wo haiyou yige **feichang** zhongyao de mudi lai dao zhege wutai, yinwei qishi wo shi ben zhou ni lai de. (如果今天晚上有一位老师能够为我转身的话, 我是当然肯定**很**高兴。但是其实我还有一个**非常**重要的目的来到这个舞台, 因为其实我是奔着你来的。If a teacher

would turn around for me tonight, I would definitely be **very** happy.
Actually, I also have an **extremely** important purpose for coming to
this stage, I'm actually coming for you.)

T3 Yang: A! (啊! Ah!)

T4 Yu: Nide. (你的。Yours.) [pointing to Yang]

T5 Yang: Wo de xiao xinzang **shaowei** dong le **yixia**. (我的小心脏**稍微**
动了**一下**。My little heart has been touched **a little**.)

In T1, Coach Yang asks politely how contestant Dai feels, by using *yixia*
('a little bit', a softener to mitigate the tone of the question). Dai replies
that, in fact, she came to the competition because of Yang and, in T2,
she uses the scalar strengthener *feichang* ('extremely') to enhance her
claim. In T5, Yang uses two scalar softeners, *shaowei* ('slightly') and *yixia*
('a bit'), to express his surprise and excitement in a veiled manner. In
T3, Yang sounds rather surprised but, in T5, he uses a metaphor to suggest that he is a little bit touched by this, in a semi-humorous way. The
reason for Yang's mitigated tone in T5 could be that he is trying to be
modest rather than appearing to be arrogant.

4.1.4 Epistemic Stretcher

Epistemic stretchers include stance markers and attitudinal devices
(Zhang, 2015). These words tend to express possibility rather than certainty, for example, *maybe, possible, I think* and *sort of*.

Excerpt 16 (6/5/6): Four speakers over four speaking turns.
Unfortunately, in this case, no coach has turned around for the contestant, perhaps because it is now the final stage of the auditions and
limited spaces are available on each team, and so the coaches are being
particularly choosy.

T1 Liu: Gei wo ganjue youdian yongli guomeng. (给我感觉有点用力过
猛。I feel a little overkill.)

T2 Na: En. (嗯。Yes.)

T3 Zhou: **Wo juede** haoting de difang zai fuge nage difang. Danshi women
bei gandong dao de, buneng zhishi yinwei fuge. (**我觉得**好听的地方
在副歌那个地方。但是我们被感动到的， 不能只是因为副歌。

I think the best part was the chorus. But we should have been moved by more than that.)

T4 Chen: **Wo juede** ni keyi shishi kan, [demonstrating how to sing the lyric in a gentle way] 'wo de ai, mingming hai zai', jiushi keyi, huozhe shi qing yidian. Bu yinggai. **Buyiding** yao zhege fangshi lai. (**我觉得**你可以试试看，'我的爱，明明还在"，就是可以，或者是轻一点。不应该 。**不一定**要这个方式来。**I think** you can try singing like this: 'my love, clearly still here', that is, sing it a little lighter. It should not be like this, [sings the lyrics in a less gentle way]. It **probably** doesn't have to be sung like this.)

The contestant is unsuccessful and so the coaches are trying to emotionally comfort him. They explain how the contestant can improve his singing, which they believe is valuable advice for him to take away from the competition. In T3, coach Zhou points out that a good singer needs to manage both the verse and chorus well. He uses an epistemic stretcher, *wo juede* (I think), to mitigate his tone and avoid sounding too authoritative. In T4, the same stretcher is used again, this time by coach Chen who wants to make his suggestion less imposing. At the end of this speech turn, another epistemic stretcher, *buyiding* ('probably don't have to'), is used to soften the tone of Chen's criticism.

Excerpt 17 (5/4/2): Three speakers over four speaking turns. The contestant belongs to the Buyi ethnic group in China. Three coaches have turned around for her, and there has been much debate between the three coaches.

T1 Yu: **Wo geren juede** ni chu le yige sou zhuyi. (**我个人觉得**你出了一个馊主意。**I myself think** you gave a bad idea.)

T2 Zhou: **Youdian** xiang bu dao. (**有点**想不到。It's **sort of** unexpected.)

T3 Wang: Shenme yisi? (什么意思? What does it mean?)

T4 Zhou: **Wo juede** zheyang bijiao haowan. Nimen sanwei yanjing bishang, ta hui momo de zou dao nide qianmian qu. (**我觉得**这样比较好玩。你们三位眼睛闭上，她会默默地走到你的前面去。**I think** it's going to be a lot of fun. You three please close your eyes, and she will go to you silently.)

When it was time to choose a coach, Wang suggested that Zhou (the only coach who did not turn around for the contestant, and therefore is a 'neutral party' in this particular 'fight over the contestant') talks to the contestant in private and then announces her choice. In T1, coach Yu uses an epistemic expression, *wo geren juede* ('I myself think'), to mitigate his disagreement with Wang's suggestion. Note that Yu adds *geren* ('personally') to emphasise the undertone of 'I am feeling this way, but you might not'. As suggested, coach Zhou walked up to the stage and the contestant whispered the name of the coach she had chosen. Upon hearing the name, Zhou utters an epistemic stretcher, namely *youdian* ('sort of') *xiangbudao* ('unexpected'). He uses 'sort of' as a stretcher (Zhang, 2019) to qualify his surprise in case it causes offence to the chosen coach. By this stage, the coaches are rather confused and thus, in T3, Wang asks Zhou for clarification. In T4, Zhou spices things up even further by proposing another intriguing idea. Zhou also resorts to using *wo juede* ('I think') to perform a similar function to *wo geren juede* ('I myself think') in T1. 'I think', in T4, mitigates the potential offensiveness of his new, and somewhat mischievous, idea to make the announcement more interesting. In the end, Yu was chosen, although Wang talks about reviving the contestant's ethnic folk songs. It was an excellent move on Wang's part, but unfortunately the idea did not interest the contestant.

Excerpt 18 (3/2/8): Three speakers over five speaking turns. The two contestants, Robynn and Kendy, are from Hong Kong and they sang as a team. Three of the four coaches have turned around for them.

> T1 Qi: Wo dangran ting dao you yixie xiaoxiao de xiaci, danshi tong-shi wei pengyou wo you ting dao le yigu, leisi **xiangshi** bijiao qing-chun de ganjue, liangge ren hezuo de feichang wu jian. Suoyi **wo juede** feichang de bang. (我当然听到有一些小小的瑕疵，但是同时为朋友我又听到了一股，类似**像是**比较青春的感觉，两个人合作得非常无间。所以**我觉得**非常地棒。Surely I heard some small flaws, but at the same time I heard something that **sounds like** a feeling of youth, between the two friends they work together so beautifully. So **I think** they are excellent.)

T2 Robynn: Xiexie, xiexie lao shi! (谢谢, 谢谢老师! Thank you, thank you, teacher!)

… …

T3 Robynn: Qishi **wo juede** women zhen de mei xiangdao, you sanwei daoshi hui wei women zhuanshen. Suoyi xianzai **women jiushi juede** … (其实**我觉得**我们真的没想到, 有三位导师会为我们转身。所以现在**我们就是觉得** … Actually, **I think** we really didn't expect three mentors to turn around for us. So now **we just feel** that…)

T4 Na: Youdian zhengzha. (有点挣扎。It's a bit of a struggle.)

T5 Robynn: Dui, youdian zhengzha. (对, 有点挣扎。Yes, it's a bit of a struggle.)

The two contestants sang one of coach Qi's songs. In T1, Qi uses the epistemic stretcher, *xiangshi* ('sounds like'), to tentatively express his judgement. Qi also uses *wo juede* ('I think'), and this epistemic stretcher appears to be evaluating in this case. In T3, firstly *wo juede* ('I think') is singular, and then secondly *women jiushi juede* ('we just think') is plural. After some struggle, the two contestants chose coach Yang primarily for his songwriting talent.

Excerpt 19 (4/3/2): Four speakers over six speaking turns. The contestant, Zhang, is a law graduate and a good singer. All the coaches have turned around for her.

T1 Yu: Ni qishi houmian you yiduan, shi bijiao qianglie de changfa. Ni weishime yi kaishi mei you xiangdao zheng shou ge zheyang chang? (你其实后面有一段, 是比较强烈的唱法。你为什么一开始没有想到整首歌这样唱? Actually, there was heightened singing towards the end of the song. Why didn't you sing that way from the start?)

T2 Zhang: Zhe **keneng** he xingge you yiding de guanxi **ba**. Zheshi Wang Feng laoshi de yuan ban, geng duo de xiang biaoda yizhong hen jinli qu kuanghuan de ganjue. (这**可能**和性格有一定的关系**吧**。这是汪峰老师的原版, 更多地想表达一种很尽力去狂欢的感觉。This **may** be related to personality. This is the original version of Wang Feng, and I want to express more a feeling of great effort to Carnival.)

T3 Wang: Dui. (对。Yes.)

T4 Zhang: Ran hou, yinwei wo shi xue faxue de, **keneng** hui bijiao man re yidian. (然后, 因为我是学法学的, **可能**会比较慢热一点。Also because I was trained in the law, **may** be taking a bit longer time to show my emotions.)

… …

T5 Zhou: Ni lai wo zheli keyi wan henduo dongxi. (你来我这里可以玩很多东西。You can have lots of fun if you join my team.)

T6 Yu: **Haoxiang** wo ye **keyi**. [laughter and applause] Ni zuo ge xuanze **ba**. (**好像**我也可以。你做个选择**吧**。It **seems** that I can also offer you that. **Could** you **please** make a choice?)

The contestant, Zhang, sings a rock song, of which coach Wang is the writer and original singer. In T2, Zhang uses the epistemic stretcher *keneng* ('may') and the sentential particle *ba* (marker for probability) to indicate that her explanation is not categorical. The same tentativeness is also manifested in T4, again with the help of *keneng* ('may'). In T5, coach Zhou plays a 'having fun' card with the contestant. Coach Yu takes over the speaking turn in T6, and says that 'It seems that I can also offer you that'. The epistemic stretcher *haoxiang* ('seem') acts as a modest marker and has humorous elements as well, and this arouses laughter and a round of applause. At the end of T6, Yu politely asks the contestant to choose a coach, which is achieved by using *ba* (a politeness marker) at the end of the suggestion. It was interesting to note that, at the end, Zhang actually chose Yu to be her coach, rather than Wang, even though she performed Wang's song.

Excerpt 20 (6/5/7): Four speakers over five speaking turns. The contestant, Huang, is from Singapore and two coaches have turned around for her.

T1 Na: Nainai kuai feng le, qi de. (奶奶快疯了，气得。Grandma is driven (by the noisy music) crazy and angry (at your loud singing).)

T2 Huang: Ta xianzai zai houmian, **wo juede ta juede** wo han de zhide. (她现在在后面，**我觉得她觉得**我喊得值得。She's in the back now. **I think she thinks** (all the suffering of) my loud singing is worthwhile.)

T3 Zhou: **Shuobuding** nainai de neixin ye shi hen yaogun. (**说不定**奶奶的内心也是很摇滚。Who knows grandma's heart is **probably** very like rock too.)

… …

T4 Liu: Wo dei bang Eason shuoshuohua, **wo juede** Eason shi tebie zhencheng, tebie tancheng de ren. Ta diyige chong xialai, yiding shi ta zhenxin xihuan ni ... (我得帮 Eason 说说话, **我觉得** Eason 是特别真诚, 特别坦诚的人。他第一个冲下来, 一定是他真心喜欢你 ... I have to speak for Eason. **I think** Eason is a very sincere and candid person. He was the first to turn his chair for you. He must be really wanting you in his team.)

T5 Zhou: Danshi **wo shi zhende juede** dui xueyuan hao de hua, wo yao geiyu ta zhengque de daolu. (但是**我是真的觉得**对学员好的话, 我要给与她正确的道路. But **I really feel** that if it is good for the students, I will provide her the right way.)

The contestant, Huang, mentions that she shares a room with her grandma in Singapore. She practices singing every night and so her grandma has got used to the noise. In T2, Huang guesses that her grandma might think that all her suffering (from her granddaughter's loud music) has been worth it. The combined epistemic expression used in T2 differs from others in this study. In this case, *wo juede ta juede* ('I think that she thinks ...') has two layers, and the speaker's expectation of others is involved here (Moxey & Sanford, 1993). In T3, Zhou uses an epistemic stretcher, *shuobuding* ('perhaps'), because he is unsure whether this is the case.

Coaches sometimes support each other for various reasons, particularly in cases where they did not turn around, and are therefore not in competition with the others. Excerpt 20 is such a case. In T4, Liu (who did not turn around) tries to support coach Chen, whose English name is Eason, by saying he thinks that Chen is very genuine and really likes the contestant. Liu uses *wo juede* ('I think') as an evaluative indicator (Zhang, 2016). In T5, Zhou proposes a different view: coaches should not turn around if they are not experts in the particular style of music in question, for otherwise he/she would not be able to offer the contestant the best coaching. Zhou's comments may cause some discomfort for the coaches, so he uses *wo shi zhende juede* ('I really think') to emphasise his sincerity.

4.2   Pragmatic Functions

This section discusses the six categories of the pragmatic functions of EL, based on Zhang (2015). These include just-right elastic, rapport elastic, mitigating elastic, intensifying elastic, self-protection elastic and evasive elastic. These categories will be investigated with the help of excerpts drawn from the data.

4.2.1   Just-Right Elastic

A just-right elastic function refers to providing vague, but an appropriate amount of, information (Zhang, 2015). In communication, there is often no need to be exact or the precise information is unavailable (Channell, 1994). Therefore, elastic expressions tend to be used to deal with these situations.

Excerpt 21 (1/1/5): Four speakers over eight speaking turns. Three coaches have turned around for the contestant, Xu.

> T1 Yang: Ni fuqin jintian mei lai ma? (你父亲今天没来吗? Didn't your father come today?)
> T2 Xu: Wo mama lai le, ranhou **wo juede** wo baba ye lai le. (我妈妈来了，然后**我觉得**我爸爸也来了。My mother is here, and **I feel** that my father is here as well.)
> T3 Na: Juede a? (觉得啊? You feel?) [long pause]
> T4 Xu: Baba sangeyue qian shengbing qushi le. (爸爸三个月前生病去世了。My father was sick and passed away three months ago.)
> … …
> T5 Liu: Ta shuo ta baba **keneng** (stressed) lai ba, women hai bu zhidao shi shenme yisi. (她说她爸爸**可能**来吧，我们还不知道是什么意思。She said her dad **might** be here, we don't know what it means.)
> T6 Xu: **Wo juede** ta zai zher. (**我觉得**他在这儿。**I think** he's here.) [Xu nods her head, and the audience applauds]
> T7 Liu: Ta tai ke'ai le. (她太可爱了。She's so lovely.)
> T8 Na: Dui. (对。Yes.)

Previously, contestant Xu said that she would dedicate the song to her father. Without knowing that Xu's father had actually passed away three months previously, coach Yang, in T1, asks whether her father was there that day. Xu answers that she feels that her father is there. When coach Na asks why Xu uses the word 'feel', Xu tells her that her father had passed away. In T5, coach Liu senses the tentativeness of Xu's tone, and people are becoming rather confused. Then, in T6, Xu reiterates that she feels that her father is there, and nods with confidence. The audience is touched by Xu's story and applauds her. Xu uses the epistemic expression, *wo juede* ('I think') twice. Coach Liu also uses *keneng* ('possibly'). These expressions are appropriate for conveying the right amount of information: Xu's father has passed away and she hopes that his spirit would be there watching over her, but this is a hope or a possibility, rather than a fact. In this situation, elastic words expressing possibility and epistemology are suitable, and provide the correct amount of information (Grice, 1975).

Excerpt 22 (3/2/4): Three speakers over six speaking turns. Three of the four coaches have turned around for the contestant, Zhao, who is a music graduate.

> T1 Na: Shouxian wo ting dao ta de shengyin you **yisisi** de Zhang Xinzhe.
> (首先我听到他的声音有**一丝丝**的张信哲。 First, I heard **a little bit** of Zhang Xinzhe in his voice.)
> T2 Yang: Haiyou yige ren. (还有一个人。 There's one more person.)
> T3 Na: Haiyou shui? (还有谁? Who else?)
> T4 Yang: Yang Zongwei. (杨宗伟。 Yang Zongwei.)
> T5 Qi: Duide, dui de. (对的对的。 Yes, yes.)
> T6 Yang: **You yidiandian**. (**有一点点**。 **A little bit**.)

Here, the three coaches discuss who Zhao sounds like. Coach Na, in T1, suggests that Zhao's voice is *yisisi* ('a little bit') similar to that of the musician Zhang Xinzhe and, in T4, coach Yang mentions another similar sounding musician, Yang Zongwei. In T6, Yang says that the similarity between Zhao and Yang is *you yidiandian* ('a little bit'). The two occasions in which 'a little bit' is used here describe the similarity in a 'just-right' manner, although they express an underspecified degree of similarity.

Excerpt 23 (6/5/14): Four speakers over four speaking turns. The contestant, Xie, is from Malaysia and only one coach has turned around for him.

T1 Na: **Wo** hui **juede** wo xihuan ta nage shengyin li shasha de, **haoxiang** zhezhong shengyin te zhi hai shi **ting** hao de. (**我**会**觉得**我喜欢他那个声音里沙沙的，**好像**这种声音特质还是**挺**好的。**I think** that I like his rustling voice, **seems** this kind of quality of voice is quite good.)

T2 Liu: Erqie shi nage dianxing de, **wo** jiu **juede** shi zaimen huayu nage R&B, jiushi **henduo** geshou yong zheyang de yige shengyin. (而且是那个典型的，**我**就**觉得**是咱们华语那个R&B，就是**很多**歌手用这样的一个声音。And the typical one, **I think** it is R&B in Chinese, **many** singers use such a voice.)

T3 Zhou: Hen shihe chang R&B de. (很适合唱R&B的。It's very suitable for singing R&B.)

T4 Xie: Xiexie! (谢谢! Thank you!)

This audition occurred towards the final selection stage of the show, and the limited number of remaining spaces forced the coaches to be more selective with their choice of contestant. In T1, coach Na likes Xie's voice, and she expresses her views by using the elastic expressions, *wo juede* ('I feel'), *haoxiang* ('seem') and *ting* ('quite'). Na has not turned around for Xie (so this particular selection is irrelevant to her) and she expresses a positive view of Xie, so therefore there is no need for her to mitigate in any way. Therefore, it is more likely that Na's use of EL is to serve a just-right elastic function, by providing the right amount of information in a straightforward manner.

Liu agrees with Na and elaborates further in T2. Liu is the only coach who has turned around for Xie, and so there is no competition for him either. Liu uses *wo juede* ('I think'), which serves an evaluative function, that is a just-right elastic function (Zhang, 2015). Liu also uses the quantifier *henduo* ('many') here, and this performs a just-right elastic function. Liu explains that Xie's voice is typical and representative of *many* Chinese signers. In this case, it is impossible for Liu to provide the precise number of people who have this kind of voice, but this is probably unimportant. 'Many' is used appropriately here to serve a just-right function, conveying the right amount of information that is neither too much nor too little.

Excerpt 24 (1/2/4): Five speakers over six speaking turns. The contestant, Liu, is popular and all the coaches have turned around for her

T1 Yang: … Ruguo ni jiaru wo de duiwu, wo jiejinquanli di wei ni xie ge … (如果你加入我的队伍, 我竭尽全力地为你写歌。If you join my team, I will try my best to write songs for you.)

[Applause]

T2 Liu: Guniang, zai zheli buzhi ta yige ren hui xie ge. (姑娘, 在这里不只他一个人会写歌。Miss, other people here can also write songs, not just him.)

T3 Yu: Wo ye hui xie ge. Wo ye xie le **ersanshi nian** le. (我也会写歌。我也写了**二、三十年**了。I can write songs, too. I've been writing for **twenty or thirty years**.)

T4 Liu: Erqie wo bu shi gei ziji xie ge, wo gei **henduo** bie de geshou xie ge. Ta de ge **daban** du shi gei ta ziji xie de. (而且我不是给自己写歌, 我给**很多**别的歌手写歌。他的歌**大半**都是给他自己写的。And I didn't write songs for myself. I wrote songs for **many** other singers. **Most of** his songs were written for himself.)

… …

T5 Contestant: Wo juede zheli tai bang le, jiu shi yiqie dou tai dui le, tai dui le! Zhe **shinianlai**, wo zai juguangdeng de beihou, yi ci ci de kan zhe naxie geshou zai juguangdeng de zhong xin, wo zhende wushu ci di hui xiangxiang huoxu you yitian wo ye hui chengwei tamen. Suo yi jintian wo jiu zhan shang wutai, wo yao gaosu dajia wo ai wutai, wo yiding hui zhongxin kaishi. (我觉得这里太棒了, 就是一切都太对了, 太对了!这**十年来**, 我在聚光灯的背后, 一次次的看着那些歌手在聚光灯的中心, 我真的无数次地会想象或许有一天我也会成为他们。所以今天我就站上舞台, 我要告诉大家我爱舞台, 我一定会重新开始。I think this is wonderful, everything falls into place, fantastic! **Over the past ten years**, I have watched from behind the spotlights the singers at the centre of the stage, and I really imagined countless times that one day I would probably become one of them, too. So today I stand on this stage, I want to tell everyone that I love the stage, and I will start again.)

T6 Na: Women huanying ni. (我们欢迎你。We welcome you.)

All four coaches are fighting over the contestant, with Coach Yang vowing to write a song for her. Coaches Liu and Yu counter Yang's proposal by highlighting that they can also write songs. In T3, Yu uses the elastic item *ersanshi nian* ('20 or 30 years') to claim that he is indeed an experienced song writer. In T4, coach Liu tries to compete with Yang, by saying that Yang's songs are *daban* ('most of') written for himself to sing, but Liu has written *henduo* ('many') songs for other singers as well. In T5, the contestant expresses how excited she feels at that moment, an expression *shinianlai* ('over the past ten years') is used to convey her long endured disappointment as a backing singer over many years. All these approximate stretchers are used to provide a just-right amount of information, because there is no need for precise information and the EL used is suitable here (Jucker et al., 2003). In the end, the contestant chose coach Liu, so apparently Liu's persuasion was successful.

Excerpt 25 (2/1/3): Three speakers over four speaking turns. The contestant, Jin, is a musician and all the coaches have turned around for him.

> T1 Na: Wo zhidao wo xianzai yijing juede ni de baowen ye ting bang de. (我知道我现在已经觉得你的豹纹也挺棒的。I know that now I think your leopard print is also excellent.)
> [laughter and applause]
> T2 Yu: Shime! (什么! What!)
> T3 Jin: Wo pingshi du xihuan **yixie** baowen, hen hua **yidian** de dongxi. 我平时都喜欢**一些**豹纹，很花**一点**的东西。I usually like **some** leopard patterns, things **a bit** bright and colourful.)
> T4 Yu: Kuangye xing de, shi ba? (狂野型的, 是吧? Wild type, isn't it?)

Contestant Jin loves funky clothing and also wears sunglasses on stage. Coach Na tries to determine what makes Jin tick by saying, in T1, that she loves his leopard print clothing. Praising Jin's appearance maintains his positive face (Brown & Levinson, 1987). However, in T2, coach Yu is not impressed with Na's tactic. In T3, Jin appears to enjoy Na's compliment, confirming that indeed he likes things with *yixie* ('some') leopard print and *yidian* ('a bit') more colour. The elastic expressions that are used here again perform a just-right elastic function, as they simply convey factual description in a vague manner. In the end, Jin chose Yu, rather than Na, as his coach, probably because Yu is renowned for his funky taste and fun-loving style of music. In this case, Na's persuasion tactics unfortunately did not work.

4.2.2 Rapport Elastic

Rapport elastic (Zhang, 2015) functions build positive and harmonious relationships, and give a sense of in-groupness (Ryoo, 2005). For example, the sentence 'Can I do *something* for you?' indicates a tone of affiliation, affection and solidarity (Fetzer, 2010). Rapport tends to be achieved through establishing common ground and enhancing interpersonal connections (Aijmer, 2002).

Excerpt 26 (5/4/2): Four speakers over nine speaking turns. The contestant, Wang, is from the Buyi ethnic group and three of the four coaches have turned around for her.

T1 Na: **Hen** zhipu, dan **hen** rongyi rang women yixiazi jiu dai jinqu le. Wo **tebie** xihuan ni zhe zhong changfa. (**很**质朴, 但**很**容易让我们一下子就带进去了。我**特别**喜欢你这种唱法。It's **very** simple, but it's **very** easy for us to be touched right away. I like your singing **very much**.)

T2 Contestant: Xiexie laoshi. (谢谢老师。Thank you, teacher.)

T3 Na: Wo **hen** haoqi a. Yinwei wo shi manzu, wo zhidao Guizhou you **haoduo** minzu, Buyi zu. (我**很**好奇啊。 因为我是满族, 我知道贵州有**好多**民族, 布依族。I'm **very** curious. Because I am Manchu, I know there are **many** nationalities in Guizhou, including the Buyi minority.)

T4 Contestant: Dui, Buyi zu ye bei ren chenwei liushui minzu, yinwei women du shenghuo zai hebian. (对, 布依族也被人称为流水民族, 因为我们都生活在河边。Yes, the Buyi minority is also known as the "flowing nationality", because we all live on the riverside.)

…… ……

T5 Na: Ruguo ni yaoshi lai dao wo de zhandui, ai [clicks her tongue, stalls to think about what to say next], ni keyi **jiaoyijiao** wo Buyi zu de **yixie** xiaoqiangdiao ma? (如果你要是来到我的战队, 哎, 你可以

教一教我布依族的**一些**小腔调吗? If you come to my team, alas, can you **just** teach me **some** folk songs of the Buyi?)

T6 Contestant: Keyi. (可以。Yes.)

T7 Na: Keyi a. (可以啊。Yes.)

T8 Wang: Wo gen ni shuo wo de xiangfa. Mei yige shaoshu minzu de gesheng, zai zhege wutai shang de shihou, women daoshi dou **tebie** chenzui. Danshi shaoshu minzu de yinyue, zai wo men zhengge de zhege (liu xing) yinyue de da huanjing limian, yizhi du shi **hen** shao bei da zhong ting dao he jieshou. Ni lai wo de zhandui, wo yao ba ni re'ai de shaoshu minzu de yinyue jie he dao liuxing yinue limian, rang **geng** duo de ren ting dao. Wo yiding yao zuo zhe jian shiqing. (我跟你说我的想法。每一个少数民族的歌声, 在这个舞台上的时候, 我们倒是都**特别**沉醉。但是少数民族的音乐, 在我们整个的这个(流行)音乐的大环境里面, 一直都是**很**少被大众听到和接受。你来我的战队, 我要把你热爱的少数民族的音乐结合到流行音乐里面, 让**更**多的人听到。我一定要做这件事情。I'll tell you what I think. We enjoy **very much** all music from the ethnic groups on this stage. However, ethnic music as a whole has been **very** rarely heard and accepted in the (pop) music world. You come to my team, I want to combine the music of your ethnic group into pop music, so that **more** people can hear it. I will definitely do it.)

T9 Yu: Wa, zhege gou hen, zhege gou hen. Xiang ni zheyang yilei xueyuan, wo **shaoshu** hui chong xialai de, suoyi ni kao lü **yixia**. Dui wo laijiang you xinxian gan. (哇, 这个够狠, 这个够狠。像你这样一类学员, 我**少数**会冲下来的, 所以你考虑**一下**。对我来讲有新鲜感。Wow, that's ruthless, that's ruthless. I **seldomly** go for students like you, so **please** consider choosing me. You bring me a sense of freshness.)

Three coaches (but not Liu) turn around for the contestant, and the battle is intense. The singer is from an ethnic minority and the persuasion tactics, quite naturally, revolve around ethnic music. In T1 and T3, coach Na employs five scalar stretchers (as highlighted) to compliment the contestant's rustic style and to express her curiosity of the ethnic group. In T5, she also uses elastic items to show her eagerness to learn from the contestant and to close the gap between contestant and coach. She says *jiaoyijiao* ('teach a bit') to me *yixie* ('some') Buyi folk music: the first elastic item is a verb duplication which makes a mitigated request;

the second one is a softener which makes Na sound quite modest. In T6, the contestant responds with a positive answer, suggesting that a harmonious relationship (Aijmer, 2002) has been established.

In T8, coach Wang joins the fray, and he uses a few elastic items to establish his connection with the contestant: *tebie* ('very much'), *hen* ('very') and *geng* ('more'). Wang tries to develop rapport with the contestant by promoting ethnic music and, more importantly, integrating it with popular music, so that the hybrid version would attract more people. Wang's strategy is appreciated by coach Yu, in T9. Yu also uses a few elastic items to close his gap with the contestant (Fetzer, 2010), namely *shaoshu* ('rarely') and *yixia* (a polite device when making a request). Yu appeals to the contestant by saying that he is fascinated by his refreshing music.

All three coaches have tried to establish rapport with the contestant in different ways, and EL plays a role in their interactions. In the end, in this case, coach Yu is the winner and the contestant chooses him.

Excerpt 27 (2/1/1): Five speakers over 16 speaking turns. The contestant, Liu, is 18 years old and three coaches have turned around for her.

T1 Yu: Suoyi ni weishenme bu chang zhezhong gelu, shi yinwei ni zhiqian meiyou zhezhong li liang **haishi zenmeyang**, hai shi bu xihuan? (所以你为什么不唱这种歌路， 是因为你之前没有这种力量**还是怎么样**, 还是不喜欢? So why don't you sing this style of song, because you don't have the power **or something**, or you don't like this style?)

T2 Liu: Yinwei wo yiqian bijiao shou, keyi yibian chang yibian tiao, nazhong **hen** ke'ai de ge. zicong wo pang le, wo jiu jueding yao zuo yige liliangxing de ren le. (因为我以前比较瘦, 可以一边唱一边跳， 那种**很**可爱的歌。自从我胖了, 我就决定要做一个力量型的人了。 Because I used to be thin, so I could sing and dance at the same time, doing that kind of **very** lovely songs. Ever since I became bigger, I decided to sing powerful songs.)

T3 Na: Zhe jiu dui le! (这就对了! You have done the right thing!)

T4 Yu: Yuanlai yinyue rang ni you le power. (原来音乐让你有了 Power. So music gives power.)

T5 Zhang: Yating [contestant's given name], juedui bu yao xiang ni ziji pang **haishi shenme de**, wo gen ni jiang, pang you shenme guanxi a?

(雅婷, 绝对不要想你自己胖**还是什么的**, 我跟你讲, 胖有什么关系啊? Yating, don't ever think that you are fat **or anything like that**, I tell you, why does it matter being fat?)

[applause]

T6 Yu: Mei cuo, hui changge **geng** zhongyao! (没错, 会唱歌**更**重要! Correct, singing is **even more** important!)

T7 Zhang: Pang, hui changge, you zixin, haobuhao, Yating? (胖 , 会唱歌, 有自信, 好不好, 雅婷? Big girl, but singing with confidence, okay? Yating?)

T8 Yu: Dangran wo xiang wen **yixia**, yinwei ta xianzai hai shi yige xiao nühai, ni shuo ni zhe ge pang hui dui ni zaocheng yingxiang? (当然我想问**一下**, 因为她现在还是一个小女孩, 你说你这个胖会对你造成影响? Of course, could I **please** ask, because she is still a little girl now, do you think that being fat will affect you?)

T9 Liu: Hui **youdian** shangxin. (会**有点**伤心。 Would be **a bit** sad.)

T10 Wang: Weishime? (为什么? Why?)

T11 Liu: Yinwei pang le jiu mei you **name** meili. (因为胖了就没有**那么**美丽。 Being fat would not be **so** beautiful.)

T12 Na: Ni kan A Mei bu mei ma? (你看阿妹不美吗? Don't you think A Mei is pretty?)

T13 Zhang: Najie, ni shuo wo pang ma? (那姐, 你说我胖吗? Sister Na, are you implying that I'm fat?)

T14 Na: Wo bu shi shuo ni pang. (我不是说你胖。 I'm not saying that you are fat.)

T15 Yu: Na Ying, ni hai shi pengyou ma? Zhezhong hua jiao Wang Feng jiang ma. (那英, 你还是朋友吗? 这种话叫汪锋讲嘛。 Are you still a friend, Na Ying? This should be said by Wang Feng.)

T16 Wang: A Mei **yidiandian** dou bupang. (阿妹**一点点**都不胖。 A Mei is not fat, not **one bit**.)

The contestant, Liu, is a large girl, and she believes that large girls are not attractive. In T1, coach Yu asks Liu why she did not sing powerful songs in the past. He guesses that she possibly did not have the physical strength *or something like that*. He uses the general extender (Terraschke & Holmes, 2007) here to indicate an intimate relationship between the speakers. This is because the understanding of a general extender is often based on the common ground between the speaker and listener. The use of such expressions indicates some form of intimacy between the interactants (Ryoo, 2005). In T1, Yu does not want to list everything that is similar to 'no physical strength'; he probably believes that there is no need to list everything here because his interactants should know what he means. Also, in this case, there would be insufficient time for him to list all similar things.

In T2, Liu answers Yu's question: she was thin in the past and so she could sing songs while also dancing. After she became larger in size, she decided to switch to singing more powerful songs. Yu and Zhang encourage her, in T3 and T4, by saying that it was the correct thing to do and music gives people power. In T5, coach Zhang advises Liu that being a large girl has no relevance to being a good singer, and to get 'I'm fat *and anything like that*' out of her mind. Zhang uses another general extender here, *haishi shenme de* ('and anything like that'). The function of this general extender is similar to the earlier one used in T1. Note that, in this turn, Zhang addresses Liu by her given name, a strategic move to make Liu feel happy about herself. Zhang's confidence in Liu wins a round of applause from the audience.

In T6, Yu emphasises that singing is much more important than appearance by using the scalar word *geng* ('even more') and, in T7, Zhang continues her argument that large girls can be confident and good singers. In T8, Yu asks a mitigated question with the help of the softener *yixia* (a politeness marker): would the young contestant be affected by being overweight? In T9, Liu admits she would be *youdian* ('a bit', an approximate stretcher) broken-hearted and, in T11, says that being fat is not pretty.

Coach Na, in T12, turns to coach Zhang, asking, 'Don't you think A Mei is pretty?' Na addresses Zhang by using her nickname to demonstrate their closeness. The question implies that Zhang is a large girl too, so Zhang asks Na, 'Are you implying that I am fat?', which Na denies. In T15, Yu fools around and asks coach Wang to be the judge on the issue. Wang appears to have no other option but to say that Zhang is not at all fat (*yidiandian*, 'not at all', 'not even one bit'), and a scalar stretcher is used here to emphasise the degree of negation. Wang's answer caters to positive politeness, by maintaining the face wants of coach Zhang (Brown & Levinson, 1987).

Between T1 and T11, EL was used to establish rapport between the contestant and coaches, and then from T12 to T16 was used to maintain in-groupness between the coaches. Excerpt 27 demonstrates that EL can create rapport not only between coach and contestant, but also between coaches.

Excerpt 28 (5/4/6): Two speakers over two speaking turns. The contestant, Wan, is a musician and all the coaches have turned around for her.

> T1 Na: Ni juede xiha de jingshen shi shenme? (你觉得嘻哈的精神是什么? What do you think of the spirit of hip hop?)
>
> T2 Wan: **Wo juede** hip hop ta de yige zhongdian, yige zhongxindian jiu shi keep real, baochi zhenshi, zuo ni ziji. Buguan shi xie ge, hai shi zuo ren ye hao, **huozhe shi zenmeyang**, jiu **duo** dian zhencheng, **shao** dian taolu zheyang. (**我觉得** hip hop 它的一个中点, 一个中心点就是 keep real, 保持真实, 做你自己。不管是写歌, 还是做人也好, **或者是怎么样**, 就**多**点真诚, **少**点套路这样。**I think** a main thing of hip hop, a central point is to keep real, keep the truth and be yourself. No matter whether writing songs or being a good person **or all that**, be sincere **more** and routine **less**.)

The contestant, Wan, is asked by coach Na to explain what hip hop means. Wan appears to be a bit uneasy talking about the concept, perhaps feeling like she is teaching a fish how to swim in front of all these well-known musical artists. Wan begins her explanation by using an epistemic stretcher (*wo juede*, 'I think') to demonstrate her modesty, which helps to close the gap between herself and her listeners. She says that keeping real and being oneself is the spirit of hip hop, and being more genuine and less routine is the key to songwriting and how to behave, *or all that*. The general extender *huozhe shi zenmeyang* ('or all that') is used under the assumption that the speaker and listeners have a common understanding in terms of what is entailed by 'or all that'. Songwriting and how to be a good person are two exemplary members of this category, with the other members of this category being similar to the two exemplary members and should be understood by all the parties involved. Therefore, the use of EL in this answer, particularly the general extension, functions to highlight the in-groupness among interactants.

Wan chose coach Zhou's song for this audition but, in the end, she chose Na to be her coach. A number of contestants chose one of Zhou's songs to perform, but then did not choose him to be their coach. One reason could be that Zhou does not come across as being as pushy or persuasive as the other coaches.

Excerpt 29 (5/4/1): Five speakers over eight speaking turns. The contestant, Li, is a university student and two of the four coaches have turned around for him.

T1 Wang: Ta **haoxiang zhishao** you sanzhong changfa … (他**好像至少**有三种唱法 … He **seems** to have **at least** three kinds of canto.)

T2 Yu: … Meiguanxi, ni jiu yong ni de fangfa chang, chang yige **shenme** "Zhengfu" a, dajia shu de ge … (没关系，你就用你的方法唱，唱一个**什么**"征服"啊，大家熟的歌。It doesn't matter, you can sing in your own way, sing **something like** "Conquest", everyone's familiar song.)

T3 Li: Wo chang **yixia** "Meng Yichang" **ba**. (我唱**一下**"梦一场"**吧**。**Allow** me to sing "All a dream".)

T4 Yu: Hao, hao. (好，好。OK, OK.)

… …

T5 Wang: Ni xuan le Jielun de ge, **wo** daoshi **juede** ru guo ni qu le Jielun duiwu limian, ta you **keneng** hui you mimi wuqi. (你选了杰伦的歌，**我**倒是**觉得**如果你去了杰伦队伍里面，他有**可能**会有秘密武器。You chose Jielun's song, actually **I think** if you go to Jielun's team, he **may** have secret weapons for you.)

T6 Zhou: Ai, zhe shi bang wo lapiao de yisi **ba**? (哎，这是帮我拉票的意思**吧**? Well, is this the way to pull the ticket for me, **right**?)

T7 Wang: A. (啊，Ah.)

T8 Na: Ni shi bu shi **youdian** jieshou bu le Wang Feng zheyang? (你是不是**有点**接受不了汪峰这样? Are you **somewhat** not able to accept Wang Feng like this?)

Coaches Zhou and Yu have both turned around for Li. Li was asked to try a singer's song. In T1, coach Wang tries to help Li by pointing out that the singer appears to have at least three singing styles.

The elastic item *haoxiang* ('seem') and *zhishao* ('at least') indicate Wang's tentative tone, who perhaps wants to create a harmonious feeling. In T2, coach Yu encourages Li to just be himself, and sing a popular song, something like 'Conquest'. The general extender *shenme* ('something like') is an indicator of in-groupness (Ryoo, 2005). 'Conquest' is coach Wang's song, and Yu's recommendation would have been appreciated by Wang. In T3, Li makes his decision in a tender tone of voice to maintain the good relationship that has been established with coaches, manifested through his use of the politeness markers, *yixia* and *ba*.

In T5, coach Wang, as an 'outsider', recommends coach Zhou to Li with the help of EL (*juede* 'think', *keneng* 'may'). Zhou, in T6, seeks Wang's confirmation by using the politeness maker *ba*. Na, in T8, jokes about this, enquiring whether Zhou finds Wang's friendly assistance rather unexpected, where *youdian* ('somewhat') highlights humour and maintains the harmonious relationship. The EL that is used here aims to show affection (Holmes, 1988) and establish rapport between coach and contestant, as well as between the coaches.

Excerpt 30 (1/1/1): Two speakers over two speaking turns. Three of the four coaches have turned around for the contestant, Huang.

> T1 Yang: Ni ruguo canjia dao wo de duiwu libian, wo jinnian you san-shier chang de quanguo xunyan de geren yanchanghui, wo yaoqing ni dang wo de jiabin. (你如果参加到我的队伍里边, 我今年有三十二场的全国巡演的个人演唱会, 我邀请你当我的嘉宾。 If you join my team, I will invite you to be my guest singer, as I am going to have 32 solo concerts in my national tour this year.)
>
> T2 Yu: "Huiluo"! Bu yao guan nage 32 chang **shenme de**. Ruguo ni zai wo de dui shang, wo hui bang ni zhege ziran de ganranli **gengjia** xuanran, rang dajia **geng** gandong. ("贿赂"! 不要管那个三十二场**什么的**。   如果你在我的队上，   我会帮你这个自然的感染力**更加**渲染, 让大家**更**感动。 Bribe! Don't pay attention to that 32 concerts **or all that**. If you are on my team, I will help you with **more** natural appeal and make the audience **more** touched by your song.)

The competition between the three coaches for contestant Huang is rather intense. In T1, coach Yang plays his trump card by inviting

Huang to sing at his 32 solo concerts that year. Yang has a tendency to do this to attract contestants during the auditions. Coach Yu, in T2, 'complains' light-heartedly. He asks Huang to ignore Yang's 'corrupted' offer and pay no heed to the 32 concerts *shenme de* ('or all that'). Yu also uses two further scalar words to persuade Huang to join his team, in T2.

The above interactions demonstrate that some 'fighting' seems to have been going on between the coaches, but only in a semi-joking way. The language, including EL, creates the feeling of a well-maintained interpersonal relationship. The use of elastic items works to establish some rapport between the parties involved. Coach Na was rather forceful and walked up to the stage to dance with Huang and, in the end, she was selected to be the coach.

4.2.3 Mitigating Elastic

The mitigating function of EL is used to soften the tone of speech and to show politeness (Zhang, 2015). Hedges are often found to serve this function, which tend to make the meaning less precise (Aijmer, 1984, 2002; Holmes, 1993; Lakoff, 1973). A typical hedge is 'sort of', which qualifies the certainty of a statement (Parvaresh & Zhang, 2019; Prince, Frader, & Bosk, 1982). EL, such as 'sort of', is also a politeness marker serving face wants (Miskovic-Lukovic, 2009). Communicating imprecisely or 'safely vague' may avoid face-violations, and EL can serve the positive face (cater to face wants) and the negative face (avoid imposing on others) (Brown & Levinson, 1987, p. 116).

Excerpt 31 (6/5/11): Five speakers over six speaking turns. Unfortunately, no coach has turned around for the contestant, Zhang, who is a songwriter.

> T1 Na: Wo shuo **yixia**. **Wo jiu juede dabufen** de shijian, wo du tao buchu **shenme** maobing. Dan shi wo jiu xiwang ni zai di'er duan de shihou, chang qilai ne, yao you qifu le. Yinwei ni yizhi du zai nage difang huang, huang lai huang qu **wo jiu juede** jiu cha name **yidiandian** de gandong. (我说**一下**。**我就觉得大部分**的时间, 我都挑不

出**什么**毛病。但是我就希望你在第二段的时候，唱起来呢，要有
起伏了。因为你一直都在那个地方晃，晃来晃去**我就觉得**就差那
么**一点点**的感动。Can I **please** say this? **I** just **feel that most of the
time**, I can't pick out **any** problems. But I was hoping that when you
sang the second part of the song, you could have made some twists and
turns. You were just tagging along, lacking, **I feel**, **a little** something
that makes people really moved.)

T2 Zhang: Mingbai. (明白。I see.)

T3 Zhou: **Wo juede** ta de shengxian na, you yizhong wennuan de ganjue.
Qishi ni ruguo chang Eason de ge, yinggai ye **ting** bucuo de. (**我觉得**
他的声线哪，有一种温暖的感觉。其实你如果唱 Eason 的歌，应
该也**挺**不错的。**I think** his voice has a warm feeling. Actually, if you
sing Eason's song, it should be **pretty** good too.)

T4 Chen: Wo ting wan zhihou, wo qishi you zhengge ren du lengzhu le.
Juede nage nühai, na ge duixiang hai **man** can de, **youdian** xixu de
ganjue. Dan bu shi wo zui xihuan de nazhong, suoyi wo jiu meiyou
an xialai. (我听完之后，我其实有整个人都愣住了。**觉得**那个女
孩，那个对象还**蛮**惨的，**有点**唏嘘的感觉。但不是我最喜欢的那
种，所以我就没有按下来。Having heard it, I actually was shocked.
I think the girl, the partner, is **quite** misfortunate, and feeling **a little**
sad. However, this performance is not my type, so I didn't choose him.)

T5 Liu: Eason jiang zhe jiu bu shi ta de cai, zui jiandan de jiangfa. (Eason
讲这就不是他的菜，最简单的讲法。Eason said it was not his type,
the simplest explanation.)

T6 Chen: Dan ni zhende meiyou shenme hao taoti. Qi shi ni chang ge
ting gandong de, zhende. Ni de yaozi **tebie** de qingchu, qishi **hen** rongyi rang wo jinru ni zai jiang shenme, zhege zhuangtai. (但你真的没
有什么好挑剔。其实你唱歌**挺**感动的， 真的。你的咬字**特别**地
清楚，其实**很**容易让我进入你在讲什么，这个状态。Honestly, you
are really good. Honestly, I was **quite** touched by your singing, really.
Your pronunciation is **particularly** clear, in fact **very** easy for me to
understand the story the song tells.)

This episode is one of the final auditions. Therefore, limited space is left
in each team and it has become very competitive: as a result Zhang has
not been selected by any coach. Under the circumstances, the coaches
comfort Zhang to make him feel better. Coach Na, in T1, begins by
asking to be allowed to explain *a bit* ('yixia', a politeness marker) why

she just feels ('wo jiu juede') that there is *not much* ('shenme') of a problem with *most* ('dabufen') of Zhang's performance. If anything, *she just feels* ('wo jiu juede') that it lacks *a little bit* ('yidiandian'). Na uses all these hedges to convey her reasons for not turning around for Zhang.

In T3, coach Zhou *feels* ('wo juede') that Zhang's voice delivers warmth, and suggests that if Zhang were to sign one of Eason's (another coach) songs, it should be *quite* ('ting') good. In T4, coach Chen (i.e. Eason, looking very sincere and smiling while he is speaking) mentions that he *feels* ('juede') he is being touched by Zhang's song, and feels *a bit* ('youdian') sorry for the *very* ('man') sad story told by the song. However, the song is not quite Chen's style, so he did not turn around for Zhang. Chen emphasises, in T6, that Zhang sang perfectly and *quite* ('ting') movingly, his pronunciation was *particularly* ('tebie') clear, and it was *very* ('hen') easy to understand the story behind the song.

All the coaches' efforts in using a combination of hedges as well as intensifiers appear to have improved the contestant's mood, and the use of EL plays a role in conveying encouragement and mitigating critical evaluation (Miskovic-Lukovic, 2009).

Excerpt 32 (5/4/3): Three speakers over four speaking turns. Three of the four coaches have turned around for the contestant, Shan, whose singing incorporated some Chinese operatic elements.

T1 Zhou: Wo xian shuo **yixia**. Wo benlai jiu shi xihuan Zhongguofeng de, ni hai yong le jia shang xiqu de yanchang, suoyi shuo ni you shou dao wo de yingxiang, **wo juede**. (我先说**一下**。我本来就是喜欢中国风的，你还用了加上戏曲的演唱，所以说你有受到我的影响，**我觉得**。Can I say something first **please**? I always like the Chinese style, you also added operatic singing, so you have been influenced by me, **I think**.)

T2 Na: **Wo juede** Zhongguofeng dui wo laishuo, yinggai bi Zhou Jielun geng dong. (**我觉得**中国风对我来说，应该比周杰伦更懂。**I think** I know the Chinese style better than Zhou Jielun.)

T3 Yu: Geng neihang. (更内行。Know more.)

T4 Na: Dui. (对。Yes.)

There is an intense battle between the three coaches over contestant Shan. In T1, coach Zhou mentions that his musical influence can be seen in Shan's performance. Zhou makes this assessment using *wo juede* ('I think') at the end of the sentence. 'I think' in the clause-final position is known to be mitigating (Zhang, 2014; Zhang & Sabet, 2016). In addition, Zhou uses a politeness marker *yixia* when saying, 'Can I say something please?' at the start of his turn, making his tone softer. In T2, Na fights back by claiming that she knows the 'Chinese style' better than Zhou. Na also uses *wo juede* ('I think') to tone down her claim slightly, perhaps to avoid sounding too arrogant.

Excerpt 33 (1/1/10): Four speakers over six speaking turns. All the coaches have turned around for the contestant, Zhang.

> T1 Na: Aya, tai gandong le! (啊呀, 太感动了! Wow, it's so moving!)
> T2 Yu: Wo tai zhenjing le. (我太震惊了。I'm so shocked.)
> … …
> T3 Yu: Ni **haoxiang** yanjing … (你**好像**眼睛 … It **seems** your eyes…)
> T4 Zhang: Dui, yinwei congxiao shishenjing weisuo, suoyi wo dou kan bu jian. (对, 因为从小视神经萎缩, 所以我都看不见。Yes, I've suffered from optic atrophy since I was little, so I couldn't see.)
> … …
> T5 Yu: Wo zai ting ta de shengyin de shihou, wo juede tai xiang Deng Lijun le. (我在听她的声音的时候, 我觉得太像邓丽君了。When I listen to her voice, I feel it seems like Deng Lijun very much.)
> T6 Liu: Tai xiang le, shizai shi. (太像了, 实在是。Very much alike, indeed.)

The contestant, Zhang, is a blind street performer. While she was singing, she also played a keyboard on stage, which earned a standing ovation from the coaches. She sang Deng Lijun's song, who is a well-known singer. The coaches were touched by her unique talent, as expressed in T1, T2, T5 and T6. In T3, coach Yu asks about Zhang's eyes in a very sensitive manner: it seems ('haoxiang') your eyes … Talking about a person's handicap is a sensitive topic, and thus Yu resorts to the elastic word 'seems' to soften his tone, and to show his care and respect to Zhang. Yu also employs the strategy of an unfinished sentence to avoid saying the word 'blind', or suchlike. Apparently, Zhang is comfortable with Yu's veiled question and answers it in T4. This interaction works out successfully with the help of mitigating EL.

Excerpt 34 (1/1/3): Six speakers over 11 speaking turns. None of the coaches has turned around for the contestant, Deng.

T1 Yu: **Kanqilai** hen wenjing de nanhai, ha. (**看起来**很文静的男孩, 哈. **Looks** **like** a very quiet boy, oh.)

T2 Na: Dui dui dui. (对对对. Yeah, yeah, yeah.)

… …

T3 Yu: Shi yiwei hen wen de gezhe, ha. Keshi zai wending zhong, **haoxiang** meiyou zhua dao daoshimen de zhongdian, hao, wo shi zheyang ganjue de, a. (是一位很稳的歌者, 哈。 可是在稳定中, **好像**没有抓到导师们的重点, 好, 我是这样感觉的, 啊。You are a very stable singer, oh. But while being stable, it **seems** that you didn't catch the emphasis of your mentors, OK, I feel that way, ah.)

T4 Liu: **Keneng** zhe shi weiyi **dagai** meiyou rang wo an zhege anniu de yuanyin. Meiyou yige di fang ciji dao wo, rang wo yixiazi zhan qilai pai zhege dongxi. (**可能**这是唯一**大概**没有让我按这个按钮的原因。没有一个地方刺激到我, 让我一下子站起来拍这个东西。**Maybe** this is **perhaps** the only reason why I didn't press this button. No particular part of the singing really touched me, making me stand up without hesitation and press this thing.)

T5 Deng: Xiexie Liu Huan laoshi. (谢谢刘欢老师。Thank you, teacher Liu Huan.)

T6 Host: Na Ying tongxue. (那英同学。Student/Young* Na Ying.) *Calling coach Na 'student' is a humorous usage here.

T7 Na: Jiayou ba, jiayou! (加油吧, 加油! Come on, come on!) [laughter and applause]

T8 Yang: Wo shi ganjue shi zheyang de, yinwei ni jintian chang zhuge de shihou, **wo juede** ting hao de. Danshi chang dao fuge gaoyin de shihou, suiran shi you qubie, danshi **wo juede** fan cha shi feichang da de. Chang dao fuge de shihou, jiu shi you, shengyin shang qu le, ye li zhu le, danshi **shaowei youdian** bian. (我是感觉是这样的, 因为你今天唱主歌的时候, **我觉得**挺好的。但是唱到副歌高音的时候, 虽然是有区别, 但是**我觉得**反差是非常大的。唱到副歌的时候, 就是有, 声音上去了, 也立住了, 但是**稍微有点**扁。Here is how I feel: today when you sang the verses, **I think** it was good. However when it came to the treble of the chorus, although there was a difference, but **I think** the contrast is very large. During the chorus, well, it reached the treble and kept there as well, but **a little bit** flat.)

… … [coaches continue to provide advice and support]

T9 Liu: Ni yinggai hui you jinbu, ni yiding hui you jinbu. Xiangxin wo. (你应该会有进步，你一定会有进步。相信我。You should make progress, you will make progress. Trust me.)

T10 Yang: Wo juede ta feichang feichang de qianxu, ta de ganjue feichang hao. (我觉得他非常非常的谦虚，他的感觉非常好。I think he is very modest. His sense is very good.)

T11 Liu: Jixu nuli, yiding hui hao. (继续努力，一定会好。Keep going, it will be good.)

The contestant, Deng, must have been devastated when no one turned around for him. Coach Yu, in T1, tries to cheer him up by praising him ('*looks like* a gentle and quiet boy'). Na agrees with Yu, and both maintain Deng's positive face (Brown & Levinson, 1987). In T3, Yu states that Deng sings in a very steady manner, but *seems* ('haoxiang') to be lacking in focus, and that was why he did not turn around. Coach Liu, in T4, seconds Yu's comments, by saying that, *maybe* ('keneng') an unfocused moment (no special moment) is *perhaps* ('dagai') the only reason why Liu did not turn around. Liu uses two epistemic items here to soften his tone to avoid further disappointing Deng.

In T6, the host asks coach Na to comment, and jokingly addresses her as 'student Na' ('Young Na'), most probably to instill some humour and light-heartedness. Na gives some general encouragement in T7; she does not make any specific comment to avoid criticising Deng. In T8, Yang gently points out Deng's weak point, realised by using EL (e.g. the downtoner 'I think' is used repeatedly). According to Yang, Deng sings the verses quite well, but sings the chorus differently, being *a little bit* ('shaowei youdian') flat, where two softeners are used to decrease the sharpness of the critical evaluation. Before Deng leaves the stage, the coaches shower him with lots of encouragement and hope, in T9–T11.

In addition to hedge-like softeners, other types of EL (e.g. intensifiers) can also be used to make emotionally devastated contestants feel better and to cheer them up after a poor audition, as illustrated in Excerpt 34 above.

Excerpt 35 (1/1/6): Two speakers over four speaking turns. Two of the four coaches have turned around for the contestant, Li.

> T1 Yu: 24 sui ya? (24岁呀? 24 years old?)
>
> T2 Li: Chang de **youdian** zhaoji. (长得**有点**着急. My appearance has grown **a little** hastily/I look older than my age.) [laughter from the audience]
>
> T3 Yu: Gan zhou chang a, man **yidian** ma, bie ji ya. (赶着长啊, 慢**一点**嘛, 别急呀。 Grow up hurriedly, slow down **a bit**, don't hurry.)
>
> … …
>
> T4 Li: Qishi siwei laoshi wo du **feichang** **feichang** xihuan. Wo **feichang** xiwang nenggou jiaru Liu Huan laoshi de duiwu. (其实四位老师我都**非常非常**喜欢。我**非常**希望能够加入刘欢老师的队伍。 Actually, I like all four teachers **very** **very** much. I **really** hope to join teacher Liu Huan's team.)

The contestant, Li, is 24 years old, but he looks slightly older. In T2, Li says, with some humour, that his look seems *a bit* ('youdian') '*in a hurry*' ('zhaoji'), implying that his appearance is somewhat more mature than his peers. This joke serves the purpose of self-face wants: to laugh off the 'unpleasant' perception, as well as to make the audience laugh. Similarly, in T3, Yu uses the elastic item *yidian* ('a bit') to ridicule Li in a friendly and humorous way. In this case, EL makes the interactions more enjoyable through its mitigating function. In T4, Li first uses the intensifier *feichang* ('very') twice to convey that he likes all four coaches very much, which foreshadows his later announcement that he wishes to join coach Liu's team. This politeness strategy works well because none of the coaches are offended.

4.2.4 Intensifying Elastic

Intensifying elastic functions increase the strength of an utterance (Zhang, 2015). For example, in 'I am *very* happy to help out', 'very' pushes the tone of 'being happy' to a higher level.

Excerpt 36 (4/3/4): Three speakers over six speaking turns. Two of the four coaches have turned around for the contestant.

T1 Wang: Wo zhidao wo yinggai zenmeyang geiyu ni **haoduo** dongxi, wo meiyou **geng** huali de ci, huozhe **hen** duo zhaor. (我知道我应该怎么样给与你**好多**东西，我没有**更**华丽的词，或者**很**多招儿。I know how I can teach you **a lot of** things; I don't have **very** fancy words, or **a lot of** tricks.)

T2 Na: Wo jiu **geng** meiyou zhaor le. Ni zhidao wo shi yige **tebie** zhipu de daoshi, wo meiyou **name** duo huali de yuyan. Wo ye jiang bu guo ta, danshi wo zhidao ni shi yiwei jianqiang de nüxing. (我就**更**没有招儿了。你知道我是一个**特别**质朴的导师， 我没有**那么**多华丽的语言。 我也讲不过他， 但是我知道你是一位坚强的女性。 I have **even** less tricks than you. You know I'm a **very** simple mentor, I don't have **so** many fussy words. I cannot win him over by arguing, but I know you are a strong woman.)

T3 Wang: Dan shishi shang ta de hua bi wo duo **haoduo** bei. Wo zhi xiang shuo ne, wo shi xi wang dui wo de suoyou de xue uan geiyu tamen **geng** duo laizi yu yinyue de xingfu. (但事实上她的话比我多**好**多倍。 我只想说呢， 我是希望对我的所有的学员给与他们**更**多来自于音乐的幸福。But in fact, she talks **much** more than me. I just want to say, I want to give all my students **much** more happiness from music.)

T4 Na: Dao wo de tuandui lai, **jihu** du shi ni xiang chang shenme, wo jiu rang chang shenme. (到我的团队来, **几乎**都是你想唱什么, 我就让唱什么。Join my team, **almost** **all** **the** **time** I will let you sing whatever you want to sing.)

T5 Wang: Wo juede an ni de xin zou ba, hao ma? (我觉得按你的心走吧。好吗? I think you just follow your heart, okay?

T6 Contestant: Ai'ya, **zhenshi** **hao** nan! (哎呀, **真是好**难! Aya, it's **indeed** **so** hard!)

The contestant is a homemaker with a three-year-old son. Competition takes place between coaches Wang and Na to win the contestant over. In T1, Wang appeals to the contestant by highlighting his ability to offer her *a lot of* ('haoduo') things, instead of *very/a lot of* ('geng', 'hen') fancy (but empty) words and strategic moves. Na strikes back in T2, stating that she has *even* ('geng') less tricks, and she is *extremely* ('tebie') unsophisticated and does not use *so* ('name') much flowery language. In T3, Wang points out that actually Na speaks *much* ('haoduo') more than he does, and his aim is simply to bring his students *much* ('geng') more happiness from music.

Na changes her tactic in T4, where she promises artistic freedom to the contestant, by allowing her to choose her own songs, *almost* ('jihu') any song she wants. In T5, Wang retreats from the battle by simply asking the contestant to go with her heart. The contestant feels *it is indeed extremely* ('zhenshi hao') difficult to decide but, in the end, she chooses Wang to be her coach, probably moved by his pitch. In this excerpt, intensifiers are used as effective weapons to win the battle by increasing the coaches' persuasive powers (Hyland, 2005; Lakoff, 1982).

Excerpt 37 (2/1/7): Three speakers over three speaking turns. All four coaches have turned around for the contestant, Zhu, and an intense battle to win over Zhu has ensued between them.

> T1 Yu: Ta de shengyin **tai** you xi le! (他的声音**太**有戏了! His voice is **extremely** rich!)
>
> T2 Wang: Ta de nage "li" zi shi wo zui xihuan ting de yinse. (他的那个 "离"字是我最喜欢听的音色。 His singing of the character "leave" is my favourite timbre.)
>
> T3 Na: Wo xiang gen ni shuo, **hen** zao nianjian ting guo Liu Huan chang "Li bu kai ni", qian yi duan shijian ting Huang Qishan chang guo, ni chang zheshou "Li bu kai ni", **geng** you hou du, **geng** you rang wo xiangxiang de kongjian, **feichang** de you neirong, **feichang** de nanren. (我想跟你说, **很**早年间听过刘欢唱"离不开你", 前一段时间 听黄绮珊唱过, 你唱这首 "离不开你", **更**有厚度, **更**有让我想象 的空间, **非常**地有内容, **非常**得男人。 I want to tell you, I heard Liu Huan sing "I cannot do without you" a **very** long time ago. I also heard Huang Qishan sing it before, but your version has **more** depth, **more** imagination, space, **extraordinarily** rich, and **very** manly.)
>
> [applause]

The contestant, Zhu, is a single father and desperately needs a professional job as a musician to support his family. He performed a song called 'I cannot do without you', which is a well-known and powerful song in China. In T1 and T2, both coaches speak highly of Zhu. In T3, coach Na uses five intensifiers (two instances of *very*, two instances of *more*, and *extraordinarily*) in a row to emphasise her appraisal of Zhu's excellence. Na believes that Zhu sings even better than the two old hands sitting before him: he has more depth, more imagination, sings with substance and is very manly. Na's extraordinarily positive comments earn a round of applause from the audience. Zhu chooses Na, in the end, perhaps because of her persuasive language which performs an intensifying elastic function.

Excerpt 38 (1/2/1): Five speakers over 10 speaking turns. All four coaches have turned around for the contestant, Dingding.

> T1 Liu: … Zhe jiu shi shengyin benshen keneng dailai de yizhong meili, wo **feichang** xihuan … (这就是声音本身可能带来的一种魅力, 我**非常**喜欢。… This is the charm that the voice itself can bring. I like it **very much**.)
>
> T2 Na: Dingding, ni ting hao le. Dao muqian weizhi, **zheme** duo geshou, youqi shi wo nage tuan dui, xuan liao **hao** duo du shi da sangzi. Jintian **tai** taoqiao le, zheng xuan dao wo xinli qu le. (丁丁, 你听好了。到目前为止，**这么**多歌手，尤其是我那个团队，选了**好**多都是大嗓子。今天**太**讨巧了，正选到我心里去了。Dingding, listen. So far, **so** many singers, especially in my team, **very** many of them have a large voice. Today I've got **really** lucky, you are exactly who I want.)
>
> … …
>
> T3 Yang: … Yige zhongyao de yuanyin shi ni gen tamen zai yikuair, ni hui gen tamen chan sheng qianglie de daigou de, yinwei tamen de nianling bi wo da **duo** le. Haiyou wo zhege dui wu limian yige nüsheng du meiyou, ni lai le du yifen, ni xiang zenmeyang zenmeyang. [audience laughs] (… 一个最重要的原因是你跟他们在一块，你会跟他们产生强烈的代沟的, 因为他们的年龄比我大**多**了。还有我这个队伍里面一个女生都没有，你来了独一份，你想怎么样怎么样。The most important reason is that if you are with them, you will have a strong generational gap with them, because they are **much** older than I am. Also, there's no girl in my team. If you come alone, you can do whatever you want.) [audience laughter]
>
> T4 Na: Wow!
>
> T5 Yu: **Geng** weixian! (**更**危险! **More** dangerous!)
>
> T6 Na: Wa, Dingding xiang hao liao! (哇, 丁丁想好了! Wow, Dingding, you'd better watch out!)

T7 Dingding: Wo xianzai xiang shuo yixie hua. Cong nin zhe kaishi [turns to Yu]. Qishi nin de ge wo ting guo **hen** duo, erqie wo **tebie** xihuan nin de fengge. (我现在想说一些话。从您这开始 [turns to Yu]。其实您的歌我听过**很**多，而且我**特别**喜欢您的风格。I'd like to say something now. I like to start with you. I've listened **quite** a lot to your songs, and I like your style **very** **much**.)

T8 Yu: Xiexie! (谢谢! Thank you!) [Yu's hands are in a prayerful position]

T9 Dingding: Ranhou Liu Huan laoshi, women yi jia ren du **feichang** xihuan nin. (然后刘欢老师，我们一家人都**非常**喜欢您。And teacher Liu Huan, my family all like you **very** **much**.)

T10 Liu: Xiexie! Bi ni **geng** jin yi bu. (谢谢!比你**更**进一步。Thank you! (talking to Yu) Love me **more** than you.) [laughs]

The contestant, Dingding, is a lovely young model, and the coaches turned around very quickly for her rather than waiting until the last minute. In T1, coach Liu loves Dingding's charming voice *very much* ('feichang'). In T2, Na emphasises that Dingding will fill a niche in her team, because among *so* ('zheme') many students so far, all have *very* ('hao') large voices. Na feels *really* ('tai') lucky today that Dingding (with a different musical talent) has come along. Yang, in T3, cleverly points out the age gap between the other three coaches and Dingding, as they are *much* ('duo') older than Yang, and so she could potentially have a problem with them because of generational differences. Yang promises Dingding that she would be the one and only female singer in his team because, to date, he has not chosen any female performers for his team. From T4 to T6, coaches Yu and Na light-heartedly 'warn' Dingding about going to Yang's team because he is single and loves beautiful girls.

From T7 to T10, Dingding uses three intensifiers to praise coaches Yu and Liu, politely paving the way to announce her decision. In the end, Dingding chooses coach Yang anyway, perhaps as a result of his pitch promising her that she will be the one and only female performer in his team. In this excerpt, the intensifying elastic function is used to maintain the positive face wants of both contestant and coaches, demonstrating the significant role that strengtheners play in communication. The coaches and contestant use the intensifying elastic function for slightly different purposes though: the former tries to increase the tone of their claim to attract the contestant, whereas the latter is trying to be polite and less offensive before rejecting some of the coaches by making them feel better.

Excerpt 39 (1/1/2): Three speakers over eight speaking turns. All four coaches have turned around for the contestant, Huang.

T1 Na: Ai, ni shi diao yanlei le? (哎, 你是掉眼泪了? Eh, are you crying?)

T2 Yang: Meiyou meiyou. (没有没有。No no.)

T3 Yu: Ku le ni? (哭了你? Are you crying?)

T4 Yang: Wo shi … (我是 … I'm…) [lowers his head and wipes his eyes]

T5 Yu: Yanjing **tai** gan le, shi ba? (眼睛**太**干了, 是吧? Eyes are **too** dry, aren't they?)

… …

T6 Yang: Wo zhen de shi xin limian **tebie** **tebie** de gandong. Wo liu de yanlei bu shi gei ni kan de, shi gei wo ziji de. Wo zhen de bu pian ni. (我真的是心里面**特别特别**地感动。我流的眼泪不是给你看的, 是给我自己的。我真的不骗你。I feel **really** **really** very touched. My tears are not for you to see, but for myself. I honestly mean it.)

T7 Na: Ou, liu gei ziji. (哦, 流给自己。Oh, tears for yourself.)

T8 Yang: Women bu neng yong yanlei qu mihuo. (我们不能用眼泪去迷惑。We can't use tears to cheat.)

Contestant Huang's song brought coach Yang to tears, by reminding him of the hard times he has experienced in the past. When asked about his tears, Yang is somewhat reluctant to admit that he is crying. Therefore, in T5, it would appear that coach Yu is trying to cover for him by pointing out that Yang is not actually crying, but that he must have *too* ('tai') dry eyes. Yu is trying to save the negative face of his fellow coach (Brown & Levinson, 1987), by ensuring that Yang is not being imposed upon. In T6, Yang explains that he is *really really* ('tebie tebie') touched by the song, and his tears are genuine and not just for show. The intensifier *tebie* is used twice to enhance the degree that Yang has been touched. He also explains further, in T8, that tears should not be used to confuse, or gain sympathy from, the contestant, as well as other people.

Excerpt 40 (1/1/7): Three speakers over five speaking turns. Two of the four coaches have turned around for the contestant, Li.

T1 Li: Jiu buyiding dou shi zhege difang, danshi mei shang du hui you zhi. Tongxuemen hui jue de youdian chaoxiao huozhe shi kan bu qi. Dan shi wo **zhende feichang feichang** di jidong. Wo yong wo de shengyin zhengming ziji bing bu bi bieren cha. (就不一定都是这个地方， 但是眉上都会有痣。同学们会觉得有点嘲笑或者是看不起。但是我**真的非常非常地**激动。我用我的声音证明自己并不比别人差。This is not always the place, but there is always a mole on the eyebrow. Students may laugh at me a little or despise me. But I'm **really very**, **very** excited. I use my voice to prove that I am not inferior to anyone.)

T2 Na: Dangran bu bi. (当然不比。Of course not.) [the audience applauds]

T3 Yu: Ni budan bu bi bieren cha, ni hai bi bieren qiang **hen** duo… Wo juede ronghe (yiban liuxing changfa he ziran shengtai changfa) de **hen** ziran **hen** qiaomiao. Rang wo zhiqian gen Yunnan shaoshu minzu zuo le **hen** duo de goutong, suoyi wo geren shi **feichang** shanchang ba zheyangzi de yuanshengtai gequ gen liuxing yinyue zuo qiaomiao de ronghe. (你不但不比别人差， 你还比别人强**很**多。。。我觉得融合 (一般流行唱法和自然生态唱法)的**很**自然**很**巧妙。让我之前跟云南少数民族作了**很**多的沟通, 所以我个人是**非常**擅长把这样子的原生态歌曲跟流行音乐做巧妙的融合。Not only are you not inferior to others, you are **much** better than others … I think fusion (popular singing and traditional singing) is **very** natural and **very** ingenious. In the past, I have interacted with the minority nationalities in Yunnan **very** often, so I am **very** good at skilfully integrating the traditional songs with pop music.)

T4 Na: Jiu shi ni ma! (就是你吗! That's you!)

T5 Yu: Jiu shi wo. Yinwei wo **hao** duo ci zheyang de jingyan. (就是我。因为我**好**多次这样的经验。It's me, because I have **many** many times worked like this.)

Contestant Li is a young prince of the Hani ethnic minority in China. In T1, contestant Li uses three intensifiers in a row to highlight his excitement at being selected by the coaches. The confirmation from coaches Na and Yu, in T2 and T3, provides much comfort to Li.

Coach Yu desperately wants Li and so he uses a series of intensifiers in T3 and T5, as highlighted above, to persuade Li to join his team. Yu emphasises that Li is *much* ('hen') better than the others and the hybrid form of popular singing and traditional singing is *very* ('hen') natural and *very* ('hen') ingenious. Yu also mentions that he knows the Yunan minorities in China *very* ('hen') well and is *especially* ('feichang') good at integrating different musical forms into a hybrid style of music. In T5, Yu confirms that he is the one coach who has *many* ('hao') many years of experience and is in the best position to supervise Li's hybrid style of music.

4.2.5   Self-Protection Elastic

The self-protection elastic function, as defined in Zhang (2015), defends the speaker against any potential risks. In a sentence such as 'I *may* be able to lend you the money, but I am not 100% sure', the speaker uses *may* to lessen his/her commitment to *you*, in case the money lending does not happen for whatever reason.

Excerpt 41 (2/1/7): Two speakers over two speaking turns. All four coaches have turned around for the contestant, Zhu.

> T1 Wang: Yiban yige geshou, xiang ni zheyang yige gehou, xuan ge yiding bu shi qingyi xuan de. **Wo juede** ni de gesheng li, **haoxiang** you sushuo de. (一般一个歌手，像你这样一个歌手，选歌一定不是轻易选的。 **我觉得**你的歌声里, **好像**有诉说的。 Generally speaking, a singer like you, does not pick songs arbitrarily. **I think** your voice **seems** to be telling us something.)
>
> T2 Zhu: Zhe shou ge tebie neng chang chu wo xianzai de xinjing. (这首歌特别能唱出我现在的心境。 This song can particularly express my mood right now.)

The song that contestant Zhu performed is a very emotional one called 'I cannot do without you'. Zhu is 41 years old, a single father and has been through a very difficult time. Coach Wang comments that Zhu is a thoughtful singer and must have a reason for choosing that particular soul touching song. Wang senses that Zhu seems to be recounting something in his performance. Wang expresses his observation tentatively by using *I think* ('wo juede') and *appear* ('haoxiang'), the reason for this being, perhaps, to protect himself in case Zhu does not concur with his observation. It is much safer for him to voice his opinion in a less authoritative way. Zhu does not confirm whether he is recounting something in his song, but what he does verify is that the song reflects his current frame of mind.

Excerpt 42 (2/1/3): Two speakers over three speaking turns. All the coaches have turned around for the contestant, Jin, who is a musician himself.

> T1 Zhang: Wo dui ni de shengyin hen you ganjue, wo shi feichang xiwang women you jihui ke yi hechang. Dangran, ni jiaru wo de zhe ge A Mei de family, zhege jiating limian, women **yexu** hui you yixie yinye de jiaoliu. (我对你的声音很有感觉，我是非常希望我们有机会可以合唱。 当然，你加入我的这个阿妹的 family，这个家庭里面，我们**也许**会有一些音乐的交流。I feel very much about your voice, I really hope we can have a chance to sing together. Of course, if you join me, this A Mei family, yeah this family, **perhaps** we can have some exchange of music.)
> T2 Yu: Zhe jiao "huilu"! (这叫"贿赂"! This is called a "bribe"!)
> T3 Zhang: Zhe bu shi "huilu". (这不是"贿赂"。This is not a "bribe".)

Contestant Jin is an excellent singer and coach Zhang is particularly keen for him to join her team, and she makes this known to him, in no uncertain terms, in the first part of T1. However, in the second part of this turn, Zhang scales this down slightly by saying that, if Jin joins her 'A Mei' (Zhang's nickname) family, *perhaps* ('yexu') they could have some exchange of music. Coach Yu immediately protests, in T2, accusing Zhang of bribery, which she denies in T3. In this case, Zhang uses EL to prevent any embarrassment if Jin does not choose her and to protect herself from accusations of 'bribery'. In fact, Jin chose Yu to be his coach, rather than Zhang.

Excerpt 43 (3/2/1): Three speakers over three speaking turns. Three of the four coaches have turned around for the contestant, Qin.

T1 Qi: Wo juede jiu shi liang ge zi "guoyin", yinwei ting ni changge, wanquan meiyou bao liu … (我觉得就是两个字"过瘾"。因为听你唱歌，完全没有保留 … I feel just two words "wonderful", because listening to you singing, you sing the best you can …)

T2 Na: Qishi wo neng ganjue dao ta yao xuan shui. (其实我能感觉到她要选谁。I can actually feel who she is going to choose.)

T3 Wang: Bu, ye buyiding. (不, 也**不一定**。No, **not necessarily**.)

Coach Qi turned around for contestant Qin, and so he speaks highly of her in T1. On the other hand, Na did not turn around for Qin, and that is probably why she risks saying that she can sense who the contestant is going to choose. In T3, coach Wang, who also turned around for Qin, has more at stake, and is therefore careful about making any categorical statement. The use of *not necessarily* ('buyiding') is possibly to shield him from being wrong, in some way. It sounds to be a good choice for Wang to use when playing it safe and not wanting to expose himself in any shape or form.

Excerpt 44 (2/1/4): Two speakers over two speaking turns. All four coaches have turned around for the contestant, Yao.

T1 Wang: Wo gangcai di yi ge zhuanshen, shi yinwei wo yijing ganjue dao ni you **keneng** jiu shi wo xiang yao de. Yinwei ni de butong shi, ni shi yige zhiye de geshou, lai zhege wutai bai fen zhi jiushijiu du shi yeyu de geshou, dui yu ni he tamen, yiding you yidian chabie. Suoyi ni keyi fazi neixin de shuo yixia, nage zhenzheng de mengxiang shi shenme. (我刚才第一个转身，是因为我已经感觉到你有**可能**就是我想要的。因为你的不同是，你是一个职业的歌手，来这个舞台百分之九十九都是业余的歌手，对于你和他们，一定有一点差别。所以你可以发自内心地说一下，那个真正的梦想是什么。Just now I was the first who turned around for you, because I already feel that you **probably** are someone I want. Because you are different, you are a professional singer, and 99% of other contestants here are amateur singers. There must be some difference between you and them, so please tell us honestly what your real dream is.)

T2 Yao: Wo zhenzheng de mengxiang, qishi tebie xiwang jiu shi xiang jitian zheyang, chuan shang niuzaiku, chuan shang pingdixie, zai yige xiang liuxing yinle jie nayang de yige da de wutai shang, he yuedui

laoshi yiqi changge. Yinwei zhende yuanlai, duibuqi [crying, the audience applauds], yinwei jiang zhenhua, zhende wo hen shao you jihui
chang zheyang de xianchang, erqie shi chang zheme haoting de gequ,
wo ziji xihuan de. (我真正的梦想, 其实特别希望就是像今天这样,
穿上牛仔裤, 穿上平底鞋, 在一个像流行音乐节那样的一个大的
舞台上, 和乐队老师一起唱歌。因为真的原来, 对不起, 因为讲真
话, 真的我很少有机会唱这样的现场, 而且是唱这么好听的歌曲,
我自己喜欢的。My real dream, in fact, is especially performing like
today, wearing jeans without high heels, singing with a band on a big
stage like a pop festival. Because I didn't, I am sorry, I honestly have
much opportunity to sing like today, and sing such beautiful songs of
my own choice.)

Unfortunately, sometime after this audition, contestant Yao passed away
from cancer when she was only in her 30s. She was a professional singer
and was very popular with all the coaches during the auctions. As every
coach wanted Yao, Wang was unsure whether he could win her over.
This is probably the reason why Wang is careful when making his pitch
and uses, 'I feel that you are *probably* ('keneng') someone I want'. In
this way, Wang is able to avoid embarrassment if he is not selected by
the contestant, that is, the EL used here serves a self-protection purpose.
In the end, Wang's strategy of self-protection was successful because Yao
chose coach Na instead.

Excerpt 45 (4/3/8): Two speakers over six speaking turns. Three of
the four coaches have turned around for the contestant, Jiang.

T1 Jiang: **Keneng** ni yijing ji bu de wo le, ni gei le wo yi zhang qian ming
CD. Danshi **wo bu zhidao** tamen shi wei le fuyan wo, gei le wo yi
zhang zhege … (**可能**你已经记不得我了, 你给了我一张签名CD。
但是**我不知道**他们是为了敷衍我, 给了我一张这个… **Maybe**
you don't remember me, you gave me a signed CD. But **I am unsure**
whether it is fake, they were just going through the motions.)

T2 Zhou: Meiyou, wo xian wen ni, zi chou bu chou? Ruguo chou jiu shi
wo xie de. (没有, 我先问你, 字丑不丑? 如果丑就是我写的。No, let
me ask this first, does the signature look ugly? If it is, then it is mine.)

T3 Jiang: Bu, buchou. (不, 不丑。No, not ugly.)

T4 Zhou: Ai, **<u>youdian</u>** qiguai, yinwei shaowei chou yidian cai shi wo qian de. (哎，**有点**奇怪，因为稍微丑一点才是我签的。 Oh, it's **<u>a little bit</u>** strange, because my signature was somewhat ugly.)

T5 Jiang: Nage bisai rang wo dui yinyue geng you xinxin le. (那个比赛让我对音乐更有信心了。 That competition made me feel more confident about music.)

T6 Zhou: Wo juede women zhen de hen you yuanfen. (我觉得我们真的很有缘分。 I think we really have a lot of fate.)

Coach Zhou is contestant Jiang's idol and, in the end, he was indeed chosen by Jiang. Jiang took part in a singing competition for a ticket for Zhou's concert, and won first prize (an autographed copy of Zhou's CD). In T1, Jiang asks whether Zhou still remembers him and if the autographed CD is genuine. Jiang uses EL ('maybe' and 'I'm unsure') to maintain both his face and Zhou's face, in the event that Zhou does not remember him or the CD was indeed autographed by Zhou.

In T4, Zhou is careful when answering whether his signature on Jiang's CD is real, because the CD was given out by Zhou's agency rather than by himself. Zhou claims that his signature is a bit ugly, which could be true, or maybe he is just being modest. He feels *a bit* ('youdian') strange, because Jiang mentions that the signature does not look ugly, which would indicate that the signature is not his own. However, Zhou is unsure what the circumstances were at that time and, therefore, it is prudent for him to make his utterances less certain to protect himself in case he makes a wrong assumption.

4.2.6 Evasive Elastic

Evasive elastic functions, according to Zhang (2015), withhold information inappropriately or can even be deceptive. In this study, evasion is defined in a broader sense: it includes cases whereby the speaker holds back some information for a variety of reasons, and is not necessarily an inappropriate action.

Excerpt 46 (5/4/8): Two speakers over four speaking turns. Three of the four coaches have turned around for the contestant, Huang.

T1 Yu: Jielun shi juedui yingan ma? (杰伦是绝对音感吗? Is Jielun the absolute best in distinguishing music notes?)

T2 Zhou: Dui, wo shi juedui yingan, danshi wo changchang chang bu zhun, dui. (对, 我是绝对音感, 但是我常常唱不准, 对。Yes, I am very good at distinguishing AP music notes, but I often sing the wrong note, yeah.)

T3 Yu: Ni yici keyi tingdao jige yin? Yige hexian xiaqu. (你一次可以听到几个音? 一个和弦下去。How many notes can you hear at a time? In one chord.)

T4 Zhou: Yige hexian xiaqu a? Bu yao dan de hen bu hexie dehua, **ying-gai dou hai keyi**. (一个和弦下去啊? 不要弹得很不和谐的话, **应该都还可以**。In one chord? It **probably should be okay** if the chord is played reasonably well.)

The contestant, Huang, performed one of Zhou's songs and, in the end, he also chose Zhou. In T2, coach Zhou confirms that he is very good at distinguishing musical notes, but often sings out of tune. Is Zhou telling the truth here or is he just being modest? He is a well-known musician, and singing out of tune, and even more so 'often' out of tune, sounds extremely unlikely. In T3, Yu asks how many musical notes Zhou can distinguish in one chord. Zhou answers, in T4, that if the chord is played harmoniously, he *probably should be okay* ('ying-gai dou hai keyi'). Zhou avoids answering Yu's question in detail and does not confirm how many notes he can distinguish in one chord. This is probably because he does not know or he does not want to give a specific number, in case the actual result does not match what he is claiming.

Following T4, Zhou was placed on the spot and had to distinguish some musical notes which, according to the other coaches, he did rather well. The peer ratification that he received is partly a result of Zhou's evasive answer in T4. Otherwise, it could have been problematic for Zhou if he had claimed he could distinguish, say, ten notes, but only ended up distinguishing nine. Zhou deliberately avoided giving a precise answer, and so distinguishing nine notes is perfectly acceptable because there is no specific number against which to measure Zhou's test result. It is therefore much easier for him to claim success in the test. This case demonstrates the advantage of using EL to perform an evasive elastic function.

Excerpt 47 (2/1/8): Three speakers over five speaking turns. Three of the four coaches have turned around for the contestant, Ye.

> T1 Na: Wang Feng ni hui houhui ma? Wo zai gei ni yici jihui. (汪峰 你会后悔吗? 我再给你一次机会。Will you regret it, Wang Feng? I can give you another chance.)
>
> T2 Wang: A, <u>you yidian</u> rang wo **feiyisuosi**, dui. (啊, **有一点让我匪夷 所思**, 对。Ah, **a little bit** beyond my imagination, yes.)
>
> T3 Yu: Haha, feiyisuosi, zhe yinggai shi kuajiang duibudui? (哈哈, 匪夷 所思, 这应该是夸奖对不对? Haha, unimaginative, this is a compliment, isn't it?)
>
> T4 Wang: Dui, zhe ju hua ni xuyao qu shenke de lingwu. (对, 这句话 你需要去深刻地领悟。Yes, you need to fully comprehend this expression.)
>
> T5 Yu: Shensi shensi, wa! "Wang lao fuzi" jianghua jiu shi zheyang. (慎思慎思, 哇!"汪老夫子"讲话就是这样。Think carefully, wow! This is the way the "Wang the old wise man" is speaking.)

Coach Wang did not turn around for contestant Ye, unlike the other three coaches. In T1, Na teases Wang by asking if he has any regrets and, if so, she would offer him a second chance. In T2, Wang's answer is 'a little bit beyond my imagination', which evades Na's question. The answer is too general to have any definite meaning. It has more than one possible reading: (1) Wang believes that he has slightly misjudged the contestant and indeed is regretting it, (2) Wang feels that the other coaches have not made the right choice because he thinks that the contestant is not particularly good. In T3, coach Yu asks for a clarification: is Wang's answer a compliment? Wang, in T4, again avoids the question by asking Yu to think carefully for himself. Whatever Wang has in mind, his answer in T2 adopts EL to withhold information (whatever it is that he has in mind) from the other interactants and to create some confusion for them, particularly for Yu.

Excerpt 48 (2/1/5): Three speakers over five speaking turns. Two of the four coaches have turned around for the contestant, Ding.

T1 Ding: Qishi zheyang de, wo zheci lai, qishi hai you yige xiao xiangfa,
jiu shi, wo canjia wan zhege, ruguo bo chuqu zhihou, wo maozi he
yanjing de xiaoliang yinggai hui zengjia.
[laughter]. (其实这样的，我这次来，其实还有一个小想法，就是，
我参加完这个，如果播出去之后，我帽子和眼镜的销量应该会
增加。As a matter of fact, I came here with a plan, that is, if I have
finished this, sales of my hats and glasses would increase after the
broadcast.)

T2 Yu: Suoyi ni de mengxiang shi yanjing he maozi mai de hao yidian,
dui ma? [laughs] Ni ying gai jiang yixia zhenzheng de mengxiang.
(所以你的梦想是眼镜和帽子卖得好一点，对吗? 你应该讲一下真
正的梦想。So your dream is to sell glasses and hats better, right? You
should tell us your real dream.)

T3 Ding: Qishi jiu shi, wo xiang zhengming zhe ji nian dangzhong,
youxie suowei de yinyue ren, bifangshuo ta xiang bang wo zuo ge,
danshi tamen hui you ge yiwen, jiu shi ni de sang yin youdian tai bu
zhuliu le. (其实就是，我想证明这几年当中，**有些**所谓的音乐人，
比方说他想帮我做歌，但是他们会有个疑问，就是你的嗓音有点
太不主流了。To be honest, I want to prove (myself). During recent
years, **some** of the so-called musicians, for example, say that they
wanted to help me produce songs, but they were concerned that my
voice is a little too non-mainstream.)

T4 Yu: Ni men juede ta de sangyin hen guai ma? (你们觉得他的嗓音很
怪嘛? Do you think his voice is weird?)

T5 Na: Wo juede ni de sangyin hen zhuliu. (我觉得你的嗓音很主流。
I think your voice is very mainstream.)

Contestant Ding sells glasses and hats at a night market and, on the
day of his performance, he is wearing colourful clothing, glasses and a
hat on stage. Coach Yu asks Ding what his dreams are, to which Ding
replies, in T1, that he just wants to sell more glasses and hats on the
back of the publicity he would receive from taking part in the show.
When Yu pushes him for a more serious answer, Ding says that he
wants to prove himself as a good mainstream musician. In T3, when
Ding mentions that *some* ('youxie') so-called musicians doubted him
and thought his voice was not mainstream, he uses an evasive approach.
Evidently, he does not want to publicly name these people to avoid

offending them. The general stretcher *some* is useful for serving an evasive function, as demonstrated in this case.

Excerpt 49 (1/3/1): Four speakers over five speaking turns. One of the four coaches has turned around for the contestant, Wu.

T1 Yu: Na women hai shi gei ta yidian jianyi … ni bu tai wen ding … A Mei de zheshou ge hen nan chang de, chaoji nan chang, ni weishime hai yao xuan? (那我们还是给她一点建议…你不太稳定…阿妹的这首歌很难唱的, 超级难唱, 你为什么还要选? Well, let's give her some advice… You are not very stable… This A Mei's song is very difficult to sing, super hard to sing, why did you choose it?)

T2 Wu: Wo xiang zhengming gei **mouxie** ren kan. Zengjing wo you yige nanpengyou, a, ta shuo yinwei wo gezi tai ai le, suoyi he wo fenshou. (我想证明给**某些人**看。曾经我有一个男朋友, 啊, 他说因为我个子太矮了, 所以和我分手。I want to prove myself to **some** people. Once I had a boyfriend, ah, he told me that the reason he broke up with me was because I was too short.)

… …

T3 Yu: … Ni zhan zai tai shang jiu shi xiao juren le, dui, ni shi yinyue xiao juren. (… 你站在台上就是小巨人了, 对, 你是音乐小巨人。… You stand on the stage and you are the little giant, right, you are a little musical giant.)

T4 Liu: Qishi gangcai **wo juede**, wo yaoshi mei ji cuo dehua, Yang Kun laoshi zhuan guolai de shihou, zhihou ta chang le yige chao gao de yin. Yi jian dao Yang Kun laoshi yin ye gao le, **wo guji** nahuir ger ye gao liang gongfen. (其实刚才**我觉得**, 我要是没记错的话, 杨坤老师转过来的时候, 之后她唱了一个超高的音。一见到杨坤老师音也高了, **我估计**那会儿个儿也高两公分。Actually, just now, **I think**, if I remember correctly, when Yang Kun turned around, she sang an ultra high note. She sang higher notes when she saw Yang Kun, **I guess** she would grow two centimetres in height as well.)

[all laugh]

T5 Yang: Buguan zenmeyang, wo juede ni jintian zhengming le ni de shili … (不管怎么样, 我觉得你今天证明了你的实力 … Anyway, I think you have proved you are the real deal today …)

In T1, Coach Yu asks contestant Wu why she chose such a difficult song. Wu, in T2, explains that she wants to prove herself to people, particularly her former boyfriend who broke up with her because she is rather small. However, she does not name anyone, but simply mentions *some people* ('mouxie'). This anonymous approach is perhaps because of issues of privacy, namely it is inappropriate to publicly name her former boyfriend in this setting.

In T4, coach Liu mentions that he *feels* ('wo juede'), if he is not mistaken, that the contestant reached a particularly high note after coach Yang turned around (he is the only coach who turned around for Wu). Liu also mentions jokingly that he *guesses* ('guji') that Wu would also be two centimetres higher after seeing Yang turning around (perhaps due to over excitement). In this instance, Liu employs EL to shield himself from making an incorrect statement or assessment.

Unlike Wu in T2 (evasive elastic strategy), Liu uses a self-protection elastic strategy in T4. As Excerpt 49 demonstrates, Wu withholds some information and hence is being evasive. Liu does not hide any information and hence is adopting a self-protection tactic. These two strategies have different foci which set the two apart. Liu reduces the certainty of his utterance to protect himself in case something turns out to be in conflict with what he has stated. On the other hand, Wu does not provide any information about who these *some people* are, not even some less detailed information about them, and is therefore being evasive.

Excerpt 50 (4/3/8): Four speakers over six speaking turns. Three of the four coaches have turned around for the contestant, Jiang.

T1 Yu: Ta ye bu gen ni duo shuo **shenme**, ta jiu xiexie ni zhuanshen. [laughter] (他也不跟你多说**什么**, 他就谢谢你转身。 He doesn't say **anything** to you, just thanks you for turning around.)

T2 Wang: Zhi shi anwei, zhi shi anwei. (只是安慰, 只是安慰。 Just some comfort, just some comfort.)

…… ……

T3 Na: Ni xianzai zai dianping wo, shi ma? [with some annoyance] (你现在在点评我, 是吗? You are commenting on me right now, aren't you?)

T4 Jiang: Meiyou meiyou, wo **tebie** x huan ni de nazhong xingge, jiu shi he ni de shuohua de fangshi. (没有没有, 我**特别**喜欢你的那种性格, 就是和你的说话的方式。 No, not at all, I like your personality **very much**, and the way you speak.)

T5 Yu: Jiu shi ta meici du peng chu ge xiao guanjun lai, ha. (就是她每次都捧出个小冠军来, 哈。 That is, she always wins the competition with someone from her team being the champion, eh.)

T6 Jiang: Dui, **hen** bang! (对, **很**棒! Right, **very** good!)

Three coaches turned around for Jiang, namely Na, Yu and Zhou. As mentioned in T1 and T2, contestant Jiang was asked to comment on coach Na's song, but he evades that question and instead thanks Na for her approval of him. However, Jiang praised the other coaches on their songs which, more than likely, rather annoyed Na. In T3, Na confronts Jiang but, in T4, he is evasive again, steering clear of commenting on Na's music. He instead praises Na's personality and the way in which she speaks. Coach Yu jumps into defuse the awkward situation by mentioning Na's impressive track record in the competition. Jiang quickly then concurs with Yu. Coach Zhou is actually Jiang's idol and, to no one's surprise, he chose Zhou to be his coach.

4.3   Overall Analysis

Having separately analysed EL at both lexical and pragmatic levels in previous sections, this section discusses the overall use of EL based on longer examples of conversation, and a wider range and variety of lexical items and pragmatic functions. This overall analysis provides an integrated picture of how and why EL is used in Chinese TV discourse.

Excerpt 51 (5/4/8): Five speakers over 12 speaking turns. Three of the four coaches have turned around for the contestant, Huang.

T1 Zhou: Lao shi shuo, wo ziji **butai** gan tao zheshou ge chang, yinwei zhege nandu ye suan **man** gao de. Ni ba ta congxin gaibian de, **wo juede** shi **hen** kaixin kan dao zhejian shiqing, yinwei zhe jiu shi ni de fengge. (老实说, 我自己**不太**敢挑这首歌唱, 因为这个难度也算**蛮**高的。你把它从新改编的,　**我觉得**是**很**开心看到这件事情, 因为这就是你的风格。 To be honest, I myself wouldn't **quite** dare to pick this song, a quite difficult song. **I feel very** happy to see you have rewritten the song in your own style.)

T2 Na: Wo, **wo juede** ni de shengyin tezhi, **tebie** shihe chang zhezhong yonglan de, ranhou xiao qingxin de, tuzi he qiangdiao du **feichang** de shufu. Wo ting qilai jiu shi bu xiang Jie Lun yuanben de nage zhuang-tai, danshi **hen** hao ting, zhineng jia fen. (我, **我觉得**你的声音特质, **特别**适合唱这种慵懒的, 然后小清新的, 吐字和腔调都**非常**地舒服。我听起来就是不像杰伦原本的那个状态, 但是**很**好听, 只能加分。I, **I think** your voice quality is **very** suitable for singing this type of lazy-like, yet slightly refreshing song, your articulation and accent are **very** comfortable to listen to. It doesn't sound like Jielun's original, but it's **very** pleasant to hear, which can only add points to you.)

T3 Wang: Na jie, ta ni shizaibide ma? (那姐, 他你势在必得吗? Sister Na, do you have to get this contestant in your team?)

T4 Na: Ou, **zheyangzi** a. (哦, **这样子**啊。Oh, **like this**.)

T5 Yu: Ni de yisi shi shuo, ruguo ta shizaibide, ni jiu keyi bang ta dao shou ma? (你的意思是说, 如果她势在必得, 你就可以帮她到手吗? Do you mean that if she wants the contestant, you can help her to achieve it?)

T6 Wang: Jilü **hen** gao, jinwei ta xuan le Jielun de ge. Ni mingbai? (几率**很**高, 因为他选了杰伦的歌。你明白? The probability is **very** high, because he chose Jielun's song. Get it?)

T7 Yu: Dui a. Zhege wo **youdian** kongbu, **wo juede youdian** jinzhang. (对啊。这个我**有点**恐怖, **我觉得有点**紧张。Yeah. I'm **a little** scared, **I feel a little** nervous.)

… …

T8 Wang: Ni dan beisi dan duojiu le? (你弹贝斯弹多久了? How long have you been playing bass?)

T9 Huang: Wo dan beisi you **sinian** le. (我弹贝斯有**四年**了。I've been playing bass for **four years**.)

… …

T10 Wang: Wan yixia. [talks to the band] (玩一下。Let's play.)

T11 Yu: Lai ge hexian hao le. (来个和弦好了。Play a chord.)

T12 Wang: Liu Zhuo [who is the musician for the show], ni jiu **dagai** dan **liuqige** yin zheyang a [Liu plays some notes]. (刘卓, 你就**大概**弹**六七个**音这样啊。Liu Zhuo, play **about six or seven** notes, that will do.)

The contestant, Huang, is a third-year undergraduate student specialising in electric bass, and he chose coach Zhou's song to perform, which Zhou believes is a difficult song to sing. In T1, Zhou says that he himself would *not quite* ('butai', a scalar stretcher) dare to choose this song. This serves a just-right elastic purpose, as Zhou is simply stating a fact. In the same speaking turn, Zhou also uses *very* twice ('man' and 'hen', scalar stretchers) as well as *I think* ('wo juede', an epistemic stretcher) to enhance the force of his praise on Huang. Zhou is particularly keen for Huang to join his team, and is trying very hard to achieve it. This is also the goal of coach Na, and she, in T2, uses four elastic items to form an intensifying strategy in order to speak highly of Huang.

Wang did not turn around for Huang, so he is in a position to assist the other coaches in their bids for Huang. In T3, Wang indicates that Na would have a slight edge in the fight to win Huang over, and asks if she has to have him. In T4, Na uses an evasive elastic term ('like this') to duck the question and to avoid sounding too arrogant. During the course of the show, a trend could be seen to be emerging: if a contestant chose a coach's song to perform, it had the result of 'cursing' that coach. This view is considered by Yu when he, in T7, agrees with the other coaches, and expresses his fears by using *a bit* ('youdian', a scalar stretcher) twice and *I feel* ('wo juede', an epistemic stretcher). Yu employs a rapport elastic strategy here to demonstrate his in-groupness with similar thinking peers. However, the 'curse' theory is not quite the case because, in this instance, Huang actually chose Zhou after performing his song. Compared with the other coaches, Zhou appears to not be forceful enough. However, in this case, Zhou fought the hardest for the contestant and achieved his goal.

In T9, Huang tells the coaches that he has been playing electric bass for four years, and on its own 'four' is precise. However, in this case, four can be a vague number because a whole number, even one that is seemingly precise, can be perceived to be a rounded number (Channell, 1994). In T12, to test Zhou's ability to recognise musical notes, Wang asks the show's musician, Liu, to play *about 6 or 7* ('dagai', 'liuqige', an approximate stretcher) notes. Wang uses a just-right elastic strategy here: he gives an inexact instruction to Liu, allowing him some flexibility. There is probably no need to be precise here because an approximate quantity adequately serves Wang's goal.

Excerpt 52 (1/2/9): Five speakers over 14 speaking turns. No coach has turned around for the contestant, Dai.

T1 Liu: Ni shi bu shi jintian ding de zhe ge diao you **yidiandian** di? Wo de ganjue jiu shi ni zai **hen** yong qing, ye zai **hen** yong qixi, danshi **haoxiang** zhe ge diao ba ni quan zai limian le. (你是不是今天定的这个调有**一点点**低？我的感觉就是你在**很**用情，也在**很**用气息，但是**好像**这个调把你圈在里面了。Have you set the tune **a little bit** low today? My feeling is that you are using your emotions **very much**, and also your breath **very much**, but it **seems** that the tune has let you down.)

T2 Dai: Xiexie Liu laoshi. (谢谢刘老师。Thank you, teacher Liu.)

… …

T3 Na: Wo **zhen** peifu ni de yongqi, you nen dang quanzhi mama, hai nen chulai canjia xi'ai de huodong. (我**真**佩服你的勇气，又能当全职妈妈，还能出来参加喜爱的活动。I **really** admire your courage, you can be a full-time mum, and you can also come out to enjoy something you love.)

T4 Dai: Yinwei **wo juede** buguan wo you duoda nianji, wo du you zhuiqiu ziji mengxiang de quanli. (因为**我觉得**不管我有多大年纪，我都有追求自己梦想的权力。Because **I feel** that no matter how old I am, I have the right to pursue my dream.)

T5 Na: Ou. (哦。Oh.)

[applause]

T6 Yang: Wo shi xiang wen **yixia**, women si ge mei you zhuanshen de guolai yihou, jintian wan shang ni de zhege mengxiang wanzhuan de shuo meiyou shixian, ni xin limian shi zenme qu xiang de? (我是想问**一下**，我们四个没有转身的过来以后，今天晚上你的这个梦想婉转地说没有实现，你心里面是怎么去想的？Can I please **just** ask, after the four of us didn't turn, it means that this evening your dream, to put it tactfully, did not come true, what is in your mind right now?)

T7 Dai: Ruguo jintian wanshang you yi wei laoshi nenggou wei wo zhuanshen dehua, wo shi dangran kending **hen** gaoxing. Danshi qishi wo hai you yige **feichang** zhongyao de mude lai dao zhege wutai, yinwei qishi wo shi benzhe ni lai de. (如果今天晚上有一位老师能够为我转身的话， 我是当然肯定**很**高兴。但是其实我还有一个**非常**重

要的目的来到这个舞台，因为其实我是奔着你来的。If a teacher could turn around for me tonight, I would surely be **very** happy. But in fact, I have a **very** important goal for coming to this stage, because I actually came for you.)

T8 Yang: A! (啊! Ah!)

T9 Yu: Ni de. [pointing to Yang] (你的。You.)

T10 Yang: Wo de xiao xinzang **shaowei** dong le **yixia**. [laughter] (我的小心脏**稍微**动了**一下**。My little heart **slightly** moved **a little**.) [laughter]

T11 Yu: Xiao xinzang! (小心脏! Small heart!)

T12 Dai: Yinwei wo shi **feichang** xihuan nin de ge. Xiwang neng gou gei ge jihui wo he nin he chang yishou ge. (因为我是**非常**喜欢您的歌。希望能够给个机会我和您合唱一首歌。Because I like your song **very much**. I hope to have a chance to sing a song with you.)

T13 Yu: Keyi, keyi. (可以, 可以。Yes, yes.)

T14 Na: Tai hao le! (太好了! That's great!)

[with everyone cheering, Yang goes on stage]

Contestant Dai is a 38-year-old home maker and she has a 5-year-old daughter. It must be disappointing for Dai that no one has turned around for her, meaning that she has to go home empty handed. In T1, coach Liu comments on the possible reasons for Dai's failure: it could be that the pitch was set *a little bit* ('yidiandian') low. He feels that Dai put in *a lot* ('hen') of emotion and used *a lot* ('hen') of energy. However, it *seems* ('haoxiang') that Dai foundered because of the very low pitch she used. The EL used by Liu is mitigating elastic in nature.

In T3, Na praises Dai: Na *really* ('zhen', an intensifier) admires her courage to be both a full-time mum and able to do those activities she enjoys. Dai, in T4, assertively states that she *feels* ('wo juede') she has the right to chase her dreams, irrespective of her age. Her answer wins a warm round of applause from the audience.

In T6, coach Yang asks a sensitive question by using a mitigating elastic strategy. He asks her, 'Can I please *just* ('yixia', a politeness marker) ask how you feel when we didn't turn for you?' Dai adopts an intensifying elastic strategy in her answer, in T7: she would be *very* ('hen') happy if someone had turned around for her. However, she actually came to the audition with another *extremely* ('feichang') important goal, to meet Yang.

While coach Yang might be very excited to hear this, he uses EL to demonstrate modesty and humour, as he does not wish to appear arrogant. In T10, he says that his 'little' heart is *slightly* ('shaowei') moved *a little* ('yixia'). Dai invites Yang, in T12, to come on stage to sing a duet together because she likes his song *very much* ('feichang', an intensifier).

Excerpt 53 (5/4/4): Four speakers over 12 speaking turns. All four coaches have turned around for the contestant, Yang.

T1 Wang: Ai, ni zhi bu zhi dao wo shi **ji nian lai** zui kuai shijian xialai de. (哎， 你知不知道我是**几年来**最快时间下来的。 Well， you should know that I was the fastest to turn over the past **several** years of this show's history.)

T2 Yang: Xiexie, xiexie! (谢谢, 谢谢! Thank you, thank you!)

T3 Yu: Lai, xian rang women renshi ni **yixia**. (来， 先让我们认识你**一下**。 Come on, let's **just** get to know you first.)

… …

T4 Yu: Ni yao bu yao **shuoshuo** kan, ni xuan zhe ge ge, ni xiang yao biaoda **yixie** shenme? (你要不要**说说**看， 你选这个歌， 你想要表达**一些**什么? Do you want to **just** talk about what kind of **things** you want to express by choosing this song?)

T5 Yang: Qishi ba, qishi wo zhiqian ye shi zou na chang na. Danshi bieren wen wo, dang wen wo, wo shi gan shenme hangye de shihou, wo jiu buhaoyisi, wo jiu bugan shuo ziji shi yige geshou. Yinwei **wo juede** wo dandang buqi zhe liangge zi. Dan **wo juede**, ruguo neng zhan zai xiang zheyang de wutai changge dehua, jiu hui chengwei yiming xiang zuanshi yiyang shanyao de zhenzheng de geshou. (其实吧， 其实我之前也是走哪唱哪。但是别人问我， 当问我， 我是干什么行业的时候， 我就不好意思， 我就不敢说自己是一个歌手。因为**我觉得**我担当不起这两个字。但**我觉得**， 如果能站在像这样的舞台唱歌的话， 就会成为一名像钻石一样闪耀的真正的歌手。 Actually, actually previously I was singing here and there. When being asked what profession I was in, I was embarrassed and didn't dare to say that I was a singer. Because **I felt** I didn't deserve the name. But **I think** if I can stand on stage like today, I will become a real singer who shines like diamonds.)

… …

T6 Na: Bushi. **Wo jiu juede** zhege laogong jiu shi yige bole, **feichang** weida de laogong, **zhen** hao. (不是。**我就觉得**这个老公就是一个

伯乐, **非常**伟大的老公, **真**好。 No. **I just think** this husband is a good judge of talent, a **very** great husband, **really** good.)

T7 Yu: Laogong zai houtai, shi ba? (老公在后台, 是吧? Your husband is backstage, isn't he?)

T8 Yang: Yinggai shi zai houbian ba. (应该是在后边吧。 He should be at the back.)

T9 Na: Ni you mei you xiang guo, dui ni **zheme** ke'ai de laogong, yao shuo **dian shenme**? (你有没有想过, 对你**这么**可爱的老公, 要说**点什么**? Have you ever thought to say **a little something** to your **very** lovely husband?)

T10 Yang: Laogong, ni jue le, wo ai ni! (老公, 你绝了, 我爱你! Husband, you are fantastic, I love you!)

T11 Yang's husband [backstage]: Wo ye ai ni! (我也爱你! I love you too!)
…… …

T12 Yu: Wo **henjiu** mei jiang zhe ju hua le, ta **buyiding** neng dang diyi, keshi ta yiding neng dang weiyi. (我**很久**没讲这句话了, 她**不一定**能当第一, 可是她一定能当唯一。 I haven't said this sentence for a long time. She **may not** be the first, but she can be the only one.)

Contestant Yang sang Rihanna's English song, and she is popular with the coaches. Coach Wang appeals to Yang by highlighting that he was the fastest (and the first) to turn around for her, indicating that he is very keen for her to join his team. He points out that this is his quickest turn around *over the past several years* ('jinian lai', an approximate stretcher) of the show. Wang uses a just-right elastic term here because there is no need for him to be precise. In T3 and T4, Yu asks Yang to introduce herself to get to know her *a little* ('yixia', a politeness marker) better and *just talk about* ('shuoshuo', a reduplication of the verb as a softener to tone down the impact of Yu's request) why she chose Rihanna's song, and what kind of *things* ('yixie') she wants to express. Yang, in T5, says that she is not confident enough to say that she is a singer because she *feels* ('juede', an epistemic stretcher) that she is not good enough. However, she also *thinks* ('juede', an epistemic stretcher) that now she can sing on this stage, she is well on her way to becoming a real singing star.

In T6, Na tries to meet Yang's husband, probably using him to make a favourable impression on the contestant. Na's request is softened by the mitigating elastic strategy she adopts, manifested through the use of the scalar stretcher *a little* ('dian') in T9.

In the end, contestant Yang chose Yu, which delights him. In T12, Yu mentions that he has not said this sentence for *a long time* ('henjiu', an approximate stretcher), that Yang *may not* ('buyiding', an epistemic stretcher) win the prize, but she is the only contestant with her own unique style.

Excerpt 54 (3/2/5): Five speakers over 12 speaking turns. All four coaches have turned around for the contestant, Zhang.

T1 Yang: Meinü jieshao **yixia** ziji **ba**. (美女介绍**一下**自己**吧**。Miss, **please just** introduce yourself.)

T2 Zhang: … Wo ganggang cong Hanguo huilai. (… 我刚刚从韩国回来。… I've just come back from South Korea.)

T3 Wang: … **Wo juede** ni shi shuyu bijiao lihai de geshou. Shishi shang ni zai yanchang fang mian, wulun shi yinzhun, qixi, haishi kongzhi ni ziji de qingxu fangmian, yijing da dao **bijiao** gao de yige shuizhun le. (… **我觉得**你是属于比较厉害的歌手。事实上你在演唱方面，无论是音准、气息， 还是控制你自己的情绪方面， 已经达到**比较**高的一个水准了。… **I think** you are a very good singer. In fact, you have already reached **quite** a high standard in singing, whether it's intonation, breathing or controlling your own emotions.)

T4 Qi: **Wo** daoshi **juede**, **keneng** ta de Intonationyinse a, shengbu shi **bijiao** zhong di **yidiandian**, xiang zheyang de shengyin xianzai **bijiao** shao jian. (**我**倒是**觉得**, **可能**她的音色啊, 声部是比较中低**一点点**, 像这样的声音现在**比较**少见。Actually **I think**, **probably** her timbre **quite** belongs to a **somewhat** middle-low range, a voice like this is **rather** rare now.)

… …

T5 Yang: Na meihao de shiwu da jia du bixu **nage shenme** ma. [laughter] Wo zhuyi de bu guang shi ta de waibiao, dangran xianzai zanshi meiyou banfa zou dao ta de neixin. Danshi ne, **wo juede** dui zheme yige cong Hanguo xueye huilai de nühair, zhan zai zhege wutai shang, bu guan jintian zenmeyang, qishi ni jiaxiang de gemi gei ni reqing shi zui relie de. Ni yao renshi dao zheyidian. (那美好的事物大家都必须**那个什么嘛**。我注意的不光是她的外表，当然现在暂时没有办法走到她的内心。 但是呢, **我觉得**对这么一个从韩国学业回来的女孩，站在这个舞台上，不管今天怎么样，其实你家乡的歌迷给你热情是

最热烈的。你要认识到这一点。When we see beautiful things, we are always all **thingummyjig**. I pay attention to not only her appearance. Of course, at the moment I am unable to get to know her fully. But, **I think** standing on the stage is the girl who studied and returned from South Korea. No matter what happens to you today, your hometown fans will be the most enthusiastic, you have to know this.)

T6 Na: Mei cuo. (没错。Correct.)

[applause]

T7 Qi: Ni jinnian ershiwusui dui ba? (你今年二十五岁对吧? You are twenty-five-years old, right?)

T8 Zhang: Dui. (对。Yes.)

T9 Qi: Fumuqin jinnian …? (父母亲今年…? How old are your father and mother…?)

T10 Zhang: Baba shi shu niu de, mama shi shu hu de. (爸爸是属牛的, 妈妈是属虎的。Daddy's animal year is the cow, and mum's is the year of the tiger.)

T11 Qi: Na du bi wo **dagai** xiao ge **liangsansui zuoyou**. Ba ma yinggai **chang** gen ni tiqi wo **ba**? (那都比我**大概**小个**两三岁左右**。爸妈应该**常**跟你提起我**吧**? That's **about** **two or three** years younger than I am. They **often** mention me to you, **don't they**?)

T12 Zhang: Dui. (对。Yes.)

[laughter]

Contestant Zhang is a beautiful and talented young woman and all the coaches are keen to have her on their teams. She chose coach Na, and then went on to win that season.

Coach Yang is single, and tends to be teased by the other coaches when a beautiful girl comes on stage. In T1, Yang invites Zhang to introduce herself. Yang uses a mitigating elastic strategy to make his tone softer, by employing *please just* ('yixia', a softener) and the clause-final particle *ba* (a politeness marker). Wang, in T3, comments on Zhang's superior singing techniques, using a just-right elastic strategy which employs the elastic items *I think* ('wo juede', an epistemic stretcher serving an evaluative purpose) and *quite* ('bijiao'). In T4, coach Qi contributes to the conversation by introducing a different aspect: he *thinks* ('juede') that *probably* ('keneng') her voice is *quite* ('bijiao') *somewhat* ('yidiandian') between mezzo-soprano and alto, and he believes that Zhang's voice is *rather* ('bijiao') rare. In this instance, Qi's tone is rather tentative, and the EL which is used primarily serves a mitigating function.

Zhang mentions that she has just returned from South Korea. She went to study music and joined the Sunny Days girl group during her time there. Yang begins T5 with a vague and general statement: 'When we see beautiful things, we are always all **thingummyjig**'. By using the placeholder *thingummyjig* ('nage shenme'), he is being evasive. As a single man, he might be afraid that people will make fun of him or accuse him of flirting with attractive female contestants. He does not provide clear information here, probably for his own protection. He then tries to impart some form of advice to Zhang (Suzuki, 2008) by using a mitigated tone. The word *I think* ('wo juede') performs as a softener in this case. Yang implies that although Zhang went to South Korea to study music, her most appreciative fans will always be from China, from her own hometown. Yang is unsure whether Zhang would appreciate receiving his advice, and so he uses *I think* ('wo juede') to make it sound less imposing.

In T7, coach Qi cleverly changes tack in an attempt to win the contestant over. He tries to achieve rapport by establishing a link between himself and Zhang, accomplishing this by discussing her parents. In T11, Qi mentions that Zhang's parents should be *about two or three years* ('dagai', 'liangsansui'and 'zuoyou' are all approximate stretchers) younger than him. An interesting point to note is that, although Qi may know the exact age difference, he chooses to use EL. In this instance, there may be no need to be precise and some EL creates more intimacy (Ruzaitė, 2007). Qi also asks Zhang if her parents mention him *often* ('chang', a scalar stretcher). The clause-final *ba* indicates a softened tone because Qi does not want to appear arrogant, or suchlike. As expected, Zhang's answer positively confirms Qi's remarks.

Excerpt 55 (4/3/6): Four speakers over 12 speaking turns. Three of the four coaches have turned around for the contestant, Michael.

T1 Yu: Women **liaoliao**, ni yong le **henduo** shenme yuyan? (我们**聊聊**, 你用了**很多**什么语言? Let's chat **a bit**, you used **many** languages in your lyrics, what are they?)

T2 Michael: Dui, butong yuyan. (对，不同语言。Yes, different languages.)

… …

T3 Zhou: Jiang zhen de, wo ting dao you ren chang Yingwen ge, wo turan dou hui juede **man** xianmu de. Erqie ta yong Yingwen raoshe, **wo jiu juede**, wa, yong wo de ge, ranhou Ying wen raoshe jia jinqu, juede **man** ku de. (讲真的，我听到有人唱英文歌，我突然都会觉得**蛮**羡慕的。而且他用英文饶舌，**我就觉得**，哇，用我的歌，然后英文饶舌加进去，**觉得蛮**酷的。To tell you the truth, I hear people singing English songs, I suddenly feel **very** envious. And he raps in English, **I just think**, wow, it's **very** cool to add some English raps in my songs.)

T4 Na: Yinwei ni genben bu hui Yingwen, shima? (因为你根本不会英文，是吗？Because you don't know English at all, do you?)

T5 Zhou: [lowers his head and nods repeatedly]

T6 Yu: Ye mei **name** cha, hao bu hao. Ni ganggang nage liuzhong yuyan, zhege shi cong ta yuanshi de geci bianhua lai de, haishi ni … (也没**那么**差，好不好。你刚刚那个六种语言，这个是从他原始的歌词变化来的，还是你 … It's not **that/so** bad, okay. Just now those six languages, have they been adopted based on the original lyrics or are you …?)

T7 Michael: Na shi wo shenghuo limian de jingyan, ranhou **yixie** jiu zai shenbian fasheng de **yixie** youqu de dongxi. (那是我生活里面的经验，然后**一些**就在身边发生的**一些**有趣的东西。That is based on my life experience, **something** happened around me, **some** interesting stuff.)

T8 Yu: Zai jiang **yixie** shenme? (在讲**一些**什么？Are you telling us **something**?)

T9 Michael: Jiu birushuo, wo you yi ci jiu shi qu le Guizhou, gen wo de hao pengyou he le **xie** maotaijiu. Suoyi **wo juede youdian** ku, suoyi wo jiu xie zai wo ge limian. (就比如说，我有一次就是去了贵州，跟我的好朋友喝了**些**茅台酒。所以我**觉得有点**酷， 所以我就写在我歌里面。For example, I once went to Guizhou, and I had **some** Maotai spirits with my good friend. So **I think** it's **somewhat** cool, so I wrote it in my song.)

T10 Na: Ao. (噢。Oh.)

T11 Zhou: Ai, wo xiang zhidao **yixia**, ni you mei you ba "kuai shiyong shuangjiegun" zhe ju gai le cheng, shi bu shi you butong de yuyan zai limian. (哎，我想知道**一下**，你有没有把"快使用双节棍"这句改了

成, 是不是有不同的语言在里面。Hello, I'd **just** like to know if you have changed the sentence "use the double bar quickly", whether there is some different language in it.)

T12 Michael: Dui, wo shi guo gai le **ji** ci, gai cheng sige butong yuyan. You Yingwen, Fawen, hai you Riyu he Hanyu. (对, 我试过改了**几**次, 改成四个不同语言。有英文, 法文, 还有日语和韩语。Yes, I have tried **several** times to turn it into four different languages. There is English, French, Japanese and Korean.)

The contestant, Michael, comes from America, and is a fan of coach Zhou. He performed a song which was a rearrangement of Zhou's 'Double bar/nunchaku' (the original song is in Chinese) using a mixture of languages. In T1, coach Yu says that he would like to chat *a bit* ('liaoliao', a reduplication of verbs, a politeness form) with Michael. He asks Michael whether he has used *many* ('henduo', a vague quantifier) different types of language in his song. In T3, the original singer and songwriter, Zhou, says that he likes that his song has been adapted into English, using *very* ('man') twice and *I think* ('wo juede'). In T6, Yu attempts to save Zhou's face after Na puts Zhou on the spot by asking him to confirm that he does not speak English. Yu says that Zhou's English is not *that/so* ('name', an intensifier) bad, thereby rescuing him from an embarrassing situation.

Michael explains, in T7, that his song reflects *something* ('yixie', a general stretcher) that has happened in his life, particularly *some* ('yixie', a general stretcher) interesting things. In T9, Michael relates that he once went to Guizhou in China and drank *some* ('yixie', a general stretcher) alcohol there. He thought that was *sort of* ('youdian', an epistemic stretcher) cool, and so he wrote about that experience in the song. Michael primarily uses a just-right elastic strategy, and the general and unspecific information that is provided here cannot be more precise, or does not need to be precise, and therefore the information that is provided is adequate for this context.

In T11, Zhou asks Michael whether he has used a mixture of different languages in the lyrics of 'use the double bar quickly', where *yixia* (a polite form in making a request) softens the tone of the question. Michael, in T12, uses *several* ('ji', an approximate stretcher) to perform a just-right elastic function.

4.4   Frequency of Lexical Items

The previous discussions are mostly qualitative in nature and include lexical and pragmatic function analysis. This section focuses on the quantitative analysis of the frequency distribution of elastic items, revealing a general picture of how EL is used in the data.

As shown in Table 4.1, the most frequently observed category of EL lexical item is that of scalar stretcher (62.7%). This is to be expected because the discourses that were analysed were primarily intended to persuade and provide comfort. The second most frequently observed category is epistemic stretcher (16.7%), and then general stretcher, with the least frequent being the approximator and quantifier category. These results very favourably reflect the purpose of the discourse analysed in this study, which was not so much about delivering information (AQ is often a carrier), but rather providing a pitch to win over contestants. Scalar stretchers are more frequently used than all of the other three types of lexical item combined, showing the need for the speaker to manipulate his/her tone by either strengthening or softening. In fact, the majority of scalar words were used to increase the degree of the claim, rather than decreasing it; see Fig. 4.1 for details.

Table 4.2 shows that for 26.6% of contestants, two coaches turned around, and this was the most frequent outcome. Therefore, approximately one in every four contestants had two coaches turning around, with one in every five contestants having either one or three coaches turning around. All four coaches turning around is slightly less frequent, with this situation occurring for approximately one in every six contestants. Failure to have any coaches turning around was the least

Table 4.1   Overall lexical frequency in the Chinese data

Category $N = 9760$	AQ	GE	SC	EP	Total
Frequency	692	1320	6116	1632	9760
Percentage	7.1	13.5	62.7	16.7	100

Note AQ = approximate stretcher, GE = general stretcher, SC = scalar stretcher and EP = epistemic stretcher

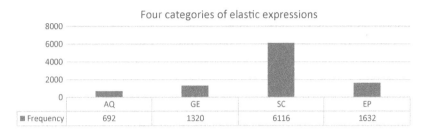

Fig. 4.1   Overall lexical frequency in the Chinese data

Table 4.2   Overview of the number of coaches that turned around for each contestant in the Chinese data

Type (N=316)	0 turned	1 turned	2 turned	3 turned	4 turned	Total
Number	37	68	84	71	56	316
Percentage	11.7	21.5	26.6	22.5	17.7	100

Table 4.3   Frequency versus the number of turned coaches in the Chinese data

Category/ no. of turns	AQ (1)	GE (2)	SC-I[a] (3)	SC-D[a] (4)	EP (5)	Total	Subtotal (3+4)
0 turned	57	84	372	78	138	729	450
1 turned	63	100	460	90	159	872	550
2 turned	180	318	1403	306	441	2648	1709
3 turned	192	368	1291	236	383	2470	1527
4 turned	200	450	1621	259	511	3041	1880
Total	692	1320	5147	969	1632	9760	6116
Chi-squared (p<0.01)	χ^2 [d.f.12, n=9760]=27.878, p=0.0057639 (significant)						

[a]SC-I: Intensifier, SC-D: Deintensifier

frequent situation and happened for approximately one in every ten contestants (Tables 4.3 and 4.4).

As Fig. 4.2 shows, in cases where two coaches turned around, the most softeners were used, which suggests that both coaches tended to adopt a soft approach to lower their tone of speech. On the contrary, in cases where three or four coaches turned around, they tended to use a

Table 4.4 Frequency versus the number of turned coaches in the Chinese data (%)

Category/ no. of turns	AQ (1)	GE (2)	SC I (3)	SC D (4)	EP (5)	Total[a] (%)	Subtotal (3+4)
0 turned N=729	7.8	11.5	51.0	10.7	18.9	99.9	61.7
1 turned N=872	7.2	11.5	52.8	10.3	18.2	100	63.1
2 turned N=2648	6.8	12.0	53.0	11.6	16.7	100.1	64.5
3 turned N=2470	7.8	14.9	52.3	9.6	15.5	100.1	61.8
4 turned N=3041	6.6	14.8	53.3	8.5	16.8	100	61.8
Total N=9760	7.1	13.5	52.7	9.9	16.7	99.9	62.7

[a]After rounding

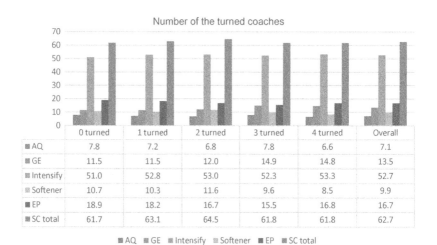

Fig. 4.2 Comparison between the number of the turned coaches and their choice of EL in the Chinese data (%)

smaller proportion of softeners and epistemic stretchers, but more general terms were used. This suggests the way in which the coaches perceive the situation: the more competition there is among the coaches, the more they have to adopt a stronger tone, to appear more confident in their efforts to win over the contestants. This is because softeners and epistemic stretchers might be seen to indicate uncertainty, less authority and less assertiveness (Carter, 2003). Expressions such as 'seems' and 'I guess' indicate the speaker's lower degree of commitment (Parvaresh, 2018; Zhang, 2013). General terms are considered to foster in-groupness (Ryoo, 2005), and "help the conversation go smoothly" (Shirato & Stapleton, 2007, p. 396). On the contrary, the AQ category is not influenced by the level of competition (how many coaches turned around) because it is more information-bearing than emotional/feelings-bearing (Zhao & Zhang, 2012).

Overall, the most frequently used category is intensifiers, such as *very* and 'extremely' which, in the data, serves the purpose of persuasion perfectly. The TV show requires the coaches to battle over the contestants, where intensifiers are useful for boosting a coach's argument. This is because intensifiers demonstrate the level of confidence with which one is making claims (Parvaresh, 2018), and the assertiveness that is required in situations where the interlocutors would be expecting it (Holmes, 1990; Hu & Cao, 2011; Hyland, 1998, 2000). By enhancing the force of the tone of speech, boosters enable the coaches to convey a sense of conviction (Hyland, 2000).

4.5 Concluding Remarks

This chapter has demonstrated how language stretching in Chinese TV discourse is manifested in the form of the lexical items and the pragmatic functions that are employed. Linguistic analyses uncovered their distributional tendencies in the Chinese discourse under investigation.

The data demonstrate that many speech acts were at play, particularly those of persuasion and mitigation.

The linguistic realisation of language stretching in the Chinese data is illustrated through the clustering of the four categories of lexical items.

The first category indicates approximation, the second generalisation, the third emphasis or mitigation, and the fourth portrays the speaker's stance and attitude. The preference for scalar words (intensifiers, in particular) in the data indicates the participants' language behaviour: for example, the frequent use of *very* implies the need for persuasion, and the use of *kind of* may imply the speaker's uncertainty or a self-protective attitude.

This chapter also discusses why language stretching is used in reality television discourse. The analysis is carried out on a pragmatic level, and the discoursal investigation focuses on the interactions between the interlocutors. The findings reveal how the participants deal with persuasion, compliments or comforting, revealing their motivations for using elastic expressions. In total, six pragmatic moves are analysed. Categories may be overlapping; for example, there may be some interconnection between the self-protection and evasive categories. If this is so, multi-functionality might be the case. Zhang (2015) discovered that, in institutional data, elastic items may perform more than one function, and one function may be realised by more than one type of elastic item. For simplicity, this study has not covered the issue of multi-functionality, but for future research the issue should be explored in non-institutional data to determine whether there are any discourse variances, and for comparison with the findings that have been drawn from Zhang's institutional data.

A note of caution: the reason why contestants chose a particular coach involves a number of factors. Some contestants had a particular coach in mind before even coming on the show and, no matter how brilliantly the other coaches pitched for these contestants, they were never going to be chosen. However, the data in this study suggest that such predetermined cases are limited in number and, in the majority of cases, the persuasive pitches delivered by the coaches do have an influence, and EL does play a role in this.

References

Aijmer, K. (1984). 'Sort of' and 'kind of' in English conversation. *Studia Linguistica, 38,* 118–128.

Aijmer, K. (2002). *English discourse particles: Evidence from a corpus.* Amsterdam: John Benjamins.

Brown, P., & Levinson, S. C. (1987). *Politeness: Some universals in language usage.* Cambridge: Cambridge University Press.

Carter, R. (2003). The grammar of talk: Spoken English, grammar and the classroom. In *New perspectives on English in the classroom* (pp. 5–13). London: Qualifications and Curriculum Authority.

Channell, J. (1994). *Vague language.* Oxford: Oxford University Press.

Fetzer, A. (2010). Hedges in context: Form and function of *sort of* and *kind of.* In G. Kaltenbock, W. Mihatsch, & S. Schneider (Eds.), *New approaches to hedging* (pp. 49–71). Bingley: Emerald.

Grice, P. (1975). Logic and conversation. In P. Cole & J. Morgan (Eds.), *Syntax and semantics. Volume 3: Speech acts* (pp. 41–58). New York: Academic Press.

Holmes, J. (1988). Doubt and uncertainty in ESL textbooks. *Applied Linguistics, 9*(1), 21–44.

Holmes, J. (1990). Hedges and boosters in women's and men's speech. *Language & Communication, 10*(3), 185–205.

Holmes, J. (1993). New Zealand women are good to talk to: An analysis of politeness strategies in interaction. *Journal of Pragmatics, 20*(2), 91–116.

Hu, G., & Cao, F. (2011). Hedging and boosting in abstracts of applied linguistics articles: A comparative study of English- and Chinese-medium journals. *Journal of Pragmatics, 43,* 2795–2809.

Hyland, K. (1998). *Hedging in scientific research articles.* Amsterdam: John Benjamins.

Hyland, K. (2000). Hedges, boosters and lexical invisibility: Noticing modifiers in academic texts. *Language Awareness, 9*(4), 179–197.

Hyland, K. (2005). *Metadiscourse: Exploring interaction in writing.* London: Continuum.

Jucker, A. H., Smith, S. W., & Ludge, T. (2003). Interactive aspects of vagueness in conversation. *Journal of Pragmatics, 35,* 1737–1769.

Lakoff, G. (1973). Hedges: A study in meaning criteria and the logic of fuzzy concepts. *Journal of Philosophical Logic, 2*(4), 458–508.

Lakoff, R. (1982). Persuasive discourse and ordinary conversation, with examples from advertising. In D. Tannen (Ed.), *Analyzing discourse: Text and talk* (pp. 25–42). Washington, DC: Georgetown University Press.

Miskovic-Lukovic, M. (2009). *Is there a chance that I might kinda sort of take you out to dinner?* The role of the pragmatic particles *kind of* and *sort of* in utterance interpretation. *Journal of Pragmatics, 41*(3), 602–625.

Moxey, L., & Sanford, A. (1993). *Communicating quantities: A psychological perspective*. Hove, UK: Lawrence Erlbaum.

Parvaresh, V. (2018). 'We are going to do a lot of things for college tuition': Vague language in the 2016 US presidential debates. *Corpus Pragmatics, 2*(2), 167–192.

Parvaresh, V., & Zhang, G. (Eds.). (2019). Vagueness and elasticity of 'sort of' in TV discussion discourse in the Asian Pacific [Special issue]. *Journal of Asian Pacific Communication, 29*(1), 1–132.

Prince, E. F., Frader, J., & Bosk, C. (1982). On hedging in physician-physician discourse. In R. J. Di Pietro (Ed.), *Linguistics and the professions* (pp. 83–97). Norwood, NJ: Ablex.

Ruzaitė, J. (2007). *Vague language in educational settings: Quantifiers and approximators in British and American English*. Frankfurt am Main: Peter Lang.

Ryoo, H. K. (2005). Achieving friendly interactions: A study of service encounters between Korean shopkeepers and African-American customers. *Discourse and Society, 16*(1), 79–105.

Shirato, J., & Stapleton, P. (2007). Comparing English vocabulary in a spoken learner corpus with a native speaker corpus: Pedagogical implications arising from an empirical study in Japan. *Language Teaching Research, 11*(4), 393–412.

Suzuki, T. (2008). *A corpus-based study of the speech act of "comforting": Naturalness and appropriateness for English language teaching*. Paper presented at the 13th PAAL Conference, University of Hawaii, Manoa, USA.

Terraschke, A., & Holmes, J. (2007). 'Und Tralala': Vagueness and general extenders in German and New Zealand English. In J. Cutting (Ed.), *Vague language explored* (pp. 198–220). Basingstoke: Palgrave Macmillan.

Zhang, G. (2013). The impact of touchy topics on vague language use. *Journal of Asian Pacific Communication, 23*, 87–118.

Zhang, G. (2014). The elasticity of I think: Stretching its pragmatic functions. *Intercultural Pragmatics, 11*(2), 225–257.

Zhang, G. (2015). *Elastic language: How and why we stretch our words*. Cambridge: Cambridge University Press.

Zhang, G. (2016). How elastic *a little* can be and how much *a little* can do in Chinese. *Chinese Language and Discourse, 7*(1), 1–22.

Zhang, G. (2019). The pragmatic use of 'sort of' in TV forums: A Chinese perspective. *Journal of Asian Pacific Communication, 29*(1), 62–85.

Zhang, G., & Sabet, P. G. (2016). Elastic 'I think': Stretching over L1 and L2. *Applied Linguistics, 37*(3), 334–353.

Zhao, X., & Zhang, G. (2012). *Negotiating with vague language: A Chinese perspective*. Beijing: China Social Sciences Press.

5

Elastic Language in the English Data

This chapter is an attempt to investigate the linguistic behaviour and realisation of EL in the English data under investigation. The data are taken from blind auditions conducted in English. The blind auditions investigated in this chapter are similar to those that were discussed in the previous chapter in terms of their general format. First, the contestant performs a song, and the coaches then turn their chairs around if they like his/her performance and/or if they see potential in his/her skills. If more than one coach turns around, then the onus is on each coach to convince the contestant to join their team. The conversations and data which are analysed in this chapter are variable in terms of how many people have chosen the same contestant, and range from situations in which no coach has turned his/her chair to situations of high competition where all four coaches have taken an interest in a contestant by turning their chairs around. As will be demonstrated, the more coaches that turn their chairs for a particular contestant, the higher the level of competition among the coaches will be. All things being equal, we would expect a contestant to join the coach who has been the most persuasive. When no coach turns their chair around for a contestant, the pragmatic functions typically change from those of persuasion

© The Author(s) 2019

G. Zhang and V. Parvaresh, *Elastic Language in Persuasion and Comforting*,
https://doi.org/10.1007/978-3-030-28460-2_5

to those of comforting. Such rich data provide us with an opportunity to look at the role that EL plays in persuasion and comforting at both lexical and pragmatic levels. In the following, the English data will be analysed at a lexical and pragmatic level, and the categorisation will follow that discussed in Chapter 4.

5.1   Lexical Items

Four lexical categories will be discussed in this section: approximate stretcher, general stretcher, scalar stretcher and epistemic stretcher. As was noted in the previous chapter, these categories are primarily based on Zhang (2015).

5.1.1   Approximate Stretcher

An approximate stretcher can be of two different but related forms. In the first, an approximator precedes a number (e.g. *about 35*), and in the second, a quantifier (e.g. *many*) is used with an unspecified meaning. The following excerpts provide illustrative examples.

Excerpt 1 (11/1/6): Three speakers over three speaking turns. The contestant, Ali, sings very well and all the coaches have turned around for her.

> T1 Miley: I'm gonna quickly jump in, only because I really do feel like you could win this show; this is just the first day, what I could bring to you sharing your story through your songs, so you don't end up just a great singer, 'cuz I got **a lot of** personalities so I would love to help you show that. I'm done!
> T2 Adam: My entire season hinges on whether or not I have you on my team!
> T3 Blake: Oh my God!

This exchange begins with coach Miley, in T1, trying to convince the contestant that she can potentially win this season given her outstanding singing ability. Miley's persuasive argument revolves around the idea that if Ali, the contestant, can sing so well even at such an early stage, she should be able to improve considerably and learn how to 'share' her stories through her songs. Miley says that she has *a lot of* personalities so she is an ideal coach for someone like Ali who, as Miley puts it, needs training in how best to share her stories with the audience. In this context, *a lot of* is without doubt an approximate stretcher in the sense that it stretches upwards the number of personalities that Miley has, without necessarily specifying how many different personalities she might possess. Of course, in this context, what is important for Miley is highlighting the idea that, as a potential coach, she has 'a lot of personality'. Indeed, the exact number or quality of these personalities is either irrelevant or even unknown. Miley's claims are then followed by Adam's pitch, who tries to win Ali over by going so far as to claim that his success in the current season *hinges on* whether or not she is on his team. This is indeed a rather grand and, at the same time, emotionally persuasive claim to make, to the extent that it even surprises Blake, in T3, who expresses his surprise at what he has just heard.

Excerpt 2 (8/1/2): Four speakers over seven speaking turns. The contestant, Lowell, has sung well, and two coaches have turned around for him with a view to convincing him to join their teams.

T1 Adam: Those guys, the Sinatras, Tony Bennett, it is about so **many** things: timing, the charismatic way that you carry yourself, how you dress, the hair in place. We feel like we were at a club in that time and we were really experiencing it with you.

T2 Christina: Blake why didn't we push our buttons? [audience laughter]

T3 Pharrell: How long have you been singing?

T4 Lowell: For **a couple of** years. I'm 19 right now, I'm new to it, I'm really excited.

T5 Pharrell: You are not new to it.

T6 Lowell: Thank you!

T7 Pharrell: You are at home with it.

Adam, in the first turn, begins by commending the contestant's singing ability and how his mastery of a combination of so *many* factors, ranging from his familiarity with singer Tony Bennett to factors such as great timing, body posture and hair style, have so impressed him that he turns around. What is important in this turn is the emphasis that is being placed on the idea that the success of Lowell's performance was a result of his mastery and execution of so *many* things at the same time, and not as much to do with the exact range or number of qualities which he mastered in his performance. In this respect, the use of the elastic quantifier *many* helps the speaker, in T1, to achieve that goal in an imprecise and elastic way.

Indeed, Adam's praise for the contestant's abilities is so great that, in the next turn, Christina, who has not turned around for this contestant, feels rather embarrassed and turns towards Blake, who has not turned around either, and enquires, 'Why didn't we push our buttons?' Pharrell, who has also turned around for the contestant, however, cuts into the conversation in T3 by asking the contestant for the number of years that he has been singing, to which the contestant replies, in T4, *a couple of* years (an approximate stretcher). The contestant's answer in T4 serves to highlight the fact that he is new to singing, so the exact number of years he has been singing prior to the competition is not relevant, or is possibly unknown. Pharrell, in T5 and T7, however, further encourages the contestant by implying that, despite the fact he has only been singing for *a couple of* years, he is not new to it and is very much at home when performing.

Excerpt 3 (11/1/2): Three speakers over six turns. The contestant, Dave, has sung well and all the coaches have turned around for him. The exchange below begins immediately after Dave has finished singing.

> T1 Miley: So I've heard **a little bit of** this one [looks and points at Adam] in there. So I got scared that there might be like a default.
> T2 Adam: I heard **a lot of** me in there!
> T3 Dave: I take that as a high compliment.
> T4 Adam: Well, other than turning around first, and believing in you first before anybody else [audience laughter]. I went there because, man Acelo is hard, but you have this way of getting into there, and it's seamless and it's perfectly on cue, but it's also soulful and smooth. I just felt instantly connected. And I want you and I need you and you are the greatest. [the audience cheers and applauds]

T5 Miley: He doesn't talk to his wife like that!

T6 Adam: I've never actually had someone on my team who I felt like almost in a way we're like similar.

Adam was the first coach to turn his chair around to express an interest in this contestant, and Miley was the second. In T1, Miley is explaining what caused her initial hesitation. As she explains, she first heard *a little bit of* Adam's style of singing in Dave's performance, which caused her to doubt her suitability to be Dave's coach. The use of the approximate stretcher *a little bit of* in this context brings to the fore the 'moderate amount' of Adam's style of singing. This is relevant to the ensuing conversation and justifies why Miley did not press her button before Adam. This causes Adam, in T2, to retort by saying that he did not hear *a little bit of* himself in Dave's performance, but rather *a lot of* it, arguably as an attempt to emphasise his interest in this contestant.

The use of the approximate stretcher *a lot of* serves to highlight the presence of an 'excessive amount' of Adam's style in Dave's performance. Adam's response is positively accepted by Dave, in T3, who regards this *as a high compliment*. Following on from this, in T4, Adam enthusiastically elaborates on Dave's singing ability and emphasises the fact that he was the first coach to turn around for him. Adam goes on to say that 'I want you and I need you and you are the greatest'. This causes Miley, in T5, to make fun of Adam's seemingly sycophantic remarks by saying that 'he doesn't talk to his wife like that', as a strategy to make the contestant doubt the truth of Adam's words. Having heard Miley's implicit criticism, in T6, Adam feels the need to further emphasise the idea that he expressed earlier: that he desperately needs Dave on his team, a wish which was not fulfilled in the end, as the contestant chose another coach, Alicia.

Excerpt 4 (8/1/6). Four speakers over eight speaking turns. Two coaches, Christina and Blake, have turned around for Treeva, the contestant.

T1 Christina: Treeva, I was so captivated as soon as you started singing.

T2 Treeva: Thank you!

T3 Christina: It was one of those smooth textures that really trigger my ear. You started with something small and sincere sounding and it then just grew. I did hear **a few** notes that were pitchy, but hey that is sort of how we work together and how to perfect those flaws. Because man at 16 for you to sound like that, so polished! It's a really really special thing!

T4 Pharrell: Well I'm disappointed that I thought about it too long. **Some of** those cracks, I mean, especially with one of these two here [looks at the two coaches who turned around for her], you are going to learn that you could use those cracks and that's Stevie Nicks' kind of way, which is really good.

T5 Blake: Have you listened to any of her records?

T6 Treeva: I haven't heard a lot. My parents are deaf, so I don't really have any sort of musical influence from them.

T7 Blake: Your parents are deaf?

T8 Treeva: Yes!

Being the first coach to turn around for this contestant, Christina expresses how impressed she was by Treeva's performance, in T1, for which Treeva shows her appreciation in T2. In T3, Christina provides more information about the contestant's performance, saying that the smooth texture of her voice *triggered* her ear. However, Christina draws the contestant's attention to the fact that, in her performance, there were *a few* notes which were not quite right. Obviously, Christina's use of the approximate stretcher *a few*, which provides only a minimum estimate of the number of relevant cases, is motivated by the fact that, for the hearer, detailed information is not necessary. What is of importance to the hearer, that is Treeva, is that there were *a few* imperfect notes which, reading between the lines, could potentially be improved if the contestant selects Christina to be her coach.

Christina's turn is followed by Pharrell who, in T4, expresses his sorrow at his inability to push the button and turn around for the contestant. He, however, reassures the contestant that the two coaches who have turned around for her are ideal and could potentially help her to improve *some of* her flaws. Obviously, in this context, the approximate stretcher *some of* provides relevant information pertaining to the ongoing discussion and serves to reassure the contestant that either one of the two coaches who have turned around for her can assist her in improving those imperfections. In the process, Pharrell draws Treeva's attention to another American singer's approach, Stevie Nicks, known for her rather distinctive voice. At this point, Blake, another coach who turned around for the contestant, seizes his opportunity by enquiring whether the contestant has heard any of Stevie's songs. Treeva replies, in T6, that both her parents are deaf and are unable to provide her with any suggestions or advice regarding which singers to listen to or to take inspiration from. This information greatly surprises all the coaches.

Excerpt 5 (10/3/7): Three speakers over four turns. Three coaches have turned around for Peyton, the contestant.

T1 Adam: Hey, what's your name?

T2 Peyton: My name is Peyton Parker; I'm 20 years old; I'm from Kennesaw Georgia but I've lived in Nashville for **about** three years.

T3 Blake: Yay!

T4 Adam: I heard country in your voice even though that was not in fact a country song. It is one of my favourite songs. If it had been changed up, the rendition that might have been more effective for me. But, clearly, I don't matter because I'm the only person who didn't turn. So, I will let these three fight over you!

Peyton's singing has been so impressive that three of the four coaches (but not Adam) have pushed their buttons for her. However, the fact that Adam did not turn around for the contestant does not prevent him from starting the conversation. Indeed, he uses this as an opportunity to explain why he did not select the contestant in the first place. Having been asked about her name in T1, Peyton then introduces herself, in T2, and provides a little information about herself. Peyton says that she is 20 years old, comes from Georgia, and has lived in Nashville for *about* three years. The approximate stretcher *about* appears to have been used by the speaker because either she is unable to pinpoint the exact number of years she has lived in Nashville, or she might feel that detailed information is not relevant. Indeed, as T3 shows, the fact that she has lived in Nashville for a while seems to be of particular interest to one of the coaches, Blake, who has also turned around for her. As T3 shows, Blake is positively excited by this news. Following on from this, Adam clarifies, in T4, why he did not turn around for the contestant.

He explains that he would not have been an ideal coach for Peyton who, having lived in Nashville, might have a tendency to sing country influenced songs, an endeavour for which Blake, given his background and extensive experience of country music, would potentially be an ideal coach.

5.1.2 General Stretcher

General stretchers include expressions such as *thing, stuff* or *something*, and are used to refer to people or things in an unprecise way.

Excerpt 6 (12/6/1): Three speakers over six turns. The contestant, Kenny, has sung fairly well and two coaches, namely Gwen and Blake, have turned around for him.

T1 Gwen: I'm curious why Nashville?

T2 Kenny: I was doing pretty good in Cleveland and felt like I was peaking. I just wanted to try and get in where everybody is at; I play a lot more country than I used to.

T3 Blake: Uhhahaha!

T4 Gwen: So do I! [audience laughter]

T5 Blake: Do you know how important Nashville is to me? And of course I want to see the best **things** that can happen to you, happen in real life, not just on this show. Gwen doesn't care about you.

T6 Gwen: [laughs mockingly] I don't really know the Nashville scene, although I have been to two billion of Blake's shows last year which I enjoyed very very much, but there's **something** theatrical about you; you have **something** to say with what you're doing; with your facial hair; with just your whole look; you know what I mean. I understand that; it is **something** I've been doing for a long time, so I'd love to work with you.

This exchange begins when Gwen asks the contestant, in T1, why he has moved to Nashville. The contestant replies that, although he was doing reasonably well in Cleveland, he moved to Nashville to improve his singing ability and that, as a result of this, he is now much more into country music. This confession excites Blake whose expertise and training is in the country music genre and, as a result, he expresses his excitement through the interjection 'Uhhahaha', in T3. Gwen, one of the two coaches who turned around for Kenny, seizes her opportunity in T4 and says *so do I*, causing the audience to burst into laughter. Indeed, this laughter makes more sense when the fact that Gwen and Blake have been dating during the show is taken into account. Therefore, Gwen's *so do I* could be taken to mean, 'I am also familiar with country music as I am in a relationship with a country music singer'.

A little later, Blake, in T5, takes his turn and talks about the importance of Nashville to Kenny and that he wants all the best *things* to happen to the contestant, arguably as an attempt to convince him to join his team. In this turn, *things* is an example of a general stretcher as it removes the onus on the speaker to provide a comprehensive list of all the good things that he wants the contestant to achieve, an endeavour which is neither possible nor feasible. In this respect, *things* stretches the category or group, which can conveniently be referred to as 'Blake's good wishes for Kenny', horizontally (Zhang, 2015), thus covering a much wider spectrum of potential items. In the same turn, Blake also says that Gwen, the other coach who has turned around, does not really care about the contestant, implying that he is the only person who truly cares and wants him to flourish, a claim which causes Gwen, in the next turn, to laugh mockingly to show her complete disagreement, and possibly even disappointment. To combat this accusation, Gwen admits that she is not particularly familiar with the Nashville scene, but she can still potentially be a good coach for the contestant in that (i) she can see *something* theatrical in him, and (ii) she believes that he has *something* to say with his performance. Gwen also further confirms that coaching is *something* she has been doing for a long time. Indeed, all instances of *something* in this turn are used as general stretchers, which enable the speaker to avoid being more precise in a context in which further information is unnecessary, or even momentarily irretrievable.

Excerpt 7 (8/1/3): Five speakers over 13 turns. The contestant, Rob, has sung very well and all but one coach are battling over him.

T1 Adam: The courage to do **something** so big, you know what I mean, it was a bold move. I have a high voice and I was like that is really high!

T2 Pharrell: That was so high I couldn't even put no vibrato on it.

T3 Rob: [laughs]

T4 Pharrell: I was like, when I was a kid, they used to do like a hearing test, like ooooooh!

T5 Rob: [laughs]

T6 Pharrell: You've got an amazing voice, you did deserve four chairs by the way, amazing voice.

T7 Rob: Thank you!

T8 Christina: [looks at Blake] I don't know, I don't know what to tell you!

T9 Rob: What's up Blake?

T10 Blake: She's upset with me 'cause I didn't hit my button!

T11 Christina: [looks at Blake] Tell him he should pick me!

T12 Blake: Well, I'm trying to think of the one time you may have said **something** like that for me, and it is not coming to my mind, sister.

T13 Christina: I have your back all the time. [audience laughter] Do you want some, some clowns or do you want **somebody** that takes you seriously? I have one star player right now and that is you!

The conversation begins with Adam praising the contestant for doing *something* impressive. The use of *something* is another example of a general stretcher which has been used in a context in which the exact word is either irretrievable or temporarily unknown. In this context, it could potentially refer to the contestant's performance during the audition. Adam also says that his voice is positively high, something which causes the contestant to laugh as a sign of appreciation (T3). The contestant's high voice is also confirmed by Pharrell in T4 and T6, for which he expresses his gratitude in T5 and T7, respectively.

In T8, Christina expresses her disappointment at Blake for not turning around for such a good singer. At this point, the contestant looks at Blake enquiringly with a friendly expression. Blake, in T10, remarks that Christina is angry at him because he did not turn around. In T11, Christina asks Blake to tell the contestant to choose her to be his coach, to which Blake replies, in T12, that he would not be doing that. It is proving difficult for him to remember the one time Christina 'may have said something like that', a claim which Christina disagrees with, in T13. The use of *something* is again an example of a general stretcher, and enables the speaker to use *something* in a generic way. Following this exchange, Christina asks the contestant whether he wants to work with some *clowns*, that is the other two coaches who have turned around for him, or *somebody* that would take him seriously, arguably as an attempt to convince him to join her team. In this turn, *somebody* is another example of a general stretcher which momentarily fills a lexical gap, a gap which is later filled in this turn when Christina implies that by *somebody* she means herself.

Excerpt 8 (10/3/2): Two speakers over two speaking turns. The contestant, Brian, has sung fairly well and two coaches have shown an interest in him.

T1 Blake: I've got so much respect for you that I did **something** so humiliating that is I hit my button when you were singing his [pointing towards Adam] freaking song. [audience laughter] That's how much respect I have for you. [audience laughter] I don't have a shot! [audience laughter]

T2 Adam: I was saying as much as I don't have a chance against a country artist, the chances for Blake on this one are literally like 10,000 times worse! [audience laughter]

The conversation begins by Blake, one of the two coaches who have turned around, telling the contestant that, in turning his chair, he did *something* rather humiliating. As he clarifies, turning his chair around was humiliating for him because the song that the contestant was performing is one of Adam's songs, who did not even turn around himself. The word *something* is a general stretcher as it enables the speaker to continue his turn without interruption. He, however, acknowledges at the end of this turn that he has little chance of being selected by the contestant. At this point, Adam, whose song has just been described as *freaking*, jumps into confirm that Blake's chances of being selected are even lower than he himself thinks, causing the audience and the other coaches to burst into laughter.

Excerpt 9 (11/1/5): Five speakers over 13 speaking turns. According to the coaches' evaluations, the contestant, Maggie, did not sing well and therefore none of the coaches turned around for her.

T1 Blake: Oh my gosh, what's your name?

T2 Maggie: Hey, I'm Maggie.

T3 Adam: Maggie you're so cute!

T4 Miley: How old are you?

T5 Maggie: Sixteen!

T6 Miley: I could feel that you were young even before turning around so that means **nothing** bad at all. You have so much time to do more **things** like this when you get to practise and you're going to be in front of people.

T7 Adam: Experience.

T8 Miley: Totally and I think you are an awesome guitar player and singer.

T9 Maggie: Thank you!

T10 Alicia: You had a beautiful execution and I think as you continue to search and play I feel like there is a lot of you to bring out and that is going to be a great, great journey.

T11 Blake: You know what, you seem like a complete package. You look like a star and I like to see you come back here and win this **thing**.

T12 Adam: Give yourself a little bit of time and seems like you've got a great attitude, 'cauz you can't wipe that smile off your face right now.

T13 Maggie: I'm talking to some amazing people whether I make it or not, thank you so much!

Maggie, the contestant, has not been successful in this audition, with none of the coaches turning around for her. Therefore, the excerpt shows that they are trying to reassure her that her singing ability is fine and she just needs further practice, after which she could return to the show another time. The conversation begins with Blake asking the contestant her name, in T1, and continues with Adam praising Maggie's cuteness, in T3. In T4, coach Miley enquires about Maggie's age, and when realising that she is only 16, begins reassuring her, in T6, that even though she was not chosen on this occasion, this means *nothing* bad, and if she practices more she can be more successful. In this case, *nothing* is an example of a general stretcher and is used to fill a lexical gap.

In T7, Adam confirms Miley's assertion that Maggie just needs more experience, and she thanks him for his comment, in T8. This is followed by Alicia, in T10, who reassures the contestant a further time, and how she would like to see her come back to the competition to win this *thing* in the future. The word *thing* is again an example of a general stretcher as it has been used to conveniently refer to the entire Voice competition and what it entails. In T12, Adam reassures the contestant another time, advising her not to be disappointed. In the final turn, Maggie expresses her thanks and appreciation for the coaches.

Excerpt 10 (8/1/1). Four speakers over six speaking turns. All coaches have turned their chairs around for the contestant, Sarah.

> T1 Adam: I want to make sure that you can be a rock and roll star, after eight seasons of doing **this** and winning twice, you wanna go with **someone** who knows how it all works …
>
> T2 Blake: Well then [Blake points towards himself]!
>
> T3 Christina: Hahah!
>
> T4 Adam: I am very good at this!
>
> T5 Sarah: [laughingly] He is doing this **thing** [referring to Blake who is pointing his finger towards himself]!
>
> T6 Adam: That's all he does, though!

The coaches have all been arguing with each other, trying to win Sarah over. In this part of the conversation, Adam begins by suggesting that he is an experienced coach as he has done *this* eight times. He suggests that Sarah should pick *someone* who knows how the competition actually works. *This* and *someone* are arguably general stretchers. The former allows the speaker to refer to the competition and what it involves in a general way, and the latter allows the speaker to avoid mentioning his own name in a context in which he assumes that the referent, that is Adam, is obvious and can be easily deduced by the contestant. In T2, Blake interrupts Adam by suggesting through, inter alia, the use of body language that if Sarah is looking for someone who can help her win the competition, it should be Blake and not Adam, which makes Christina laugh, in T3. In T4, Adam continues his pitch by reiterating that he is successful in this competition, while Blake is still pointing towards himself. While still continuing to point towards himself, Sarah laughingly remarks that Blake is doing this *thing* (a general stretcher), which is a convenient way of referring to what Blake is actually doing (i.e. pointing his finger towards himself). In the final turn, Adam reassures Sarah that this is what Blake always does, implying that she should not pay attention to Blake and should instead choose him.

5.1.3   Scalar Stretcher

Scalar stretchers are those expressions whose main function in an utterance is to strengthen or weaken the degree of the claims being made (Zhang, 2015). They can be conveniently classified as intensifiers (e.g. *very*) or softeners (e.g. *a bit*).

Excerpt 11 (8/1/1): Five speakers over six speaking turns. All the coaches have turned around for Sarah, who has sung very well, and every coach is going to great lengths to win her over.

> T1 Blake: I mean between the Nashville, the camouflage shirt and those cowboy boots and jeans, I **really** think we have a connection here.
>
> T2 Christina: It was undeniable, and I was like 'you're going for it'. I was **so** curious to see what the heck was going on behind me. He's getting up, I can see Adam over there, he's like **all** in with his Starbucks just all up on the button. Enthralled in you. Then Blake turned around and I felt like I had to go check it out. And I am **so** ready and **so** refreshed. Let's do it.
>
> T3 Sarah: Thank you **so** much!
>
> T4 Pharrell: You had my hand here for **so** long!
>
> T5 Adam: Little longer than my hand!
>
> T6 Blake: Hahaha!

The contestant has just said that she lives in Nashville, which greatly excites Blake, given that city's long history of country music. In T1, Blake elaborates on what he considers to be the range of items that could potentially link him to the contestant (e.g. the camouflage shirt she is wearing, the cowboy boots). In this turn, *really* is a scalar stretcher which enables Blake to strengthen his claim. In T2, coach Christina begins playing her cards. She recalls how she felt when the contestant was singing. She uses the scalar stretcher *so* on three occasions with a view to strengthening the claim that she is *curious, ready* and *refreshed,* respectively. Also, in this turn, she uses another example of a scalar stretcher, that is the word *all,* to describe Blake's behaviour when the contestant was performing. In T3, the contestant's reply to these words of praise also includes another example of the scalar stretcher *so.* Pharrell implies, in T4, that although he was not the first coach to turn around for this contestant, his hand was right on the button and ready to push, for *so* long. This is another instance of the use of a scalar stretcher to emphasise and highlight a point, and to imply that he was interested in this contestant right from the beginning. In T5, Adam seizes his opportunity by reminding everyone that he turned around before Pharrell, causing Blake to burst into laughter.

Excerpt 12 (10/3/4): Three speakers over 12 speaking turns. Two coaches, namely Blake and Pharrell, have turned around for the contestant, Brittany.

T1 Pharrell: Welcome to Voice Brit! That was a great performance.

T2 Brittany: Thank you!

T3 Pharrell: And you **definitely** have different tone and your vibratos are one of those crispy classic vibratos of the past that we don't get a chance to see these days.

T4 Brittany: Thank you **very** much!

T5 Pharrell: What brought you to Nashville?

T6 Brittany: Writing; I love to write!

T7 Pharrell: But for whatever reason you still came out here to California for the rest of the world to hear you. I know that your propensity **might** be with the guy who knows his way around Nashville [points towards Blake] but I have a GPS! [audience laughter]

T8 Blake: Have you been writing **a lot** with a lot of other writers?

T9 Brittany: I write with Buddy Owens.

T10 Blake: I love Buddy Owens.

T11 Brittany: I love Buddy Owens too.

T12 Blake: I like you even **better**, though!

Pharrell begins this exchange by saying that Brittany has given a great performance. He continues, in T3, to commend the contestant on her voice quality and performance, saying that she *definitely* has a different voice quality, which provides an example of a scalar stretcher being used to strengthen the claims being made. In T4, Brittany uses another scalar stretcher *very* to thank Pharrell for his comments. Over the course of the conversation, Pharrell continues to enquire as to the reasons why the contestant has moved to Nashville. Having heard the contestant's motivation, Pharrell tentatively suggests, his suggestion being modified by a scalar stretcher, that Blake *might* be a better coach for her, in T7. However, he immediately forwards an alternative opinion suggesting that he has got a GPS and would be a better coach for her than Blake. In T8, Blake enquires about the contestant's songwriting activities, and uses the scalar stretcher *a lot* to gauge the extent of her involvement in writing. The contestant confirms that she has been writing with Buddy Owens, whom Blake apparently admires. In T12, Blake says that although he admires Buddy Owens, he likes Britney, the contestant, even *better*. In this context, *better* is another example of using a scalar stretcher to extend the strength of an utterance upwards.

Excerpt 13 (11/1/11). Five speakers over eight speaking turns. All the coaches, with the exception of Miley, have turned around for the contestant, Christian.

T1 Adam: You did not turn around!

T2 Miley: I'm trying to help you! He [i.e. Adam] paid me to not turn around on **really** good ones!

T3 Adam: That cannot be proven!

T4 Miley: I felt like I was not the right coach for you or for your voice.

T5 Blake: I was **absolutely** hypnotised by this guy's personality that is coming through. The one thing that the record industry looks for is a voice that doesn't sound like anybody else, man! You sold me dude. Whether you choose me as your coach or not, which I hope that you do, I am a fan…

T6 Alicia: Where did you get that emotion?

T7 Christian: Thinking about my dad who passed away about a year ago, every day I think about the idea of how am I supposed to live without my dad.

T8 Alicia: I **really** felt you, when I first came out I was 19 years old, I just could tap on all these emotions and when I saw you I was like wow I know you, you know you've got it or you don't got it, and you got it! And I **really really really** felt you man!

Despite the fact that the contestant has sung well, coach Miley did not turn around for him, a fact that, in T1, Adam is bringing to everyone's attention. In response, Miley jokingly claims that Adam has asked her not to turn around on *really* (a scalar stretcher) good performances like those of the current contestant, a claim which Adam denies, in T3. Miley further explains, in T4, that she was not the right coach for Christian's voice. T5 includes another example of a scalar stretcher, that is *absolutely*, which helps the speaker emphasise the good qualities of the contestant's personality. In the remainder of the conversation, in response to her earlier enquiry about the nature of Christian's emotions, Alicia replies, in T8, that she *really* felt the singer. Indeed, she repeats the scalar stretcher *really* on four occasions to demonstrate how impressed she is by the contestant's personality and singing ability, amongst other things.

Excerpt 14 (12/6/9): Five speakers over 11 speaking turns. No coach has turned around for the contestant, Casey.

T1 Gwen: I had a hole in my chest, I was like wow …

T2 Adam: You have an amazing power to your voice.

T3 Gwen: What I **really** love was that you could say you were owning the room; you had a real presence about you; I wish I could have seen it; I'm sorry I didn't turn around; I regret it!

T4 Casey: I wanted you to turn around **so bad**!

T5 Gwen: I'm sorry; oh God I hate that!

T6 Blake: You screw the pooch!

T7 Gwen: If I could say that I would, but I would never use that term!

T8 Adam: Everything sounds grosser when you say it, Blake. [mockingly] Screw the pooch!

T9 Alicia: I just recommend as an arranger because I see you're an artist, make sure that there's a part that breaks down **a little bit** so that people can **really** understand the masterfulness and the variety of your voice.

T10 Gwen: You should come back!

T11 Adam: **Hell** yeah!

In the first three turns, Gwen and Adam are commending the contestant on her great voice and performance. In T3, Gwen says that what she *really* loves about the contestant is that she owned the room when she was singing. The use of the scalar stretcher helps the speaker to tone the utterance either up or down to make it more emphatic and comforting. In T4, however, given the praises she has just received and the fact that no coach has turned around for her, Casey addresses Gwen, telling the coach that she wanted her to turn around for her. The confession includes a scalar stretcher, namely *so bad*, which adds to the strength of her claim. Gwen apologises for not having turned around and, in T6, Blake, using a slang term (i.e. *screw the pooch*) criticises Gwen for not having turned around for Casey. However, both Gwen and Adam criticise Blake for having used this term. Towards the end of the conversation Alicia, in T9, recommends that the contestant ensures that a part of her voice breaks down *a little bit* to help people *really* understand her. Both *a little bit* and *really* are scalar stretchers which help the speaker to, respectively, lower and increase the tone of the utterances. In T10, Gwen recommends that Casey should return to the show, a sentiment that Adam strongly agrees with when he says *hell yeah*, another scalar stretcher which stretches the tone of his utterance upwards.

Excerpt 15 (12/6/4): Two speakers over three speaking turns. No coach has turned around for the contestant, Austin.

> T1 Blake: I **do really** think you're a **really** great singer. I feel like that performance was **extra** laid back for me; I'm looking for people that come out here with a sense of urgency and some desperation in their performances; and probably it is not stylistically what you even do.
>
> T2 Austin: I'm **a little** chilled!
>
> T3 Blake: Nothing wrong with that man. I think it's probably just a matter of timing with me!

In this short exchange, Blake is clarifying for the contestant why he did not turn around for him. In T1, Blake uses the scalar stretchers *do* and *really* (used twice) to underscore the fact that Austin is a great singer. In the same turn, he also explains the reason why he did not turn around, namely that Austin's singing was *extra* laid back for him. The word *extra* is another example of a scalar stretcher and assists the speaker with communicating the idea that the laid back quality of Austin's voice exceeded the threshold of what Blake was comfortable with. In T2, the contestant agrees with Blake that his voice and performance are *a little* chilled; another use of a scalar stretcher to tone down the utterance and also probably to save 'face' (Brown & Levinson, 1987).

5.1.4 Epistemic Stretcher

Epistemic stretchers (also called epistemic stance markers), as the name suggests, reveal information pertaining to the speaker's stance and attitude towards the propositional content (Hu & Cao, 2011). In principle, these expressions are devices that can help the speaker express what he/she thinks to be the possibility of something, and examples include *sort of*, *possible* and *I think*.

Excerpt 16 (8/1/6). Two speakers over eight speaking turns. Two coaches have turned around for Treeva, the contestant.

T1 Treeva: I haven't heard a lot. My parents are deaf, so I don't really have any **sort of** musical influence from them.
T2 Blake: Your parents are deaf?
T3 Treeva: Yes!
T4 Blake: Both parents?
T5 Treeva: Yes!
T6 Blake: **I think** I've just heard something that I've never heard before! Your voice just completely just drapes over the ***. It's not something you can do by design. You were born to sing that way. And **I think** I'm a **really** good coach for you!
T7 Treeva: Haha!
T8 Blake: So who are you going to pick?
[Note: *** stands for inaudible speech]

This excerpt, the continuation of the conversation given above in Excerpt 4, features Blake who, upon hearing the confirmation that the contestant's parents are deaf, in T1, T3 and T5, further reassures the contestant, in T6, that he believes he has heard a unique voice.

In this turn, *I think* is arguably an epistemic stretcher which helps the speaker express the possibility of something—in this particular case, the possibility that Treeva's voice is the most unique that Blake has ever heard. This is indeed a big claim, which serves to further persuade the contestant to choose him as her coach. Blake uses another epistemic stretcher (*I think*) towards the end of the same turn to indicate the possibility of him being 'a really good coach' for this particular contestant. In this context, the scalar stretcher extends the tone of the utterance downwards, although the presence of the scalar stretcher *really* immediately following this tends to balance things out at the end of T6.

Excerpt 17 (10/3/1): Three speakers over four speaking turns. Three coaches have turned around for the contestant, Hannah.

> T1 Christina: You're subtle, and sweet and kind. I **feel like** you need somebody that understands your sassiness and that fire you have in there, because I really want to be a part of that because it's your time Hannah!
>
> T2 Hannah: Thank you!
>
> T3 Blake: Thanks for sealing the deal for yourself and then handing it over to me!
>
> T4 Christina: I can only hope!

As part of her attempts to persuade this contestant to choose her as her coach, Christina lists a number of favourable characteristics about the contestant, including her sweetness and kindness, in T1. She then goes on to say, by using the epistemic stretcher *feel like*, that the contestant needs someone who can understand the sassiness and fire in her voice. This epistemic stretcher appears to have been used to portray Christina's modest attitude, an endeavour which could be potentially taken as an attempt to close the gap between the coach, the audience and other potential viewers, including the contestant. When Blake takes his turn, in T3, he begins by mocking Christina's attempts to win the contestant over and the fact that she went to great lengths to convince Hannah. This is followed, in T4, with Christina's reply that she can only *hope* (an epistemic stretcher) that Hannah will choose her, paving the way for the possibility that she is not chosen.

Excerpt 18 (14/1/6): Four speakers over four speaking turns. The contestant, Kelsey, has sung well and three coaches have turned around for her.

> T1 Kelly: Hands down, you **could** make a record right now and release it and have a career. As your coach **I would** love to focus on songs that really get you further in this competition to have that airtime to reach as many people as you **possibly** can, 'cause I didn't hear any head voice from you yet; I didn't hear any intimacy yet, which **I think** you have. That is gonna be the important thing just because I've been you and I've had to navigate through a competition. How do you stay on but not give it all away? So when you make that finale, you're like just I can have this one too!
>
> T2 Kelsey: Yes!
>
> T3 Adam: Of the three of us there is one person that's done that 13 times. I'm literally the most experienced.
>
> T4 Alicia: Hold on! I'd like to get a word to …

In T1, coach Kelly is explaining how the contestant *could* (an epistemic stretcher) potentially produce a record even at this stage of the competition, given her excellent singing ability. Kelly also uses two other examples of epistemic stretcher, namely *would* and *possibly* with a view to expressing her interest in becoming the contestant's coach, and highlighting the possibility that the contestant's voice could reach many potential audiences. Kelly's turn also includes a further example of an epistemic stretcher, namely *I think*. This appears to have been used to express the positive attitude that, although the contestant's singing is lacking in a number of crucial ways (e.g. intimacy), there is still potential and possibility for improvement. During the remainder of the conversation, Adam and Alicia also take the floor, with each trying to persuade the contestant in their own ways.

Excerpt 19 (13/1/2): Four speakers over seven speaking turns. The contestant, Mitchel, has three coaches turning around for him and the competition between them is intense.

T1 Adam: **I believe** that someone like you, a strong singer where there is no BS [refers to Blake Sheldon, one of the coaches] or the other term! [audience laughter] **I think** you can go really, really far on this show. You are a good looking dude; ladies are gonna love you.

T2 Miley: I love you!

T3 Jennifer: Yes, yes!

T4 Adam: Which never hurts, and **I think** 'cause we've got a similar style kind of tune. If Blake tried to wear jeans like that, it **would** look super funny! [audience laughter]

T5 Miley: Have you always been a singer?

T6 Mitchel: No! Actually I was supposed to be a dentist.

T7 Jennifer: I **would** feel really uncomfortable in your dental chair and my dentist looks like that! Come on, you'd be like I can't have you looking at me like that in my mouth! [audience laughter]

Adam begins this exchange by explaining that he *believes* the contestant to be a strong singer. This is an example of an epistemic stretcher which reveals a clue (or two) about the speaker's attitude about what he is discussing. In the same turn, Adam also explains how he *thinks* the contestant can potentially go far in this competition, another epistemic stretcher, which illustrates the speaker's stance regarding the claims being made. Adam also speculates that someone like the contestant will be popular with ladies, an assertion which both Miley and Jennifer confirm in T2 and T3, respectively. In T4, Adam continues the theme of his earlier turn by including a further two examples of epistemic stretcher, namely *I think* and *would*, with the latter highlighting the possibility that Blake would appear absurd. As soon as the contestant reveals that he had intended to become a dentist, Jennifer, in T7, jokes about the possibility of him being a dentist and her being one of his clients. Indeed, this possibility is expressed through the use of *would*, another example of an epistemic stretcher.

Excerpt 20 (9/1/2). Two speakers over five speaking turns. The contestant, Kota, has sung well, and three coaches have turned around for her.

T1 Blake: Kota, you're like a modern-day Cyndi Lauper!

T2 Kota: I love Cyndi Lauper!

T3 Blake: Your voice just made me smile, when I heard you sing, it sounded like fun.

T4 Kota: Thank you!

T5 Blake: On paper I don't **seem like** the best coach for you.

In this exchange, after a couple of turns in which he commends the contestant, Kota, on her singing ability and voice quality, Blake confesses that he does not *seem like* a good coach for this contestant, in T5. The epistemic stretcher *seem like* has obviously given Blake's proposal a rather tentative tone, which suits the purpose of the competition. In other words, by being slightly tentative in his assertion (i.e. by using an epistemic stretcher) Blake does not completely rule out the possibility of himself being a potential coach for this contestant.

5.2   Pragmatic Functions

The pragmatic functions that are performed by using EL can be classified into the six following categories, adopted from Zhang (2015), which are convenient for the discussion in this section.

5.2.1 Just-Right Elastic

Just-right elastic refers to situations in which the speaker provides only underspecified information, but the information is, despite its elasticity, appropriate given the context. The reason for using EL in these contexts might be due to the fact that exact information is not required.

Excerpt 21 (10/3/2): Two speakers over three speaking turns. Two coaches have turned around for the contestant, Brian.

T1 Pharrell: Clearly, you sing the song much better than I do.

T2 Blake: Nooo!

T3 Pharrell: I'm not fishing. He did **some** rhymes that I know I can't do. How long have you been singing?

Blake and Pharrell have turned around for this contestant and both coaches are trying to win him over. In this short, but revealing, excerpt, Pharrell goes as far as to claim that the contestant has sung the song 'Happy', originally performed by Pharrell, much better than himself. However, in T2, Blake is surprised by this claim, and implies through his use of the elongated *no* that this is nothing but an exaggerated claim to convince the contestant to join Pharrell's team. Pharrell has found himself in the position of being implicitly accused by Blake of making unsubstantiated claims. Therefore, in T3, he states that he is not fishing and that, in the contestant's performance, there were *some* (an approximate stretcher) rhymes which he, as the original singer of the song, would not be able to perform as well as the contestant. The use of the elastic stretcher *some*, in this context, provides the minimum information relevant to the ongoing conversation and is an example of 'go just-right' elastic. Just quite what the nature or quantity of these 'rhymes' were is really not important in this context. However, what is important is that those rhymes which the contestant outperformed Pharrell on, actually did exist. Further accurate information is either unavailable or does not need to be provided on this occasion.

Excerpt 22 (10/3/10): Three speakers over four speaking turns. The contestant, Kristen, has been successful in getting Blake and Christina to turn around for her.

> T1 Blake: You're not like **anybody else** on this show. I'm damn sure I'm not like **anybody else** on this show. [audience laughter] I think that people like us need to stick together to navigate through this **stuff**.
>
> T2 Christina: All right, all right, all right! I heard **a little** Adele in there; I heard **a little bit of** SIA. What type of music are you interested in doing?
>
> T3 Kristen: Like exactly that!
>
> T4 Christina: Oh oh, that just nailed it on the head! I love those singers!

Blake, in T1, is trying to convince Kristen to join his team. He tells her two things: she is not like *anybody else* (a general stretcher) on this show, and that Blake himself is not like *anybody else* (a general stretcher) on this show either. Indeed, these two instances of general stretcher help the speaker to provide information which is relevant to the context, and not more than is needed. In this context, it is important for Blake to tell the contestant that she is better than other performers and that he, himself, is also better than the other coaches. In what sense this contestant is better than other singers, or Blake is better than the other coaches, is not relevant or required. The identity or information of the other contestants is not required, either. What is important is that the superiority of both Kristen and Blake should be emphasised. In this sense, *anybody else* provides the hearer with just about the right information.

Towards the end of the turn, Blake refers to the competition, and what it involves, as *stuff*, another general stretcher, which helps him to go just-right as it is not possible, in this context, to specify what taking part in the competition actually involves. In T2, Christina tells the contestant that her singing had *a little* Adele and *a little bit of* (an elastic quantifier) SIA in it. In this context, what is important for the speaker (Christina) is to let the hearer (Kristen) know that this quality exists, and further information would therefore not be necessary. As the remainder of the conversation shows, the contestant agrees with Christina, in T3, and says how much the songs performed by SIA and Adele interest her.

Excerpt 23 (15/7/2): Two speakers over three speaking turns. Two coaches have turned around for the contestant, Josh.

> T1 Kelly: I have a lot of female power on my team, and I need a man that can sing and hang out with women, and that is your voice. Your runs are so effortless, and then you went for that high **stuff**. I mean it's sexy, yeah! I liked it!
>
> T2 Jennifer: Well I would like to work with you, **everything** you [looks and points towards Kelly] just said, I think we're kind of, we're similar
> …
> T3 Kelly: It's kind of hard, it is a hard season for us!

Both the coaches who have turned around for this contestant are trying to convince him to join their teams. In this part of the conversation, both coaches are making a last-ditch attempt to win the contestant over. In T1, coach Kelly describes why she needs a man to join her team and that Josh, the contestant, can fulfil this role with his superior voice quality. In addition, she elaborates on why she thinks this contestant would be ideal for her team. She tells Josh that his runs are effortless, particularly when, during his performance, he went for that high *stuff* (a general stretcher). Indeed, Kelly does not feel that she has to be any more specific in this context. The contestant, and arguably the audience, given the contextual information and the blind audition they have just watched, are able to establish what *stuff* actually means here. In T2, coach Jennifer is also trying to convince the contestant to join her team. She tells him that she agrees with *everything* (a general stretcher) Kelly has just said. For Jennifer, there is arguably no need to specify and repeat what Kelly has just said, as both the audience and contestant have been listening and are therefore able to understand what she means by *everything*. This is further evidenced by Kelly's confirmation in the next turn.

Excerpt 24 (9/2/1): Three speakers over three speaking turns. All four coaches have turned around for the contestant, Blind Joe, who has sung very well.

> T1 Gwen: … I really appreciate your performance. There was **something** so honest about it; and raw; I grew up on bluegrass and folk music and I had that feeling of my childhood when I heard you sing. I'm happy to be witnessing it.
> T2 Blind Joe: Thank you so much! [the audience cheers and applauds]
> T3 Blake: Hey Joe, how cool it would be to see you and Ronnie Milsap jamming out at the CMA award **or something**, right after you win this freaking **thing**. Dude, you overcame so much, it is time to start reaping some rewards.

All the coaches have been trying to convince Blind Joe to join their teams. In this part of the conversation, Gwen tells the contestant that there was *something* (a general stretcher) about his voice. Quite what *something* actually refers to is not relevant in this context, but what is important is the fact that it was *special*. Gwen does not feel the need to be any more specific in this context as the addressee, that is the contestant, can easily relate to the claim being made. This is evidenced in T2, where the contestant acknowledges what he has just been told. In the final turn, Blake tells the contestant that it would be nice if he could jam with Ronnie Millsap, a famous country singer, at the CMA award *or something* (a general stretcher) after he has won this *thing* (a general stretcher). Again, there is no need for Blake to provide more information: the audience and the contestant, based on previous knowledge and the ongoing conversation, can easily decide what other music awards *or something* might include, and what the word *thing* refers to.

Excerpt 25 (15/5/2): Two speakers over three speaking turns. Two coaches have turned around for the contestant, Natalie.

> T1 Adam: You are a phenomenal Rock 'n' Roll, **and everything else** probably under the Sun, singer. If Heart called tomorrow and was like Uh-oh, Wilson sisters hate each other and we need a singer, like, you could be that one that did that.
> T2 Natalie: Thank you so much!
> T3 Adam: Oh my God! Like crazy, wow! The Rock 'n' Roll community that still exists, they need you!
> [contestant laughs] [the audience cheers and applauds]

In T1, Adam praises the contestant on her excellent singing ability and performance. He goes so far as to claim that she is a phenomenal Rock 'n' Roll *and everything else* (a general stretcher) singer, which provides information relevant in this context. Adam does not feel the need to be more specific on this occasion, as the purpose of his praise is self-evident and the hearer knows what could potentially be included as *and everything else*. It can indeed include positive qualities. Adam also claims that the contestant's voice is so powerful that he would not be surprised if, one day, she could potentially be a member of the famous rock band, Heart.

5.2.2 Rapport Elastic

EL can be used to build interpersonal relationships and give the hearer a sense of in-groupness (Overstreet, 1999; Parvaresh & Tayebi, 2014).

Excerpt 26 (15/7/2): Four speakers over five speaking turns. The contestant, Josh, has been successful in getting two coaches to turn around for him.

T1 Kelly: It's **kind of** hard; it is a hard season for us!
T2 Jennifer: Right, we like similar **things**! [audience laughter]
T3 Adam: It's **kind of**, like, these fights get more pathetic every day. [audience laughter]
T4 Blake: Could I fight for Jennifer and you fight for Kelly?!
T5 Adam: Yes that would be, oh my God! OK Blake let's go! [audience laughter]

Previously the two coaches, Jennifer and Kelly, have been praising the contestant and trying to persuade him to join their teams (see Excerpt 23). However, they are basically in agreement with each other about the contestant and his performance. In T1, Kelly says that the fact that they both have a similar taste in music has made the season *kind of* (a scalar stretcher) hard for both of them. The use of the scalar stretcher *kind of*, while toning down the strength of the proposition, allows the speaker to create a sense of in-groupness by tentatively suggesting an idea which needs the other speaker's confirmation. This, by itself, is also complimentary for the contestant because he is witnessing a battle between two strong contenders for his choice of coach. In T2, Jennifer uses the general stretcher *things* to refer to what they both like. Obviously, it could include a wide range of performance and music-related characteristics, but by referring to these as *things*, Jennifer creates a more relaxed atmosphere, thus enabling the conversation to move forward in a frictionless manner.

Having witnessed Kelly and Jennifer fighting over the same contestant without really challenging each other, Adam, in T3, suggests that these *fights* have become more *kind of* (a scalar stretcher) *pathetic* recently. While *kind of* tones down the force of Adam's utterance, it also creates a sense of in-groupness by relying on an idea that people are already familiar with. This is evidenced by the audience's laughter that follows his comments. Having heard Adam's implicit criticism of Jennifer and Kelly, Blake enters the fray in T4 and suggests that, considering the other two coaches are not challenging each other properly, Adam and himself should try to fill the gap by each fighting for one of the other coaches, a suggestion which is warmly welcomed by Adam in the final turn.

Excerpt 27 (14/1/8): Three speakers over six speaking turns. The contestant, D. R. King, has sung well, and two coaches have turned around for him.

> T1 Kelly: I love that you brought your soul to that song, killed that! It was **so** well executed. Your runs were sick! I think you've got **way more than** we just heard.
>
> T2 Alicia: Oh my God!
>
> T3 Kelly: Where did you start singing?
>
> T4 D. R. King: I grew up singing in a church.
>
> T5 Kelly: Yes!
>
> T6 D. R. King: And then I went to college, then I was a school teacher.

In this exchange, taken from the very beginning of the conversation, one of the coaches who has turned around for the contestant, Kelly, praises him for bringing his soul to the song that he has just performed. She goes on to comment that it was *so* (a scalar stretcher) well executed. Of course, the scalar stretcher *so* strengthens the force of the praise being made, but on a different level. By highlighting the positive aspects of the contestant's performance, it serves to increase the sense of in-groupness, thus establishing solidarity and rapport with both the contestant and, possibility, the audience. Towards the end of this turn, Kelly also claims that the contestant has got *way more than* (a scalar stretcher + a quantifying stretcher) they have just heard, which adds to the sense of rapport being created in this utterance. The sense of positivity and in-groupness created makes Alicia confirm what Kelly has just said, in T2, despite not having turned around for the contestant. In T3, Kelly enquires about the contestant's background and establishes that he grew up singing in a church (T4) and has been a school teacher (T6), and this background may have influenced the way in which the contestant sings.

Excerpt 28 (14/1/1). Five speakers over six speaking turns. Two coaches have turned around for this contestant, Britton.

> T1 Adam: Oh look! **I think a hundred per cent** you gotta go with Alicia Keys, 'cause … [audience laughter]
> T2 Blake: Oh my God [laughing]
> T3 Adam: I'm such a fan of hers! I'm **a little** nervous. I'm sitting next to her right now because I love her **so** much! [audience laughter]
> T4 Kelly: She is **pretty** cool Britton!
> T5 Alicia: Your voice has **so much** honesty in it and there is **something so** genuine about you.
> T6 Britton: Thank you!

Although Adam has not turned around for this contestant (he had been blocked by the other coaches),[1] in T1 he is suggesting that the contestant choose Alicia and not Blake. He says that he *thinks* (an epistemic stretcher) *a hundred per cent* (a scalar stretcher) that the contestant will be better off with Alicia. The stretchers, by giving a sense of subjectivity and assuredness, allow the speaker to establish personal grounds and rapport with the contestant. Of course, this takes Blake somewhat by surprise, in T2. In T3, Adam continues by saying that he is a fan of Alicia's and that, although he is *a little* (a quantifying stretcher) nervous, he loves her *so much* (a scalar stretcher). In this case, these elastic expressions serve to not only tone down or boost the utterance, respectively, but also establish rapport and a sense of in-groupness with both the contestant and the audience.

In T4, Kelly also recommends that Britton chooses Alicia as she is *pretty* (a scalar stretcher) cool. The stretcher here highlights the positive aspects of Alicia's personality and adds to the positive atmosphere being created. In T5, Alicia takes to the floor and praises the contestant for having *so much* (a scalar stretcher) honesty and that he has *something* (a general stretcher) *so* (a scalar stretcher) genuine. In this turn, the first and third stretchers serve to not only strengthen the positive claim being made about the contestant, but also to create a sense of friendship

---

[1]Note that Adam had been blocked by the other coaches.

and solidarity with him. The second stretcher (*something*) also refers to positive aspects of the contestant's performance, but rather vaguely, thus enabling the contestant and audience to rely on the knowledge of the context and the ongoing discussion to understand what Alicia has in mind, which all contributes to the feeling of solidarity being created here.

Excerpt 29 (9/1/2): Four speakers over five speaking turns. The contestant, Kota, has impressed the coaches and three of them have turned around for her.

> T1 Blake: On paper I don't **seem like** the best coach for you.
>
> T2 Adam: Let's be fair, though, Blake is not just a bad coach on paper, Blake is just a bad idea for a coach just in general, **in all ways**! [audience laughter]
>
> T3 Blake: Give me a freaking chance, man! Come on!
>
> T4 Kota: I love you Blake! I love you!
>
> T5 Gwen: I know about trying to find your own path and I **feel like** we can have fun talking about that, to take it to the next place.

This excerpt is the continuation of that given in Excerpt 20. Previously Blake, who has turned around for this contestant, has been commending her on her singing ability and voice quality. However, in T1, Blake confesses that he does not *seem like* a good coach for this contestant. The epistemic stretcher *seem like* makes Blake's proposal sound rather tentative in tone, thus enabling Blake to not completely rule out the possibility that he could be a potential coach for this contestant. Having heard Blake's confession, Adam, who has not turned around for this contestant, interrupts him by saying (perhaps jokingly) that Blake is not only unfit to serve as a coach for this particular contestant, but is unfit to be a coach *in all ways* (a general stretcher). This causes the audience to burst into laughter. Indeed, the general stretcher creates a feeling of solidarity and rapport with both the contestant and audience. In response, in T3, Blake expresses his frustration by asking Adam to allow him to finish his sentence. Having heard this, the contestant expresses her positive feelings towards Blake, in T4. In the final turn, one of the other coaches who has turned around for this contestant, Gwen, takes to the floor, telling the contestant that she *feels like* (an epistemic stretcher) she could be a good coach for her. This stretcher serves two purposes: it allows the speaker to refrain from sounding too self-assured and it maintains interpersonal relationships.

Excerpt 30 (14/1/10): Three speakers over four speaking turns. No coach has turned around for the contestant, Mackenzie.

> T1 Adam: There is **so much** magic in your voice. However, it got **a little bit** away from you. Honest to God, the good parts, Makenzie, were fantastic! [audience applause]
> T2 Makenzie: Thank you!
> T3 Kelly: I'm just going to be real. You are **so** unexpected which **I think** is fabulous about you. It's what's gonna make you stand out.
> T4 Makenzie: Thank you!

Makenzie has not been successful in impressing any of the coaches, and none of them have turned around for him. In T1, Adam is reassuring him that there is *so much* (a scalar stretcher) magic in his voice. The elasticity of *so much* moves the tone of the utterance upwards, thus enabling the speaker to make his praise even stronger, an endeavour which, in this context, can establish a good interpersonal relationship and solidarity with the speaker. In the same turn, however, Adam confesses that he got *a little bit* (a scalar stretcher) distracted because the song was not as good as it could have been. In this context, *a little bit* makes the tone of the utterance somewhat cautious, thus ensuring that the speaker does not harm the contestant's 'face' (Brown & Levinson, 1987). In T3, Kelly also tells the contestant that he is *so* (a scalar stretcher) unexpected, which she *thinks* (an epistemic stretcher) is fabulous. Obviously, these two stretchers serve to stretch the tone of the claim being made (i.e. *positively unexpected*) upwards, and the general claim more personal, thus helping to maintain and establish rapport.

5.2.3 Mitigating Elastic

The mitigating function of EL involves decreasing the tone of the speech and showing politeness (Drave, 2002; Parvaresh & Eslami, 2009). While a wide range of elastic expressions can be used to fulfil these functions, hedges are the most common devices used for this purpose.

Excerpt 31 (11/1/6): Three speakers over four speaking turns. The contestant, Ali, sings very well, and all the coaches have turned around for her.

> T1 Adam: Last season and the season before two very different winners; Jordan Smith, I supported, and I remember vividly where I was and what I was feeling when I turned around for those two people. Both of those people, I said, you guys are winning. I am **so** blown away. I'm not speechless because I won't shut up!
>
> T2 Blake: Clearly, you're not speechless [audience laughter]. Hi Ali, I work with all different types of artists. I won this show with Alicia's ex-backup singer, Jermaine Paul. **Sometimes** the right combination happens and **maybe** it's not the most obvious **thing** but **sometimes** it can create magic, and sister I'm feeling **a little bit of** magic [Blake points towards himself]. [audience laughter]
>
> T3 Miley: So the way they've been planning is that they are **kind of** braggy about how you won and how many times you won.
>
> T4 Blake: We are proud of it!

The contestant's singing ability and performance have been so impressive that every coach wants her on their team. In T1, Adam is bragging about his coaching ability and how he has previously managed to win the show with the contestants he has coached, with a view to convincing Ali to join his team. Towards the end of this turn, he expresses his great interest in the contestant's singing ability, and he uses *so* to increase the tone of the utterance. At this point, Blake seizes the opportunity and explicitly, and rather sarcastically, highlights the fact that Adam speaks rather a lot to get attention, which causes the audience to burst into laughter. Blake's persuasive comments are rather similar to those of Adam's, in that he also discusses how successful he has been with a previous contestant with whom he ultimately won the show.

Blake states that *sometimes* the right *thing* happens and *sometimes* it can create magic, referring to the possibility that the right coach working with the right contestant, or the right contestant choosing the right coach, can be successful. Here, both cases of *sometimes* have helped the speaker to tone down the utterance in a rather conservative way. Blake also suggests that, for the other coaches and contestants, this *may* not be the most obvious *thing*, with a view to toning down the force of the utterance, or at least balancing it out, to avoid sounding too self-assured. Blake also suggests that he feels *a little bit of* (quantifying elastic) magic in this situation, again trying to encourage Ali to join his team. Having heard Blake's remarks, Miley, in T3, takes to the floor and argues that the previous coaches' arguments are *kind of* (a scalar stretcher) boastful. The use of this elastic expression serves to lessen the strength of the assertion, to avoid imposing on the listener's face and to maintain politeness. However, in T4, Blake retorts by saying that both Adam and he are proud of their achievements.

Excerpt 32 (9/2/1): Two speakers over four speaking turns. The contestant, Blind Joe, has great singing ability and all the coaches have turned around for him.

> T1 Adam: Oh man I don't expect this to go my way! I see the cowboy hat!
> T2 Blind Joe: [laughs]
> T3 Adam: Every time there is a flare they **may** lean country, I lose, Joe, and I'm sick of losing!
> [audience laughter] I wanna win and I'm not going to give up until I have **someone** that does **something** that is **completely completely** unique. And I'm hoping that I **could** have you to be that person for me.
> T4 Blind Joe: Thank you! [the audience cheers and applauds]

The contestant is wearing a cowboy hat, and as soon as coach Adam catches sight of him, he jokes that the contestant might not choose him to be his coach, given the fact that wearing a cowboy hat could potentially imply that the contestant is a country music singer; something which would appeal to coach Blake. This confession makes Blind Joe laugh. In T3, Adam further confesses, in a humorous tone, that each time the contestants *may* opt for country music as their favourite genre, he loses the battle to sign them to his team to the other coaches.

The use of a mitigating expression, such as *may*, enables Adam here to not only express the general possibility that contestants will favour the country music genre, but also to indirectly broach the question as to whether the contestant is really into country music. In other words, besides *may* referring to actual situations which have happened prior to the current blind audition, it also serves as a hedge that serves to indirectly ask the contestant whether or not he might consider not leaning towards country music. In the remainder of this turn, Adam encourages Blind Joe to consider joining his team as he is looking for someone to do *something* (a general stretcher) *completely* (a scalar stretcher) unique. Adam also states that he is hoping that he *could* (a possibility stretcher) have Blind Joe on his team. *Could* makes the tone of the utterance more hypothetical, thus enabling the speaker to make the offer less imposing.

Excerpt 33 (14/1/8): Five speakers over five speaking turns. The contestant, D. R. King, has sung well, and two coaches have turned around for him.

T1 Kelly: … You can't teach just **something** that is so innate because it's your gift, and so **I think** that we **could** do **something** fantastic together.

T2 D. R. King: Thank you! [audience applause]

T3 Alicia: You are super special man and I'm **very very** glad that Kelly and Blake turned around because there is **something** magical that's gonna happen.

T4 Adam: It's **really really really** hard to fill a room with your voice like that. That's that special quality and **I think** that you are gonna be happy with Kelly. [audience laughter]

T5 Blake: Man, I gotta tell you, your voice is explosive, and I **have a feeling** that no matter whose version of **whatever** you sing, it's going to sound like D. R. King because you just have this natural gift.

Kelly, one of the coaches who has turned around for the contestant, is telling him, in T1, that his singing ability is a gift and that she *thinks* (an epistemic stretcher) that they *could* (an epistemic stretcher) work together. In this case, both elastic expressions serve to mitigate the tone of the utterance, thus making it less imposing for the contestant. In T3,

Alicia says that she is *very* (a scalar stretcher) happy that two coaches have turned around for the contestant. Both instances of *very* serve to boost the tone of the utterance, thus reassuring and comforting the contestant in the situation where he has been chosen by only two coaches. Alicia goes on to say that *something* (a general stretcher) magical is going to happen. One could guess that, in this situation, *something* could potentially mean a 'great improvement', a 'great performance' or even 'the possibility of winning the competition', thus comforting the contestant even further.

In T4, Adam also commends the contestant on his singing ability, and what he has achieved during his performance is *really* (a scalar stretcher) difficult to achieve. Adam also suggests that he *thinks* (an epistemic stretcher) the contestant would be better off with Kelly as his coach, and not Blake. The use of *I think* enables the speaker to not only mitigate the force of the advice being given, but also to avoid imposing on him, thus maintaining negative face (Brown & Levinson, 1987). In T5, Blake, one of the coaches who has turned around for this contestant, tells him that he *has a feeling* (an epistemic stretcher) that *whatever* (a general stretcher) he sings, it is going to feel original. The first stretcher obviously serves to lessen the strength of the proposition, thus allowing the speaker to avoid potential criticism during any future performance if the prediction does not come true. The second stretcher *whatever* indicates that, because it is indicative of some future event, this general stretcher is well suited to the context, because it is impossible to predict future events, a feature termed 'displacement' by Channell (1994).

Excerpt 34 (14/1/1): Four speakers over 11 speaking turns. Two coaches have turned around for this contestant, Britton.

> T1 Alicia: I go on emotion, I **feel like** that's what makes music real and I'd love to help you **really** bring that out for people to be moved.
> T2 Kelly: You're good [looking at Alicia], you're good!
> T3 Britton: I appreciate it!
> T4 Alicia: You're welcome! [audience applause]
> T5 Blake: Britton, I just want to talk to you for a minute buddy.
> T6 Britton: You go ahead!

T7 Alicia: You may as well just not!

T8 Kelly: He always uses the word 'buddy', he is like …

T9 Blake: I mean, do I get blamed for **stuff**! Listen! You're **so** intense.

T10 Britton: Thank you!

T11 Blake: It's **almost** **like** you're angry at the song; you're playing that guitar with such strength …

Alicia, one of the coaches who has turned around for Britton, is telling him how she *feels like* this kind of emotion, an emotion which is apparently found within this particular contestant, makes music real. The epistemic stretcher allows Alicia to avoid sounding too self-assured or opinionated. She goes on to reassure the contestant that, if they work together, they can *really* (a scalar stretcher) bring real music to people. In this respect, this turn can be seen as evidence to suggest how a combination of elastic boosters and mitigatory devices, such as *feel like*, can balance out the tone of the utterance. Alicia's comments are so powerful that they influence Kelly, another one of the coaches, who acknowledges this about Alicia, in T2.

Blake, who has also turned around for this contestant, and having been teased by Kelly in T8 about his frequent use of intimate words such as 'buddy', tells the contestant, in T9, how intense his voice is, while at the same time criticises the other coaches for taking issue with what he says, which he refers to as *stuff* (a general stretcher). He uses the elastic booster *so* to stretch the tone of the utterance upwards. In the final turn, he continues by saying that it is *almost like* (a scalar stretcher) the contestant is angry at the song, to avoid sounding too imposing or self-assured about the claim being made.

Excerpt 35 (13/6/2): Two speakers over seven speaking turns. One coach has turned around for the contestant, Michael.

T1 Jennifer: I felt the soul; it shows in your music. Again I'm always listening for the instrument and the way he was executing those notes.

T2 Adam: That's a hard song.

T3 Jennifer: I **almost** had to turn around myself!

T4 Adam and Jennifer: That's a hard song!

T5 Adam: And he's doing it stripped down.

T6 Jennifer: Yeah!
T7 Adam: … it was tough, so I'm **super** excited man, **I think** you did a great job!

Coach Jennifer has not turned around for this contestant but, in T1, she is commending him on his performance and ability. She continues, in T3, by saying that she *almost* (a scalar stretcher) turned around for him. The mitigating stretcher *almost* enables the speaker to achieve two goals simultaneously: to reassure the contestant that his singing ability is good, and to avoid being accused of lying in a context in which she did not turn around for the contestant, or at least she did not turn around in time. In this case, *almost* could be taken to be an example of a positive politeness strategy, which is used to encourage the contestant even further. In the final turn, Adam, the only coach to turn around for this contestant, tells Michael how *super* (a scalar stretcher) excited he is and that he *thinks* the contestant did a great job. *I think* is obviously a mitigating device which allows the speaker to avoid sounding too self-assured, by highlighting the subjectivity of the opinions being presented.

5.2.4 Intensifying Elastic

This function is used when the speaker wishes to boost or increase the tone of the utterance (Hyland, 1998, 2000).

Excerpt 36 (14/1/5): Four speakers over seven speaking turns. No one has turned around for this contestant, Blaise.

T1 Kelly: The one **thing** that made me think about pushing the button was you have a **very** round tone. It would just get pitchy **in certain places** and I just felt the nerves **a little bit**.
T2 Blake: There was **a lot** going through your mind; and **a lot** happening up there, and it doesn't take much **a lot of** the time for us just to go mmmm [points to the button], like it wasn't **completely** put together as tightly as it could be. You're **really** close, dude!
T3 Blaise: Thank you!
T4 Blake: I mean **so** close!
T5 Blaise: Absolutely!

T6 Alicia: Try to just sing with your heart. That **would** really transcend the situation; **so**, **super** proud of you, I think you did a great job and I'm excited for your future.

T7 Blaise: Thank you all!

No one has turned around for Blaise, but the coaches are trying to explain why and to comfort him. In T1, Kelly tells him that the one *thing* (a general stretcher) that almost persuaded her to push the button is that he has a *very* (a scalar stretcher) round tone, but it was pitchy *in certain places* (a general stretcher) and she felt he was affected by nerves *a little bit* (a scalar stretcher). The elastic booster *very* serves to increase the tone of the utterance, possibly to make the contestant feel good about his voice. In T2, Blake elaborates on some of the flaws in the contestant's singing but, at the same time, he reassures him that he is *really* (a scalar stretcher) close despite the fact that it was not *completely* (a scalar stretcher) put together correctly and *a lot* (a quantifying stretcher) was happening at the same time. In T4, Blake reassures him another time by saying that he is *so* (a scalar stretcher) close. Alicia, in T6, suggests that if the contestant tries to sing with his heart, he *would* (a possibility stretcher) be more successful, and reassures him that she is *so/super* (a scalar stretcher) proud of him. All the boosters in this exchange boost or increase the tone of utterance.

Excerpt 37 (13/3/14): Two speakers over three speaking turns. The contestant, Moriah, has been successful in getting all four coaches to turn around for her.

T1 Blake: Look, **somebody** like you that comes out here that has **so much** talent; it is not fair **almost** for the rest of the world; that God, you know, when he was sprinkling out talent like **somebody** was talking to him and he forgot, and he sprinkled **extra** amounts on you!

T2 Moriah: Thank you!

T3 Blake: You know, you got all that but when you're on this show it's all a matter of having **somebody** in your corner that believes in you. That's my favourite part of being a coach and this show is to get a chance to work with young people, because you're **most likely** to come out of this show and be a star. And that's what keeps me coming back here to coach, so come on! Join team Blake!

All the coaches have turned around for Moriah and the competition is intense. In this exchange, Blake is trying to win the contestant's favour by telling her, in T1, that *somebody* (a general stretcher) like her who has *so much* (a scalar stretcher) talent is *almost* (a scalar stretcher) being unfair to others. The intensifier *so much* boosts the tone of the utterance upwards, thus emphasising the superiority of the contestant in question. Blake claims that she is so good that it appears that when God was distributing out talent, he gave *extra* (a quantifying stretcher) to this contestant because *somebody* (a general stretcher) distracted him at the same time. In T3, Blake continues to suggest that *somebody* (a general stretcher), meaning Blake himself, believes in her. He also suggests that the contestant is *likely* (a scalar stretcher) to be a star and increases the tone through the use of *most* (a scalar stretcher).

Excerpt 38 (10/3/12): Two speakers over two speaking turns. Three coaches have turned around for the contestant, Nate.

> T1 Christina: **Thoroughly** confused because for **some** reason in my head I thought there was more than one person out there, but I am **so** excited to watch what's about to happen because you have a coach, you are on The Voice. …
>
> T2 Blake: Hit my button because listening to you is **so much** fun. There is a vibe to what you do. The other reason that I hit my bottom was your chest voice … our jobs as coaches is to see the potential in people and then get them to the finale and you've got three of us to do that …

All the coaches, except for Christina, have turned around for this contestant. In the first turn, Christina is telling the contestant how confused she is by the performance. She says that she is *thoroughly* (a scalar stretcher) confused because she thought that more than one person was singing. The booster is therefore an attempt to increase the tone of the utterance and, in a way, to reassure the contestant that there is nothing wrong with his voice. She also tells him that she is *so* (a scalar stretcher) excited that the other coaches have turned around for her. The booster *so* serves to increase the tone of the utterance, possibly to make the contestant feel better and to save Christina's face from any possible criticism. In T2, Blake also tells the contestant that listening to his singing is *so much* (a scalar stretcher) fun in an attempt to not only reassure him about the quality of his voice, but also to convince him to join his team.

Excerpt 39 (9/2/2): Three speakers over four speaking turns. Ivonne has sung well and two coaches have turned around for her.

> T1 Pharrell: … The control that you have is **very very very** impressive.
>
> T2 Gwen: I loved how creative you were, making it your own; I wasn't thinking about Taylor, you were **so** in the lyrics and delivering that emotion I was **so** blown away by it. I can't believe you're 17, I mean that's **really** incredible. [the audience cheers]
>
> T3 Ivonne: Thank you so much!
>
> T4 Pharrell: Your voice is amazing, and you do have glasses and braces, and you are a special **super** unique **thing** that we don't have on this show …

In T1, Pharrell, one of the coaches who has turned around for this contestant, is telling her that she has a *very* (a scalar stretcher) impressive voice. The booster, which is repeated three times, stretches the tone of the utterance upwards, thus highlighting the impressiveness of the contestant's voice even more emphatically. Indeed, the stretcher allows the speaker to make a claim about the quality of Ivonne's voice with more confidence and assurance. In T2, Gwen is also commending the contestant on her singing ability, telling her that she was *so* creative (a scalar stretcher) in the lyrics, to the extent that Gwen, as a hearer, was *so* (a scalar stretcher) impressed. The two stretchers also serve to stretch the tone of the utterance upwards. Towards the end of the turn, Gwen uses another scalar stretcher, that is 'really', which helps her spell out, even more emphatically, how highly she thinks of the contestant's abilities. Pharrell, in T4, uses '*super* (a scalar stretcher) unique *thing* (a general stretcher)' to highlight how young and special the contestant is, the elastic meaning of *thing* indicating the loveliness and uniqueness of this young participant. The use of EL most certainly helps the speaker to increase the tone of the utterance.

Excerpt 40 (9/2/7): Three speakers over three speaking turns. Unfortunately, in this case, no one has turned around for the contestant, Bryan.

T1 Adam: Bruno is a maniac; like trust me, I'm a dude with a high voice and he makes me mad because his range is crazy; he is unbelievable; pisses me off! [audience laughter] … by the end you were nailing those notes; the problem was, it was just **a little** squirrely up until that point; but, man, you **really** should come back because I want you to start where you ended it.

T2 Bryan: Thank you! [audience applause]

T3 Gwen: You know, there was **too many I think**, **too many** moments to take the risk for us; because we only get 12 people, but on the chorus, you locked in in a way that was like whoa this guy is **actually** a **really** good singer, those top notes are **really really** strong. [the audience cheers]

In T1, Adam tells the contestant, who has just performed a song by Bruno Mars, how good that American singer is, implying that it is always difficult to sing one of Mars's original songs. He commends the contestant on his performance, but also reminds him that some of the notes were *a little* (a scalar stretcher) *squirrely*. Towards the end of the turn, he recommends that he should *really* (a scalar stretcher) take part in this competition again. The booster helps the speaker increase the tone of the utterance, thus encouraging the contestant to consider coming back another time. Following on from this, Gwen tells the contestant, in T3, that there were *too many* (a scalar stretcher) moments when the contestant was a little squirrely for the coaches to take the risk of turning around. She completes the turn by repeating the booster *really*, which helps to increase the tone of the praise she is bestowing on the contestant.

5.2.5 Self-Protection Elastic

The self-protection function of EL involves communicative strategies which are aimed at shielding the speaker from any potential risks (Cheng & Warren, 2003; Ruzaitė, 2007), that is 'She might have done that, but I could be wrong'.

Excerpt 41 (13/3/14): Two speakers over seven speaking turns. The contestant, Moriah, has been successful in getting all four coaches to turn around for her.

T1 Miley: OK, I am still the youngest one on the panel, OK? So **I think I'd** be able to give you big sister advice, because you're getting to experience this at such a young age and that's **something** that I was gifted with. And I just like to be the one because you are **so** talented.

T2 Moriah: Thank you!

T3 Miley: To keep your head on your shoulders; keep you knowing that it is important to be a great singer but it's more important to be a great person.

T4 Moriah: Thank you!

T5 Miley: So **I'd** love to be your coach.

T6 Moriah: Thank you so much!

T7 Miley: **I think** we can relate to each other a lot.

As all the coaches have turned around for Moriah, Miley is trying her best to persuade her to join her team in this part of the conversation. She says, in T1, that she *thinks* (an epistemic stretcher) that she *would* (a possibility stretcher) be able to help her. Although Miley is doing her best to convince the contestant to choose her, she does not want to sound overly intrusive, so these two stretchers appear to have been used for that purpose, particularly when it is considered that, in this turn, the claim that the contestant is talented is also scaled up by using the booster *so*. In T5 and T7, *would* (a possibility stretcher) and *I think* (an epistemic stretcher) are used another time, respectively, with a similar function. Note that there is also a general stretcher, namely *something*, in T1, which facilitates the smooth flow of the conversation.

Excerpt 42 (16/6/4): Two speakers over two speaking turns. No coach has turned around for this contestant, although by this time, both Adam and Blake had their full complement of team members and were unable to select any more contestants.

T1 Adam: That vocal is, like, I found myself married to that song the way I know it for all these years, and so it messes with my head; that's not fair, but sometimes it does do that so just to let you know you're fantastic. [audience applause]

T2 Kelly: I loved your voice, I kept looking and am going, Okay, I'm just waiting for the next level; I just wanted you to do something like **a little** higher, head voicer, you know whooooo, I was just looking for

a little more variety. That's the only reason why I didn't turn around.
I think you are a great singer.

The contestant has sung 'What You Won't Do for Love' by Bobby Caldwell and Adam mentions, in T1, how the song 'messes with' his head and how great the contestant's performance was. This is followed by Kelly, in T2, who by resorting to EL such as *a little* (a quantifying stretcher) manages to explain why she did not turn around without providing more information. Towards the end of the turn, Kelly reassures the contestant that she *thinks* (an epistemic stretcher) he is a great singer. The use of the stretcher *I think* makes the claim sound less confident, without necessarily making it so weak that it is not acceptable.

Excerpt 43 (9/2/1): Three speakers over three speaking turns. The contestant has great singing ability and all the coaches have turned around for him.

> T1 Pharrell: I press my button at the very very very last moment, but I'm glad that I turned around to give support to **someone** who is original and has their own **thing** like you do.
> T2 Blind Joe: Thank you so much man!
> T3 Gwen: **I think** that there is a thing called the country mafia and Blake [audience laughter], and Blake is in charge of that! [audience laughter]

Pharrell is telling the contestant, Blind Joe, how happy he is now that he has turned around for *someone* (a general stretcher) who does their own *thing* (a general stretcher). This is followed by Gwen who, based on the fact that the contestant is wearing a cowboy hat, jokes about one of the other coaches, Blake—who is a country singer—by suggesting that she *thinks* (an epistemic stretcher) that there is a 'country mafia' run by Blake in this competition. Although this is nothing but a joke, the use of *I think* seems to not only reassure the audience that this is a personal thought, but also scales down the tone of the utterance to a personal and friendly level.

Excerpt 44 (14/2/9): Four speakers over 14 speaking turns. All the coaches have turned around for the contestant, Pryor.

T1 Kelly: You look like a man; like a sexy man!

T2 Pryor: Well, thank you!

T3 Kelly: I love all of it, just the soulfulness. It's innate, but you are rock-
ing out of it as well. It separates you from what is happening in music
right now, so I **would** love to have you on my team.

T4 Pryor: Thank you!

T5 Adam: I'm **so** happy I turned first, the way that you make that guitar
sound is **absolutely** singular and unique and amazing.

T6 Pryor: That's a big compliment coming from you; likewise.

T7 Adam: … I don't usually hear **someone** sing the way you do, and
play the way you do, that is a rarity. And I know that instrument, that's
my heart and soul so I believe that this is home right here on my team.

T8 Pryor: All right, all right! [audience applause]

T9 Blake: Hey Pryor speaking of your guitar playing I instantly thought
that sounds like Pete Anderson back there. He made all of Dwight
Yoakam's early records.

T10 Pryor: Yes!

T11 Blake: Cuz it's **a little bit** wild, it's **a little bit** loose, it is in the
moment, so … [someone from the audience says 'whoa']

T12 Pryor: I can hear my dad yelling in the background. [all the coaches
laugh]

T13 Blake: Is that right? Dude you are an incredible vocalist, **sounds
like** you smoked a pack of cigarettes and drank a bottle of whiskey
right before you got on stage!

T14 Pryor: It is not true mum, it is not true! [audience laughter]

As all the coaches have turned around for this contestant, the competition between them is intense as they are all trying to persuade him to
join their teams. In T3, Kelly is telling him that she *would* (a possibility
stretcher) love to have him on her team. This stretcher makes the utterance slightly hypothetical and leaves some room for being rejected by
the contestant. It is a strong suggestion, but not to the degree that it
sounds too imposing or too certain. In T5, Adam commends the contestant on his ability, saying that his guitar playing is *absolutely* (a scalar stretcher) singular and he is *so* (a scalar stretcher) happy that he was
the first person to turn around for him. In T7, Adam says that he does
not usually hear *someone* (a general stretcher) sing like this contestant.
In T9, Blake continues by telling the contestant that his guitar playing

is similar to Pete Anderson's style, in the sense that it is *a little bit* (a scalar stretcher) loose and wild (T11). This elastic expression allows the speaker to remain vague, to tone down the utterance, in case his comments come under attack from the other coaches. In T13, Blake also compliments the contestant's raspy voice by saying that it *sounds like* (an epistemic stretcher) he has 'smoked a pack of cigarettes and drank a bottle of whiskey'. This is a rather controversial claim, as evidenced by the contestant's immediate denial in T14, and so it needs to be toned down. The use of *sounds like* is therefore a step in this direction, namely a self-protection strategy.

Excerpt 45 (14/2/8): Four speakers over seven speaking turns. One of the coaches has turned around for the contestant, Dylan.

> T1 Alicia: So how did you start singing?
> T2 Dylan: I was an actor at first, and then I picked it up when I hit puberty. [Kelly laughs/audience laughter]
> T3 Alicia: That's a good time to pick it up.
> T4 Adam: I hate puberty, man, that's the worst, huh?
> T5 Dylan: Mm-hmm!
> T6 Blake: [towards Adam] You think you will ever get past it? [laughter]
> T7 Adam: But yo man you're great! I love that song. It's a classic, and that's nostalgia, can **kind of** cause me some trouble with this button, but it doesn't matter cos you got Kelly Clarkson!

Only coach Kelly has turned around for this contestant and, in T1, Alicia is trying to find out more about him. The contestant says that he started singing when he reached puberty. In T5, Adam confesses that he hates puberty because it is the worst time of one's life. Blake, in T6, jokes that Adam is still in puberty and will never grow out of it, which causes the audience to burst into laughter. Pretending that he is unperturbed by Blake's remarks, Adam continues, in T7, by telling the contestant that the song he has just performed *kind of* (a scalar stretcher) caused him to be ambivalent about whether or not to press his button. The use of *kind of* enables the speaker to scale down the utterance, making it less face-threatening.

5.2.6 Evasive Elastic

Elastic expressions can be used to withhold information from others (Drave, 2002; Rowland, 2007; Ruzaitė, 2007; Trappes-Lomax, 2007; Zhang, 2015). The following excerpts illustrate how evasive function has been employed in the English data.

Excerpt 46 (14/1/10): Two speakers over four speaking turns. No coach has turned around for the contestant, Mackenzie.

> T1 Alicia: You have **such** a vibe; such energy and you are **totally** not what I expected to turn around to; that's what makes this show incredible.
>
> T2 Makenzie: Thank you!
>
> T3 Alicia: So keep doing what you do 'cause you're on to **something so** good.
>
> T4 Makenzie: Thank you so much! [audience applause]

No coach has turned around for Makenzie and, therefore, each coach is trying to comfort him. In this part of the conversation, Alicia is telling him how she admires his energy, as he has *such* (a scalar stretcher) a vibe, and that he is *totally* (a scalar stretcher) different from what she thought he would be. In T3, she further reassures Makenzie by telling him that if he continues to perform in the way that he is doing, he will be on to *something* (a general stretcher) *so* (a scalar stretcher) good. While the stretcher *so* moves the tone of the utterance upwards making it sound more confident and reassuring, the elastic expression *something* is sufficiently vague that it enables the speaker to remain positive and encouraging, without necessarily providing any further details as to what *something* might eventually turn out to be. In this case, therefore, the use of *something* seems to be motivated by a need to sound positive without necessarily having to specify how, and in which direction, the contestant will flourish.

Excerpt 47 (14/2/2): Four speakers over nine speaking turns. Two coaches have turned around for the contestant, Jaclyn.

T1 Blake: … for the first time in my life I pictured myself while you were singing; me riding a unicorn, the kind that has, like, wings. [audience laughter] The kind that has, like, wings.

T2 Jaclyn: That's the vibe I was trying to get. [audience laughter]

T3 Blake: And I was holding a Care Bear and a Care Bear right here [points to his heart].

[audience laughter] It was like, your voice is like what is happening to me? [audience laughter] Here am I? Like you did that to me.

T4 Kelly: You made a grown man do that!

T5 Adam: It's amazing how one man's dream is another man's nightmare! [audience laughter]

T6 Blake: Even though there is vocalists in this competition, that **literally** blow the roof of this place; **I think** what you do is more powerful than that.

T7 Jaclyn: Thank you!

T8 Blake: I've got to have you on my team, Please Jaclyn I love you!

T9 Adam: Let me take over before you say any other strange **things**. [audience laughter]

Blake is one of two coaches who have turned around for the contestant, Jaclyn. He begins this conversation by telling her how, during her performance, he was dreaming that he was riding a unicorn. This is arguably an attempt to show the contestant how pleasant her singing and performance were. These comments are so overly emotional that Kelly and Adam, in T4 and T5, make fun of him. However, Blake continues with his story and confirms how highly he regards the contestant by saying, in T6, that he *thinks* (an epistemic stretcher) that her voice is even stronger than those of other vocalists in the competition because it *literally* (a scalar stretcher) blew the roof of the arena. At this point, Adam, in T9, interjects by saying that he wants to take over before Blake says any other strange *things*. In this case, the use of *things* appears to have an evasive function: while it allows the speaker to refer to all Blake's earlier comments, it also allows him to refrain from specifying what these strange *things* are.

Excerpt 48 (14/2/9): Three speakers over four speaking turns. All the coaches have turned around for the contestant, Pryor.

T1 Pryor: Those days are **long** gone, long gone!

T2 Blake: I did that **stuff** for years in order to try to sound like you, and I still didn't get there, You just sound …

T3 Adam: Why you want to be led down the path of addiction right now? [audience laughter]

T4 Blake: You were born with that weathered sound. That's what makes you rare. That's what separates you from the rest of the pack; that's why you gotta pick me as your coach man, I need you on my team I want you on my team, Pryor. [the audience cheers and applauds]

Previously Blake has told the contestant that it sounded like he had smoked a pack of cigarettes and drank a bottle of whiskey before going on stage. While obviously Blake meant this to be a compliment, the contestant responds by shouting 'it is not true, mum' as an attempt to distance himself from drinking whiskey and smoking cigarettes. In T1, the contestant continues by claiming that it has been quite some time since he last consumed whiskey or smoked cigarettes by saying that those days are *long* (a scalar stretcher) gone. Having heard this, Blake replies, in T2, by saying that he did that *stuff* (a general stretcher) for years to improve the quality of his voice. In this context, the use of the word *stuff* appears to be motivated by Blake's decision not to reveal much information regarding the nature of the *stuff* he used to smoke/drink. Of course, it might not be any more serious than *whiskey* or *cigarettes*, but publicly mentioning it is clearly something that Blake would prefer not to do. However, this does not prevent Adam from making fun of him, in T3.

Excerpt 49 (14/1/11): Four speakers over seven speaking turns. Three coaches have turned around for the contestant, Justin (Blake had been blocked).[2]

T1 Kelly: How did you start singing? Like what made you go for country music?

T2 Justin: Reba McEntire, I was obsessed with her when I was a little kid.

---

[2]Blake had been blocked.

T3 Kelly: That is so weird [audience laughter] 'cause she is my mommy-in law! I'm just saying! [audience laughter] Do you all know Reba McEntire? [the audience cheers and applauds] I've done a duet with her; we've had, like, a hit!

T4 Adam: I can't wait for the GIF that's gonna exist of the dance you just did over there. [audience laughter] I'm going to send it to you all the time!

T5 Kelly: And it's gonna, and they're going to say 'Drop it like it's hot'. [the audience cheers and applauds] Her grandchildren are my children, I'm just saying, I'll call her!

T6 Alicia: I will call Reba McEntire, too, I will call Bonnie Raitt.

T7 Adam: I will call Meryl Streep [audience laughter] I will call **anybody**, **anybody** you want me to call, I'm calling. [audience laughter]

All the coaches have turned around for this contestant, with the exception of Blake, who was not able to participate because he had been blocked by the other coaches. The contestant reveals that he was inspired by Reba McEntire who just happens to be Kelly's mother-in-law. This greatly excites Kelly and she uses this, in T5, as an opportunity to tell the contestant that she can ring and ask for Reba's help. As a result, the other two coaches each mention people who they could contact for help if the need arose. In T7, Adam goes as far as to claim that he could call *anybody* (a general stretcher). The use of *anybody* no doubt serves an evasive function: while it gives the audience the impression that Adam has many connections in the cinematic and music industries, it allows the speaker to refrain from further name dropping.

Excerpt 50 (8/1/1): Three speakers over seven speaking turns. Four coaches have shown an interest in the contestant, Sarah.

T1 Pharrell: You know what, look …

T2 Sarah: We are like necklace twins!

T3 Pharrell: I know **things** about like green motorcycle jackets, pearls just like you! I'm caught up in the moment.

T4 Christina: Work Pharrell!

T5 Sarah: Hi Adam, I keep waiting to wake up in my bed in Nashville and be like oh I woke up! My God it is a dream! Adam is holding me, but Pharrell came and we are necklace twins. Blake was he there too? Christina she was back.

T6 Christina: Yes!
T7 Sarah: It was 'wow'!

No sooner has Pharrell started speaking than the contestant tells him, in T2, that they are necklace twins. Pharrell seizes his opportunity by saying, in T3, that he knows *things* (a general stretcher) about, say, the green motorcycle jacket that the contestant is wearing. This is an example of the use of EL for an evasive purpose. What Pharrell knows about, for example, *green motorcycle jackets*, is not known to us, but arguably *things* enables him to mention that he knows about these items without providing any further information.

5.3   Overall Analysis

Having analysed EL at lexical and pragmatic levels individually, it is now time to look at these expressions when they occur in longer stretches of conversation.

Excerpt 51 (15/2/4): Five speakers over 17 speaking turns. Three coaches have turned around for the contestant, Michael.

T1 Blake: You **literally** beat me to death with that vocal performance; I was thinking the whole time, it's soulful, it is the blues; then I was like screw it, I can coach this guy man! **I think** this **would** be a match made in heaven as a matter of fact!

T2 Adam: What a vote of confidence! [audience laughter] You know I was just sitting here, and I was listening; I was like '**might** as well turn'! [audience laughter] Great pitch Blake!

T3 Blake: **Actually** he is **exactly** right. I know you deserve to get all the buttons pushes you could get, man, **I'd** be honoured to be your coach. [the audience cheers and applauds]

T4 Adam: That song choice says **a lot** about **someone** and what they want to accomplish.

T5 Michael: Yeah!

T6 Adam: When I turned around first, [audience laughter] you know I am **maybe** the only one who's worked with a solo guitar player who plays solos, who plays the blues who plays that style of music.

T7 Blake: Well, I've also worked with **a couple of** guitar players on this show!

T8 Adam: Solo, like solo guitar player? Guys that play the blues?

T9 Blake: Yes, last season, remember that?! [audience laughter]

T10 Kelly: **I think** we just need to add mud and just like let them go at it! [audience laughter] I will tell you as a Texas sister, choose a team that you feel you are going to stick out in.

T11 Blake: Oh! [points to himself]

T12 Kelly: And not a team that **maybe** isn't like 'I have all the guitarists on my team'; 'I have all the guitarists on my team'. [audience laughter] So, I'm team JHUD, all the way!

T13 Jennifer: There it goes!

T14 Kelly: Ain't **nobody** on her team like you!

T15 Jennifer: **Nobody**!

T16 Adam: First of all there is **nobody** on any team like him.

T17 Kelly: That's what he said to all the people to make them feel special! [audience laughter]

As Michael has sung well and three coaches have turned around for him, the competition is intense, and every coach is trying their best to persuade him to join their team. In T1, Blake uses the booster *literally* to stretch the tone of the utterance upwards to highlight the fact that the contestant *beat him to death* with his great performance. At the end of this turn, he also states that he *thinks* (an epistemic stretcher) that if they were to collaborate, it *would* (a possibility stretcher) be a match made in heaven. The use of both *think* and *would* enables the speaker to forward an idea without necessarily sounding too brazen or imposing. In T2, Adam makes fun of Blake's attempts by claiming that his pitch was not a particularly good effort. He mocks Blake's comments by saying that 'I might as well turn', in which *might*, as a mitigating elastic device, stretches the tone of the utterance downwards, which serves to remind Blake that what he said in T1 was not strong enough.

In T3, Blake imposes his own interpretation of what Adam has just said in T2, by saying that *actually* he is *exactly* (booster stretchers) right for the contestant. Blake argues that the contestant deserves *to get all the buttons pushes* he can get. In T4, Adam continues by saying that the right choice of song says *a lot* (a quantifying stretcher) about *someone* (a general stretcher) who wants to achieve *a lot*. In this context, *a lot* stretches the utterance upwards and *someone* enables him to speak generally in ways which can be understood by both the audience and contestant. In T6, Adam states that *maybe* (a possibility indicator) he is 'the only one who's worked with a solo guitar player who plays solos, who plays the blues who plays that style of music'. This is a big claim, and so the use of *maybe* appears to have been motivated by the need to tone down the utterance slightly. In T7, Blake jumps in by saying that he has also played with *a couple of* (a quantifying stretcher) guitar players. *A couple of* is arguably a quantifier which serves to emphasise the fact that he can also be a good coach, experience-wise, without necessarily having to specify how many guitar players he has actually coached.

In T7 to T9, Blake and Adam continue to question each other's suitability to the point that, in T10, coach Kelly, who has not turned around for the contestant, comments that she *thinks* (an epistemic stretcher) that 'they just need to add mud and just like let them go at it'. This is a rather humorous proposal, and the use of *I think* tones it down and makes the proposal less serious. In T12, Kelly uses another instance of *maybe* in her attempt to convince the contestant to join Jennifer Hudson's (JHUD) team. The use of the possibility indicator *maybe* tones down the suggestion and makes it more friendly. Kelly, in T14, claims that *nobody* on Kelly's team is like this contestant, where *nobody* is a general stretcher which enables the speaker to avoid naming the other contestants on Jennifer's team. Jennifer confirms, in T15, that she agrees with Kelly's claim, whereas Adam, in T16, disagrees by saying that there is *nobody* like the contestant on any of the other teams, either. In this turn, *nobody* is a general stretcher and enables the speaker to refer to others without being explicit.

Excerpt 52 (15/1/1): Five speakers over 33 speaking turns. Three coaches have turned around for the contestant, Sarah Grace.

T1 Adam: What is your name?
T2 Sarah: My name is Sarah Grace and I'm from Houston, Texas. And I'm 15 years old.
[the audience cheers and applauds]
T3 Adam: Fifteen years old?!

T4 Sarah: Yes sir, yes sir!

T5 Kelly: From Texas?

T6 Adam: From Texas!

T7 Sarah: Yeah!

T8 Adam: Not Oklahoma!

T9 Sarah: Not Oklahoma!

T10 Adam: All right well, I get to be **kind of** an MC **of sorts** right now!

T11 Sarah: [chuckles]

T12 Adam: You got two great choices! [laughter] And I'm **really** excited to watch the sparks fly as they all fight over your adorable face…

T13 Sarah: Thank you so much!

T14 Adam: … and incredible talent!

T15 Sarah: Thank you so much!

T16 Kelly: Speaking of her face, my favourite part is 'You had stank face for days'; she was like, she was like [moves her head] [audience laughter]

T17 Adam: I'm not sure that's a nickname, that's gonna stick!

T18 Blake: Hey there is old Stank Face!

T19 Adam: There is old Stank Face Grace. [audience laughter]

T20 Sarah: I like it, I like it!

T21 Jennifer: She likes it!

T22 Sarah: Oh no, I don't like it! I was just kidding [audience laughter]

T23 Jennifer: See here at JHUD Productions we call that sass, I felt it with my chair back you know.

T24 Kelly: Wow!

T25 Jennifer: Like, I was like, **somebody** got **some** presence up in here; I **would** call you sassy.

T26 Sarah: I like that better!

T27 Adam: By the way don't blame me for the stank face; that's her idea! [points to Kelly] [audience laughter]

T28 Kelly: It is a compliment! That's like my girlfriends and I we are always like oh she has a stank face; like I loved it … I **really** do want to say I did **actually** win *The Voice* last year with a 15 year old.

T29 Sarah: That's true.

T30 Kelly: I'm just saying I can do it! [audience laughter]

T31 Jennifer: Just curious! What kind of record do you want to make?

T32 Sarah: **Probably** a blues rock roots album, pulling from Etta James, Janis Joplin.

T33 Kelly: I'm a big fan man! I was surprised you were **so** little with such a big like old soul voice!

The contestant has sung very well, despite her young age, and all the coaches have turned around for her, with the exception of Adam. In the first few turns, the coaches ascertain that she is just 15 years old and from Texas. Much to Adam's surprise, the contestant confirms that she is not from Oklahoma, coach Blake's home city. Having heard this, Adam says that he gets to be *kind of an MC of sorts*, in T10, because he did not turn around for this contestant and is therefore not in competition with the other coaches. This utterance involves two uses of EL: *kind of* and *of sorts* which, as a scalar stretcher, slightly tones down the force of the utterance making it appear more inclusive. In T12, Adam also puts on record his excitement, and stretches the tone of the utterance upwards by using the stretcher *really* (a scalar stretcher) to enhance the degree of his excitement. In T16, Kelly, in an attempt to compliment the speaker, says that she has got a *stank face*. Although Sarah at first, in T20, says that she likes this term, she changes her opinion, in T22, and says that she was only joking, earlier.

At this point in the conversation, Jennifer takes to the floor and compliments the contestant on the quality of her voice and performance. Jennifer goes as far as to claim that *somebody* has *some* presence in this competition. The word *somebody* is a general stretcher which enables the speaker to refer to the contestant without actually mentioning her name. This strategy, discursively speaking, might have different motivations, including the idea that by referring to people as *somebody* the statement can be made more emphatic. The quantifying stretcher *some* also enables the speaker to talk vaguely about the singing qualities, that is the performance, of the contestant without going into detail. In T27, Adam again criticises Kelly for using the term *stank face*, which causes Kelly to retort, in T28, by saying that it was only meant to be a compliment. Kelly also stretches the tone of her utterance upwards by using the stretchers *really* and *actually* in an attempt to win over the contestant. In T31, Jennifer asks the contestant what kind of record she wants to make, to which Sarah, in T32, replies that she would like to record *probably* a blues rock roots album. The use of the possibility stretcher *probably* tones down the utterance making it less emphatic and more hesitant. In this case, EL appears to have been used by the contestant to convey her uncertainty and avoid sounding too self-assured. In T33, Kelly again says that she is surprised at how small, physically speaking, the contestant is. The use of the elastic booster *so* in this turn not only stretches the utterance upwards, but also creates a sense of solidarity and rapport with the contestant.

Excerpt 53 (13/1/8). Five speakers over 21 speaking turns. Two coaches have turned around for the contestant, Esera.

T1 Adam: Dude, the way you fell off on the moments that are normally **really** big in the song didn't sit well with me at first but then I **actually** grew to like it **a lot**. So I'm a **total** moron! [Esera laughs]

T2 Blake: That's why you are in my phone as Total Moron when you call me! [audience laughter]

T3 Adam: I can't even say on TV what you are on my phone! [Blake and the audience laugh]

T4 Miley: Well, what is your name and where are you from?

T5 Esera: My name is Esera Tuaolo and I'm from Hawaii, but I currently live in Minnesota.

T6 Miley: Aloha! [audience laughter]

T7 Jennifer: That is one of my favourite songs and that's **probably** part of what caught my attention. The way you executed the soaring notes, they were great, and **sometimes** those notes are **so much** easier than the notes that don't soar. And when you start to sing, the pullback notes as Adam was talking about, you were losing your air.

T8 Esera: Yeah!

T9 Adam: Was that a choice?

T10 Esera: You know I played nine years in the NFL, so it's like [the audience cheers] you get coached to take short breaths. Then you come here and take deep breaths **and stuff like that**.

T11 Adam: So what you're saying is singing is **actually kind of** tough?

T12 Esera: Oh it is!

T13 Adam: So you could tell all your football buddies like 'ya'll singers are badass'! [Esera laughs]

T14 Blake: I **almost** asked if that was a Super Bowl ring you are wearing?

T15 Esera: It is the NFC championship ring.

T16 Jennifer: That's amazing! [the audience cheers and applauds]

T17 Blake: When I turned around I could see that you were **so** focused on Jennifer; I do that too! Even when she doesn't know I'm staring at the side of her face, she's like looking and I'm just like … [Blake turns his head and looks at Jennifer]

T18 Adam: It's **kind of** creepy; it's **real** creepy [audience laughter]

T19 Blake: I know, I am a country singer, but I've got **a lot of** experience doing this with **a lot of** different types of artists. I'm a fan of great singers and you are one of them. I'm **such** a football geek and if I was your coach I would **probably** drive you nuts! You've **definitely** got two servings of talent man so congratulations **whatever** coach you go with man.

T20 Esera: I appreciate that.

T21 Blake: I'm happy for you.

In the first turn, Adam tells the contestant why he did not turn around. He says that, at the beginning of the song, the way in which the contestant 'fell off' on moments that are usually *really* (a scalar stretcher) big, did not initially impress him. The word *really* highlights the importance of those moments in a vague way. However, Adam also acknowledges that, as the contestant continued singing, he *actually* began to like it *a lot* (a scalar stretcher). The epistemic stretcher *actually* renders the proposition vague by enabling the speaker to remain unclear about the truth or facts of the situation. Adam calls himself a *total* (a scalar stretcher) moron by not turning for this contestant, a fact which motivates Blake to make fun of him, in T2.

Having heard the contestant's background, coach Jennifer tells him, in T7, that the song he performed was *probably* one of the reasons that she turned around for him. This probability stretcher *probably* enables the speaker to say something without necessarily being fully committed to it (Channel, 1994). In the remainder of the turn, Jennifer argues that soaring notes are *sometimes* (a general stretcher) *much* (a scalar stretcher) easier to produce. The former allows the speaker to make a point without necessarily providing more information, while the latter helps the speaker to stretch the tone of the claim being made upwards. These are all probably used to convince the speaker that there were some flaws in his singing that needed to be perfected.

In T10, the contestant explains the reason for these flaws, arguing that he had been used to taking short breaths in his previous career as an athlete, but when he is singing, he is now in the position where he has to breathe deeply *and stuff like that*. This general stretcher seems to have been used to save the speaker from having to detail all the differences between his previous athletic training and his current singing career. In T11, Adam uses another epistemic stretcher, that is *actually*, as well as a possibility stretcher, that is *sort of*, when confirming the fact that singing is tough. In T14, Blake confirms that when the contestant was talking, he *almost* asked him if he was wearing a Super Bowl ring. This scalar stretcher makes the claim less strong and can potentially prevent him from being criticised by those who believe he is not telling the truth. In T17, Blake states that he is *so* focused on Jennifer. This epistemic booster serves to highlight the fact that he admires Jennifer, in an attempt to suggest that the contestant has two good coaches to choose from.

As Blake turns towards Jennifer, Adam, in T18, describes it as *kind of* and *real* creepy. *Kind of* is obviously an epistemic stretcher which makes the claim less strong, but *real* appears to correct *kind of* as it stretches the tone of the utterance upwards. This combination of opposing stretchers might indicate the speaker's change of mind during the utterance, an interesting phenomenon in the use of EL. Adam begins his exchange with *kind of* creepy, then changes his mind to say that, actually, it is not merely *kind of* creepy, but *real* creepy. In T19, Blake tells the contestant that he has got *a lot of* experience and has worked with *a lot of* artists. These two quantifying stretchers help to present Blake as a suitable coach without going into detail. He also suggests that if he was chosen to be the coach, he would *probably* drive the contestant crazy. *Probably* is a possibility stretcher which makes the claim less strong. However, this is followed by a booster, that is *definitely*, which stretches the tone of the claim upwards. He also congratulates the contestant on *whatever* coach he decides to choose. The general stretcher *whatever* helps the speaker to refer to both coaches in a general way, without the necessity of naming them again.

Excerpt 54 (15/1/4): Four speakers over five speaking turns. None of the coaches have turned around for the contestant, Ayanna.

T1 Blake: I'm sorry that I didn't hit my button! It was just enough out of my lane, that I just **probably** overthought **a little bit** to be honest with you.

T2 Ayanna: It's OK; thank you!

T3 Kelly: I **really** hope that you come back and, like, sing **something** just with **a little more** space. You do have a **really** cool tone.

T4 Jennifer: I was **so** close; you have an amazing voice but **some** of the notes were **a bit** under and then I was waiting for the big 'whistle' tone; it never came! I do **think** you should come back'cos you do have a great voice.

T5 Kelly: Thank you so much for coming, Ayanna.

None of the coaches has turned around for the contestant, Ayanna, and in this exchange three of them are explaining their reasons for not doing so. Having apologised for not turning around, coach Blake, in T1, tells Ayanna that he did not press his button because he felt that her singing and style of music were not what he usually prefers. He further explains that *probably* he, as a potential coach, had overthought the decision *a little bit*. Both the possibility indicator *probably* and the quantifying stretcher *a little bit* seem to have been used to show the speaker's hesitation: on the one hand, EL serves to convey the idea that he might have made a mistake by not turning around for this contestant and, on the other hand, it reassures the contestant that she might have been good enough. In T3, Kelly says that she *really* hopes that the contestant will consider returning to the competition sometime in the future. The use of the elastic booster *really* strengthens this wish and encouragement, thus comforting the contestant. Kelly hopes that if the contestant returns, she will sing *something* sweet with *a little* more space. The use of the general stretcher *something* saves the speaker both from having to find the correct word and from suggesting how she would expect the contestant to perform the next time. The quantifying stretcher *a little* enables the speaker to remain vague as to how much more space the contestant is expected to incorporate into her performance. In addition, she also commends the contestant on having a *really* cool tone (a booster stretcher).

In T4, Jennifer also tells the contestant that she was *so* close to pushing the button and turning around. The use of a booster, such as *so*, increases the tone of the claim and further comforts the contestant. She also confirms that she did not turn around because *some* of the notes in the contestant's performance were *a bit* under. The use of quantifiers, such as *some* and *a bit*, enables the speaker to remain vague as to exactly which notes were *under* and to what extent. In the remainder of the turn, Jennifer also confirms that she *thinks* the contestant should return to the show sometime in the future. The use of *I think* makes the proposition appear to be personal advice, although the use of the emphatic marker *do* makes it slightly stronger.

Excerpt 55 (12/1/3): Five speakers over 15 speaking turns. Three coaches have turned around for the contestant, Johnny.

> T1 Alicia: Your energy pops through the whole place and your tone is outrageous.
> T2 Johnny: **Really** appreciate that; just been playing in bands my whole life; started in a garage moved to Nashville, and …
> T3 Blake: But you are **mostly** rock though, right?
> T4 Johnny: Yeah, I'm a rock guy! My band, we were out opening for Rod Stewart last summer. [all coaches say 'wow!']
> T5 Alicia: I **kind of** hear **a little** Rod Stewart.
> T6 Gwen: You know, I want to say it makes sense because you have **such** presence up there. Your voice is incredible.
> T7 Alicia: Yeah!
> T8 Gwen: I **feel like** out of the three choices that you have, like it's obvious.
> T9 Adam: It's **so** obvious.
> T10 Gwen: I mean it's just **so** obvious. [audience laughter]
> T11 Adam: It's **so** obvious you don't even have to say; but it's, yeah.
> T12 Gwen: I mean it's **so** obvious! [audience laughter]
> T13 Adam: It's **so painfully** obvious! [audience laughter] Johnny, I just want to say this, because just hearing anyone sing that song it's always such an amazing **thing**. Thank you for doing that!
> T14 Johnny: Dude I appreciate that!
> T15 Adam: I love that song, I love it. [the audience applauds]

Johnny sounds like a talented and experienced singer, and all three coaches who have turned around want him on their teams. In this conversation, Alicia begins, in T1, by commending Johnny on his *outrageous* voice. In response, in T2, Johnny says that he *really* appreciates the praise he has received. The scalar stretcher *really* stretches the tone of the utterance upwards, making the appreciation stronger. In T3, Blake, who turned around for this contestant, tells him that despite the fact that he has spent some time in Nashville, his voice is *mostly* rock and not country. The quantifying stretcher *mostly* enables Blake to make a general claim, while at the same time protecting himself from the risk of being challenged or refuted. In T4, however, Johnny agrees with Blake confirming that he is indeed a *rock guy*.

In T6, Gwen, another of the coaches who turned around for the contestant, also praises him and says that he has *such* presence on stage. The scalar stretcher moves the claim upwards, and thus allows Gwen to appear more confident in her description. Following this, in T8, Gwen says that she *feels like* (an epistemic stretcher) it is obvious who will be chosen to be Johnny's coach. The expression *feels like* makes the utterance appear less imposing. At this point, Adam, the only coach not to have turned around, modifies Gwen's claim by saying that the choice is not just obvious, but *so* obvious (T9, T11 and T13). It is obvious who will be chosen to be the coach because, like the contestant, coach Gwen began her career as a garage singer. The scalar stretcher *so* not only stretches the tone of the utterance upwards, but also establishes solidarity and rapport. In T13, Adam uses another stretcher when he maintains that the choice is *painfully* obvious. The word *painfully* almost serves the same purpose as *so*, but further establishes a relaxed atmosphere with both the contestant and audience. In the same turn, Adam also uses a general stretcher, that is *thing*, which has arguably been used to refer to the pleasure that he derives from hearing that particular song performed well. Thus, a general stretcher is a convenient and unspecific way of referring to something without going into any detail.

5.4   Frequency of Lexical Items

This section discusses the findings of EL use in the English data set from the perspective of frequency analysis. This provides a general picture of the distribution of EL use, and the relationship between the level of competition between the coaches and its possible impact on their choice of elastic expressions.

As shown in Table 5.1 and Fig. 5.1, the most frequently observed category of EL lexical item is that of scalar stretchers (46.3%). This should not be surprising, given the fact that persuasion appears to be the main motivation behind the interactants' choice of words in this study. The second most frequently observed category in the English data is epistemic stretcher (24.6%), followed by those of general stretcher and approximate stretcher, respectively. As was previously discussed, the order in frequency of the elastic categories investigated in this study is not unexpected, given that the purpose of communication in this study is not so much about delivering information, but rather about persuading the contestants. The fact that the use of scalar stretchers is just slightly less than the use of all the other three categories combined, can be taken as evidence to suggest that, in the discourse domain under investigation, speakers tend to prioritise the manipulation of the tone of the speaker, either by strengthening or softening, over other things.

Table 5.1 Overall lexical frequency in the English data

Category $N = 4238$	AQ	GE	SC	EP	Total
Frequency	378	854	1964	1042	4238
Percentage	8.9	20.2	46.3	24.6	100

Note AQ = approximate stretcher, GE = general stretcher, SC = scalar stretcher and EP = epistemic stretcher

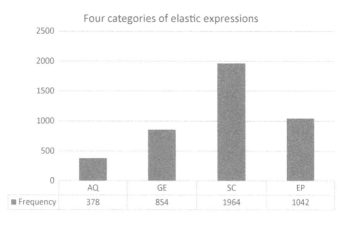

Fig. 5.1 Overall lexical frequency in the English data

Table 5.2 Overview of the number of coaches that turned around for each contestant in the English data

Type N = 298	0 turned	1 turned	2 turned	3 turned	4 turned	Total
Number	66	22	114	54	42	298
Percentage	22.1	7.4	38.3	18.1	14.1	100

Table 5.3 Frequency versus the number of turned coaches in the English data

Category/ no. of turns	AQ (1)	GE (2)	SC-I[a] (3)	SC-D[a] (4)	EP (5)	Total	Sub-total (3+4)
0 turned	70	84	252	85	174	665	337
1 turned	16	28	84	24	14	166	108
2 turned	126	348	626	132	424	1656	758
3 turned	92	176	362	47	216	893	409
4 turned	74	218	322	30	214	858	352
Total	378	854	1646	318	1042	4238	1964
Chi-squared ($p < 0.01$)	χ^2 [d.f.12, $n = 4238$] $= 78.963$, $p = 0.001$ (significant)						

[a]SC-I: intensifier, SC-D: deintensifier

It should also be mentioned that within the category of scalar stretchers, scalar boosters were used much more frequently than scalar downtoners. See Tables 5.2 and 5.3 for more details.

Table 5.2 shows that the majority of contestants managed to have at least two coaches turning around for them. For approximately one in every three contestants, two coaches turned around, but for approximately one in every five contestants, no coaches turned around. As Table 5.2 further highlights, approximately one in every three contestants had either three or four coaches turning around. Having only one coach turning around is the least frequently observed scenario, with approximately one in every fourteen contestants in this situation (Table 5.4).

The data in Fig. 5.2 show the following trends:

a. It appears that the use of an approximate stretcher is not influenced by the number of coaches that have turned around, as the proportional use of approximate stretcher fluctuates only very slightly.

Table 5.4 Frequency versus number of turned coaches in the English data (%)

	AQ	GE	SC-I	SC-D	EP	Total (%)	Sub-total
0 turned N=665	10.5	12.6	37.9	12.8	26.2	100	50.7
1 turned N=166	9.6	16.9	50.6	14.5	8.4	100	65.1
2 turned N=1656	7.6	21.0	37.8	8.0	25.6	100	45.8
3 turned N=893	10.3	19.7	40.5	5.3	24.2	100	45.8
4 turned N=858	8.6	25.4	37.5	3.5	24.9	100	41.0
Total N=4238	8.9	20.2	38.8	7.5	24.6	100	46.3

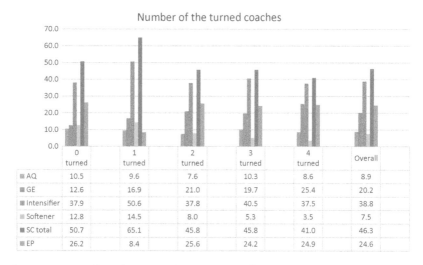

Fig. 5.2 Comparison between the number of the turned coaches and their choice of EL in the English data (%)

It could be tentatively claimed that an approximate stretcher has less to do with the emotive/persuasive functions of language than with the informative functions. This supports the findings in Jucker, Smith, and Ludge (2003) and Moxey and Sanford (1993), where approximators and vague quantifiers tend to serve informative functions.

b. It appears that the proportion of softeners and epistemic stretchers becomes either less frequent or is unchanged as the number of turned coaches increases. One reason for this tendency could be the fact that, as more coaches turn around, the competition between them intensifies, and they might be more willing to adopt a larger proportion of intensifiers than boosters or epistemic stretchers.

c. In all situations, intensifiers comprise the largest proportion of the EL used. This can be taken as evidence to suggest that, due to the nature of the competition, coaches tend to make more use of intensifiers with a view to winning over more contestants.

d. The highest proportion of general stretchers used is found in situations where all the coaches have turned around. This suggests that when competition between the coaches is greatest, solely using intensifiers may not be enough. Other strategic devices are also useful, for example, using general stretchers to create in-groupness and solidarity among the interactants (Fetzer, 2010; Overstreet, 1999; Ryoo, 2005).

e. The highest proportion of softeners is found in situations where either no coach or only one coach has turned around. This finding is in line with the expectations of the study: softeners are used to decrease the tone of the utterance, and are particularly useful when coaches feel that they need to comfort the contestants or explain why they did not turn around for them. This finding is in line with the conclusions of previous studies (e.g. Drave, 2002) that softeners tend to mitigate the force of an utterance and make an unpleasant situation more tolerable.

5.5   Concluding Remarks

This chapter sheds some light on how language stretching is manifested in the form of the lexical items and pragmatic functions that were employed in the English data. The linguistic analyses demonstrated how the different categories of EL were used throughout the interactions under investigation. The wide variety of excerpts which were analysed in this chapter highlight the fact that, in the discourse domain under investigation where many different speech acts are at play, the two speech acts of persuasion and mitigation appear to be the more relevant.

As far as the qualitative analysis is concerned, it was clarified how the four functions of approximation, generalisation, mitigation and stance marking are at work in the English data. The results of the quantitative analysis also revealed that the majority of contestants were successful in getting at least two coaches to turn around for them, and that situations involving head-to-head competition between only two coaches are the most frequent. As was noted in the previous chapter, the way in which contestants choose a particular coach depends on various factors, not necessarily the coaches' use of EL. Indeed, some contestants may have a favourite coach in mind before even entering the competition. However, as this chapter shows, EL appears to play an important role in this context.

References

Brown, P., & Levinson, S. C. (1987). *Politeness: Some universals in language usage*. Cambridge: Cambridge University Press.

Channell, J. (1994). *Vague language*. Oxford: Oxford University Press.

Cheng, W., & Warren, M. (2003). Indirectness, inexplicitness and vagueness made clearer. *Pragmatics, 13,* 381–400.

Drave, N. (2002). Vaguely speaking: A corpus approach to vague language in intercultural conversations. In P. Peters, P. Collins, & A. Smith (Eds.), *Language and computers: New frontiers of corpus research*. Papers from the Twenty-First International Conference of English Language Research and Computerized Corpora (pp. 25–40). The Netherlands: Rodopi.

Fetzer, A. (2010). Hedges in context: Form and function of *sort of* and *kind of*. In G. Kaltenbock, W. Mihatsch, & S. Schneider (Eds.), *New approaches to hedging* (pp. 49–71). Bingley: Emerald.

Hu, G., & Cao, F. (2011). Hedging and boosting in abstracts of applied linguistics articles: A comparative study of English- and Chinese-medium journals. *Journal of Pragmatics, 43,* 2795–2809.

Hyland, K. (1998). Persuasion and context: The pragmatics of academic metadiscourse. *Journal of Pragmatics, 30*(4), 437–455.

Hyland, K. (2000). Hedges, boosters and lexical invisibility: Noticing modifiers in academic texts. *Language Awareness, 9*(4), 179–197.

Jucker, A. H., Smith, S. W., & Ludge, T. (2003). Interactive aspects of vagueness in conversation. *Journal of Pragmatics, 35,* 1737–1769.

Moxey, L., & Sanford, A. (1993). *Communicating quantities: A psychological perspective.* Hove, UK: Lawrence Erlbaum.

Overstreet, M. (1999). *Whales, candlelight, and stuff like that: General extenders in English discourse.* Oxford: Oxford University Press.

Parvaresh, V., & Eslami Rasekh, A. (2009). Speech act disagreement among young women in Iran. *CLCWeb: Comparative Literature and Culture, 11*(4), 11.

Parvaresh, V., & Tayebi, T. (2014). Vaguely speaking in Persian. *Discourse Processes, 51*(7), 565–600.

Rowland, T. (2007). 'Well maybe not exactly, but it's around fifty basically?': Vague language in mathematics classrooms. In J. Cutting (Ed.), *Vague language explored* (pp. 79–96). Basingstoke: Palgrave Macmillan.

Ruzaitė, J. (2007). *Vague language in educational settings: Quantifiers and approximators in British and American English.* Frankfurt am Main: Peter Lang.

Ryoo, H. K. (2005). Achieving friendly interactions: A study of service encounters between Korean shopkeepers and African-American customers. *Discourse and Society, 16*(1), 79–105.

Trappes-Lomax, H. (2007). Vague language as a means of self-protective avoidance: Tension management in conference talks. In J. Cutting (Ed.), *Vague language explored* (pp. 117–137). Basingstoke: Palgrave Macmillan.

Zhang, G. (2015). *Elastic language: How and why we stretch our words.* Cambridge: Cambridge University Press.

6
Comparison Between the Chinese and English Findings

Drawing on the empirical evidence revealed in previous chapters, this chapter compares the similarities and differences between the Chinese and English findings. In particular, the lexical patterns, contextual influences (impact of the level of competition between the coaches), collaboration versus competition and trends in the manifestation of elasticity are investigated.

6.1 Patterns of Lexical Items

The Chinese and English data are illustrated in Table 6.1, which shows the distribution of the four categories of lexical item.

As shown in Table 6.1, the most frequently observed EL category in the Chinese data is scalar stretcher (62.7%). The same pattern, albeit with much less frequency (46.3%), is found in the English data. Furthermore, a similar frequency ranking emerged between the two languages which, from the most frequent to the least frequent is as follows: scalar stretcher, epistemic stretcher, general stretcher and approximate stretcher. This ranking is in keeping with the context of this study,

© The Author(s) 2019
G. Zhang and V. Parvaresh, *Elastic Language in Persuasion and Comforting*,
https://doi.org/10.1007/978-3-030-28460-2_6

Table 6.1 Comparison of lexical items between the Chinese and English data

Category	AQ	GE	SC	EP	Total
Chinese					
Frequency	692	1320	6116	1632	9760
Percentage	7.1	13.5	62.7	16.7	100
English					
Frequency	378	854	1964	1042	4238
Percentage	8.9	20.2	46.3	24.6	100

where persuasion and comforting are the two main speech acts in use. Scalar stretchers, together with epistemic and general stretchers, serve their intended functions very well (e.g. Channell, 1994; Cheng, 2007). Another observed trend is the greater variation between the four categories in the Chinese data. For example, in the Chinese context, the most frequently employed category (scalar stretcher) accounts for 62.7% of EL use, with the second most frequently used category accounting for only 16.7%, a 46% difference between the two categories. However, the corresponding value for the English data is 21.7%, a much smaller difference.

As shown in Table 6.2, for approximately one in every four Chinese contestants, two coaches turned around, and for approximately one in every five Chinese contestants, either one or three coaches turned around. In English, a similar pattern was found in that the majority of contestants were successful in getting at least two coaches to turn around for them. For approximately one in every three contestants, two coaches turned around, but for approximately one in every five contestants, no coach turned around.

Table 6.2 shows that for both Chinese and English contexts, it was most common to have two coaches turning around (26.6 and 38.3%, respectively). This also indicates that there is a difference of 11.7% between the two figures, which could imply that coaches in the English data set tended to differ more in their opinions of the contestants than their Chinese counterparts. For all the other coach-turned cases, the following is the ranking (highest to lowest) for the number of Chinese coaches turned: 3 turned, 1 turned, 4 turned and 0 turned.

Table 6.2 Comparison between the number of turned coaches in the Chinese and English data

No. turned	0 turned	1 turned	2 turned	3 turned	4 turned	Total
Chinese						
Number	37	68	84	71	56	316
Percentage	11.7	21.5	26.6	22.5	17.7	100
English						
Number	66	22	114	54	42	298
Percentage	22.1	7.4	38.3	18.1	14.1	100

The corresponding ranking for the English data set is: 0 turned, 3 turned, 4 turned and 1 turned. The English data have twice as many 0 turned cases than the Chinese data, which demonstrates that the contestants in the English context had a much harder time impressing the coaches than those in the Chinese context. The scenario with the largest frequency difference is when only one coach turned around, with the Chinese data displaying three times more cases than the English data (21.5% compared to 7.4%). However, when the three and four coach turning scenarios are examined, both languages produce similar trends. Overall, the variance within the Chinese data is much less than that found in the English data: the gap between the most frequent and least frequent coach turning in the Chinese data is 14.9%, but is 30.9% in the English data, twice the difference.

In cases where either one coach or no coaches have turned around, the competition between them is expected to be less than in the other cases. Given that the combined number of 0 and 1 coach-turned cases is similar (approximately 30%) in the Chinese and English contexts, the use of EL is also expected to be similar, which can be seen in Table 6.3. In the case of 3 and 4 coaches turning, the expectation would be for greater competition between them. Given that the total number of 3 and 4 coach-turned cases is approximately 8% more in the Chinese context, competition between the Chinese coaches was perhaps slightly more intense.

As shown in Table 6.3, in both Chinese and English contexts, fewer approximate stretchers were used compared to other categories, although they were used slightly more often in the English data,

Table 6.3 Comparison of frequency versus the number of turned coaches (%)

Category/ no. turns	AQ (1)	GE (2)	Intensifier (3)	Softener (4)	EP (5)	Subtotal (3+4)
Chinese						
0 turned	7.8	11.5	51.0	10.7	18.9	61.7
1 turned	7.2	11.5	52.8	10.3	18.2	63.1
2 turned	6.8	12.0	53.0	11.6	16.7	64.5
3 turned	7.8	14.9	52.3	9.6	15.5	61.8
4 turned	6.6	14.8	53.3	8.5	16.8	61.8
English						
0 turned	10.5	12.6	37.9	12.8	26.2	50.7
1 turned	9.6	16.9	50.6	14.5	8.4	65.1
2 turned	7.6	21.0	37.8	8.0	25.6	45.8
3 turned	10.3	19.7	40.5	5.3	24.2	45.8
4 turned	8.6	25.4	37.5	3.5	24.9	41.0

particularly in cases where 0, 1 and 3 coaches turned around. In the case of general stretchers, both languages showed an overall correlation between the frequency of general stretchers and the number of coaches that turned around: the higher the level of the competition, that is the more coaches that turned around, the more general stretchers were used. More general stretchers were used in the English context than the Chinese context, particularly as the number of coaches turning around increased. In terms of the use of intensifiers, the Chinese data did not show much difference across the five cases, a similar finding to the English data, except for the 1-coach-turned situation in the English context, where approximately 10% more intensifiers were used compared to the other coach-turned situations. On average, intensifiers were used approximately 12% more in the Chinese context as a whole. This suggests that Chinese speakers tended to use an enhanced speaking tone, as shown in the data.

Overall, softeners tended to be used more in the Chinese context, particularly as the number of coaches turning around increased. A consistent trend which emerged in both languages is that as the number of coaches that turned around decreased, the more softeners were used, as a result of contestants needing more reassurance and comforting when they were rejected by the coaches. The findings support the claims that softeners serve the function of mitigation (Aijmer, 1984, 2002; Holmes, 1993; Lakoff, 1973). Moreover, as the last column of Table 6.3 shows, approximately 10% more scalar stretchers (both intensifier and softener) were used in the Chinese context, suggesting that Chinese speakers might be more motivated to adjust their tone of speech. The general pattern of 'a decrease in the number of coaches turning around equates to an increase in the use of softeners' was replicated in the case of epistemic stretchers (although there are some exceptions), namely the higher level of competition between coaches when more of them have turned around leads to a decrease in the use of epistemic stretchers, as they tend to give the impression of an uncommitted attitude (Carter, 2003; Channell, 1994; Zhang, 2016). This would be detrimental in a heated competition where coaches need to appear confident and assertive.

An overall pattern that is displayed in Table 6.3 is that the Chinese used all five categories of EL consistently over all the five coach-turned situations, yet this is not the case in the English context. This might suggest that the Chinese coaches did not take the level of competition into much consideration, and thus the language usage remained the same regardless of how heated the competition became. On the other hand, the coaches in the English context took much more notice of contextual influences (e.g. the level of competition), and therefore adjusted their EL strategies to suit the particular situation.

Another striking similarity between the two languages is that scalar boosters were used much more frequently than scalar downtoners. This can be taken as evidence suggesting that, in both contexts, persuasion (supposedly achieved through the use of boosters) was the most sought-after function.

In the Chinese context, the more coaches that turned, the less softeners and epistemic stretchers were used. One possible reason for this could be that, as more coaches turn around, the level of competition between them increases and, as a consequence, the coaches feel the need to adopt a stronger tone and be more confident. A similar pattern is found in the English data in that the proportion of softeners and epistemic stretchers that are used becomes either less frequent, or remains unchanged, as the number of turned coaches increases.

6.2   Elasticity in Collaborative and Competitive Moves

In both the Chinese and English data, a similar pattern is found: the coaches used EL with a view to appealing to the contestant's positive and negative faces (Brown & Levinson, 1987). In the case of positive face, the coaches praised the contestants to make them feel good and reassured them that they were highly thought of, with a view to encouraging them to join their teams. With regards to negative face, the coaches highlighted some shortcomings in the contestants' performance, implying that they can improve with coaching and supervision.

Another common strategy in both languages is discrediting the other coaches with a view to portraying oneself as the most credible coach (e.g. Excerpt 2 in this chapter). A number of coaches also accentuated personal attributes (e.g. 'fellow countryman', 'you are a mother, I am a mother too, my children can play with yours' and 'I am the only female coach here'), professional attributes (e.g. 'my long time experience in the music industry', 'you can be my guest singer for one of my 32 music tours this year' and 'your music style fits my expertise'), and so on.

Some strategic EL moves in the data make the use of EL comparable between the Chinese and English contexts. Of particular importance are collaborative and competitive moves, which will be elaborated on further in this chapter.

6.2.1   Chinese Collaborative/Competitive Moves

The following Chinese excerpts demonstrate the EL roles in interactants' collaborative/competitive moves among themselves.

Excerpt 1 (6/5/2): Two speakers over two speaking turns. No coach has turned around for the contestant.

T1 Chen: Wo gangcai zuozai shangmian, wo jiu **ganjue** zhe shi yige nüban de Lao lang. Liu lao shi de yisi jiu shi shuo buyao mofang, yao you ziji de gexing. **Youdian tai** keyi. (我刚才坐在上面, 我就**感觉**这是一个女版的老狼。刘老师的意思就是说不要模仿, 要有自己的

个性。**有点太**刻意。 I just sat up there, I **felt** literally this is a female version of The Old Wolf. Teacher Liu's meaning is not to imitate, but to have your own personality. It's **a little too** deliberate.)

T2 Contestant: Xiexie gewei laoshi. (谢谢各位老师。Thank you all teachers.)

Coach Liu commented on the performance before coach Chen provided his comments. In T1, Chen says that he *feels* ('ganjue', an epistemic stretcher) that the contestant is a female version of Lao Lang (a famous male Chinese singer). Chen mentions that coach Liu suggested to the contestant that she should not simply copy other singers, but should have her own individuality. Chen indicates that the contestant's performance was *a little bit* ('youdian', a vague quantifier) *too* ('tai', an intensifier) much of an imitation, and lacked creativeness. In this case, Chen supports his fellow coach Liu, by agreeing to his assessment of the contestant. Supporting one another is an important strategy adopted by the coaches in this study, which enhances the high regard in which they are held by both the audience and contestants.

Excerpt 2 (5/4/5): Four speakers over 12 speaking turns. No coach has turned around for the contestant, Chen.

T1 Yu: Qishi ni zhe gesheng, youqi zai qian duan, hai **man**, **zenmejiang**, tuosu de. Keshi zai houmian zhege ge, zai zhege jiqing de chuli shang, **wo juede** jiu meiyou ni de qianduan chu li de hao. (其实你这歌声，尤其在前段，还**蛮**，**怎么讲**，脱俗的。 可是在后面这个歌，在这个激情的处理上， **我觉得**就没有你的前段处理得好。Actually, your voice, especially in the beginning part, is **quite**, **what's the name**, refined. But in the latter part, your treatment of passion, **I think** you didn't do it as well as the early part.)

… …

T2 Chen: Jielun laoshi dui ta **tebie** hao, dao shi ta [Hu] you **yixie** kuijiu. Yinwei you yici wo ji de tamen shuo yiqi da dianzi youxi … (杰伦老师对他**特别**好, 倒是他有**一些**愧疚。因为有一次我记得他们说一起打电子游戏 … Teacher Jielun is **very** nice to him, but he (Hu) has **some** guilt. Because once I remember they said they were playing video games together …)

T3 Na: You da youxi. Ai, ni yuanlai dai Jiang Yuandong, ni dai xueyuan du shi banye da youxi, zhe shenme daoshi! (又打游戏。哎, 你原来带江源东, 你带学员都是半夜打游戏, 这什么导师! Play games again. Hey, you mentored Jiang Yuandong, you led students to play games at midnight, what mentor is this?)

T4 Yu: Bu jiao renjia yinyue de! (不教人家音乐的! Do not teach students music!)

T5 Na: Guaibude Jiang Yuandong chang de **zheme** cha dao zui hou. (怪不得江源东唱得**这么**差到最后。 No wonder Jiang Yuandong sang **so** badly in the end.)

T6 Zhou: Nali you a! (哪里有啊! That's not true!)

T7 Na: Jiang Yuandong ganggang shangtai de shihou, chang ge **nage** dongting. (江源东刚刚上台的时候, 唱歌**那个**动听。 When Jiang Yuandong sang at the beginning, he sang **very** beautifully.)

T8 Zhou: Dui a. (对啊。 Yeah.)

T9 Na: Dao le houqi jieduan, ta de shengyin quan shi ya de. (到了后期阶段, 他的声音全是哑的。 At the later stage, he had a hoarse voice.)

T10 Yu: Bian yansang le. (变烟嗓了。 Changed to a smoky voice.)

T11 Zhou: Meiyou, meiyou, **hen** bang, **hen** bang. **Zhege** … (没有, 没有, **很棒**, **很棒**。 **这个**… No, no, **great**, **great**. **Eh**…)

T12 Yu: Shenme?! Ziji jiang **hen** bang **hen** bang. (什么?! 自己讲**很棒很棒**。 What?! He praises himself **very** great, **very** great.)

Contestant Chen was unsuccessful, and therefore all the coaches are being supportive and helpful to him. In T1, coach Yu comments on Chen's performance, saying that the first part is *quite* ('man', a scalar stretcher), *what's the name* ('zenmejiang', a placeholder), refined. However, Yu *thinks* ('juede', an epistemic stretcher') that the second part is not as good as the first part in terms of expressiveness. The placeholder here is a general stretcher, providing Yu with some time to search for words and continue his comments. Yu uses a mitigating elastic item to reduce the impact of his critical comment in the latter part of his utterance. Contestant Chen's friends, Yuandong Jiang and Sihan Hu, were former students of the coaches, and he was asked what they had said about them. In T2, Chen says that Hu (Zhou's student) mentioned that Zhou was *extremely* ('tebie', an intensifier) nice, but Hu felt *a bit* ('yixie', a scalar stretcher) guilty (perhaps because he did not please Zhou by winning the competition).

Between T3 and T10, coach Na firmly lays the blame on her fellow coach Zhou, and coach Yu joins Na in her endeavours. Na says that Zhou's former student, Jiang, had a *very* ('nage', an intensifier) beautiful voice in the early stages of the competition. She accuses Zhou of encouraging Jiang and the other students to play computer games until midnight, rather than teaching them music. The lack of sleep and training resulted in Jiang's hoarse/smoky voice and *extremely* ('zheme', an intensifier) poor performance.

Facing the blunt criticism from Na and Yu, Zhou, in T11, defends himself by saying 'No, no, great, great. Eh …' Zhou appears to be struggling to find the words to explain himself. Yu, in T12, disapprovingly asks why Zhou seems to be so pleased with himself. Zhou then argues that he treats his students as his friends, together they enjoy laughter, playing computer games and performing at Zhou's concerts. Later on, when being asked by coach Na if he intends to return for next year's audition, Chen confirms that he will do so, signalling that Chen likes Zhou's easy-going and fun-loving approach.

Coach Na and Yu employ a direct form of criticism in this case. This strategy aims to possibly tarnish Zhou's image and credibility. Excerpt 2 demonstrates a competitive strategy used by the coaches, as opposed to the collaborative approach used in Excerpt 1. These findings support Zhang's (2015) conclusions that EL plays an important role in both competitive and collaborative communication. Zhang's observations were drawn from data based on the encounters between Australian custom officers and passengers.

In unsuccessful cases, patterns have emerged that coaches tend to comfort the contestant, gently providing some advice for improvement and plenty of encouragement (Suzuki, 2008). Coaches go to great lengths to make the contestants feel better and continue their love of music, and in these situations, coaches tend to be very helpful and supportive, as shown in the following excerpt.

Excerpt 3 (4/3/7): Four speakers over 17 speaking turns. No coach has turned around for the contestant, Pu.

T1 Wang: Ni de qingchun shi yijing yilanwuyu, danshi **yexu** limian de zai **shaowei** yaoqiu feng fu **yidiandian** de biaoxianli. (你的清纯是已经一览无余，   但是**也许**里面的再**稍微**要求丰富**一点点**的表现力。It is absolutely clear that you have a pure voice, but **maybe slightly** richer and **a little bit** more expressive force.)

T2 Na: Mei fa fengfu a, ta **tai** nianqing le. (没法丰富啊，她**太**年轻了。It can't be rich, because she's **too** young.)

T3 Wang: Shi, shi, mei cuo. (是，是，没错。Yes, yes, that's right.)

T4 Na: Ni zhidao women shiba sui de shihou, yizhi bei ma, chang shenme du chang bu jinqu. (你知道我们十八岁的时候，一直被骂，唱什么都唱不进去。You know, when we were eighteen years old, we were always being scolded and didn't sing anything right.)

T5 Wang: [nodding]

... ...

T6 Wang: **Xiangdang** hao, you mei you **shenme** xiang gen women **shuoshuo** de? (**相当**好，有没有**什么**想跟我们**说说**的? **Extremely** good, is there **anything** you want to tell us?)

T7 Pu: Jiushi juede **hen** jidong nen zhan zai zhe. [red eyed] (就是觉得**很**激动能站在这。Just feel **very** excited to be able to stand up here.)

T8 Wang: Shui pei ni lai de? (谁陪你来的? Who came with you?)

T9 Pu: Wo bama. (我爸妈。My parents.)

T10 Wang: You shenme xiang gen ni bama shuo de ma? (有什么想跟你爸妈说的吗? Is there anything you want to tell your parents?)

[long pause, Pu is crying]

T11 Pu: Jiu (shi shuo) xinku le. (就 (是说) 辛苦了。Just want to say thank you for working hard for me.)

T12 Na: Ni shuo shui, bama xinku le, shi ma? (你说谁，爸妈辛苦了，是吗? Who do you talk about, mum and dad working hard, right?)

T13 Yu: Bama xinku le. (爸妈辛苦了。I am talking about my parents.)

T14 Pu: Hai you wo ziji ye **hen** xinku. [laughter] Yinwei tebie jidong nen zai zheli, **juede**. [weeping] (还有我自己也**很**辛苦。因为特别激动能在这里，**觉得**。And I'm working **very** hard too. Because especially excited being here, **I feel**.)

T15 Na: **Tai** bu rongyi le, ha? (**太**不容易了，哈? It is **very** hard, huh?)

... ...

T16 Pu: Qishi jintian nen zhan shang zhege wutai, tebie kaixin [weeping]. Ranhou cong diyi ci pailian dao xianzai, jiu **juede**, quan

Zhongguo ma, **wo juede** ye **meiyou duoshao** ren (nen zou shang zhege wutai). Wo **juede** ou yijing **hen** bucuo le. (其实今天能站上这个舞台, **特别**开心. 然后从第一次排练到现在, 就**觉得**, 全中国嘛, **我觉得**也**没有多少**人 (能走上这个舞台)。**我觉得**哦已经**很**不错了。Actually standing on the stage today, **extremely** happy. And from the first rehearsal to the present, **feel like**, that all of China, **I think not many people** (can go on this stage). **I think** I am **very** good.)

T17 Wang: Zai you **liangsan** nian, ni kending hui chang de **feichang** lihai. (再有**两三**年, 你肯定会唱得**非常**厉害。In **two or three** years, you will sing **very** well.)

The contestant, Pu, is a 17-year-old high school student. She is obviously disappointed by the fact that no coach has turned around for her. In T1, Coach Wang praises Pu on her pure voice. He gives this advice to improve her performance: *maybe* ('yexu', an epistemic stretcher) just *slightly* ('shaowei', a scalar stricter) richer and *a little bit* ('yidiandian', an approximate stretcher) more expressiveness in her voice. A mitigating elastic strategy is employed to soften the tone of Wang's advice, making it very gentle and more appropriate for a teenager. Even so, coach Na, in T2, still tries to defend Pu by telling her that she is too young to make her voice more expressive. Na says that when she and the others were 18 years old, they were reprimanded for not knowing how to sing in a way that would touch people. Wang immediately agrees with Na's comments on this.

In T6, Wang again praises Pu for being *extremely* ('xiangdang', a scalar stretcher) good. He then asks politely (using a reduplication of the verb *speak* 'shuoshuo') whether Pu would like to say *anything* ('shenme', a general stretcher). Pu, in T7, says that she is *very* ('hen', an intensifier) excited to be able to stand on stage. Her parents are here with her as well, and she thanks them for their dedication. In T14, Pu is in tears, as she *feels* ('juede', an epistemic stretcher) that she also works *very* ('hen') hard. Na feels for Pu, saying it must be very difficult for the teenage girl, in T15.

In T16, Pu *feels* ('wo juede', serves an evaluative function here) very happy and is proud of herself, as *not many* ('meiyou duoshao', a vague quantifier) people have the opportunity to take part in this prestigious competition. In T17, Wang encourages Pu by saying that in another *two to three* ('liangsan', a vague quantifier) years, Pu will definitely sing *very* ('feichang', an intensifier) well.

6.2.2 English Collaborative/Competitive Moves

Excerpt 4 (10/3/6): Five speakers over 27 speaking turns. The contestant, Malik, has been successful in getting three coaches to turn around for him.

T1 Christina: **I think** the two of us together **would** make a great team; I **would** love to share thoughts and get inside your head. I **really** believe that we can do **this** together.
T2 Malik: I love you Christina!
T3 Christina: I love you!
T4 Malik: Pharrell you're amazing too!
T5 Christina: Oh oh, he's going to make him sweat!
T6 Pharrell: I guess my question to you is who are your influences?
T7 Malik: Sam Smith, Bruno Mars, Justin Timberlake.
T8 Christina: Well, you **could** do **all of that**, so yeah!
T9 Pharrell: And the **thing** is you can do **all that** with either one of us. I would have to compete, because I'm not that kind of vocalist; I'm a producer.
T10 Blake: There he goes!
T11 Adam: There is the drop! Right there!
T12 Pharrell: No, but she has produced as well, so like she can do it but the **thing** is that I **would** love to be a part of this point going forward in your life, but if not you're going to be a **very** lucky artist on team Christina, because she is an amazing coach.
T13 Christina: And Pharrell as well, … I've been in this business since I was seven, OK, and I've grown up on stage **pretty much** and I am just all about nurturing an artist.
T14 Pharrell: I've been making records since I was like 18. I didn't grow up in the public eye but I worked with Justin when he was your age. [the audience cheers]
T15 Christina: Oh oh oh!
T16 Pharrell: Justin… and Britney too!

T17 Christina: Oh oh oh!

T18 Blake: Justin who?!

T19 Pharrell: And Britney too by the way!

T20 Blake: Britney who?

T21 Christina: Oh oh oh! You know what? I worked with both of them **before** he ever met them on the Mickey Mouse Club. [cheers and applause]

T22 Blake: Here we go!

T23 Pharrell: She's an artist that's lived it since she was 19, but I've been making records since I was 19; I was also producing artists that were 19.

T24 Christina: But I lived it, I lived it!

T25 Pharrell: So it's different, you have the growing plant and then you have the greenhouse!

T26 Christina: Wait what what! Oh oh oh, I am the tree that blossoms up and breaks the greenhouse'cause it's **so** big!

T27 Blake: Whoah! [the audience cheers]

Both Christina and Blake have turned around for Malik. In this excerpt, Christina is encouraging the contestant to join her team as she *thinks* (an epistemic stretcher) they *would* (a possibility stretcher) make a good team, in T1. Christina also entertains the idea of being in the situation where she *would* (a possibility stretcher) be able to share thoughts with, and get inside, the contestant's head. Christina continues by saying that she *really* (a scalar stretcher) believes they can do *this* (a general stretcher) together. In T8, having heard the names of the artists who have influenced the contestant, Christina tells him that he *could* (a possibility stretcher) do *all of that* (a general stretcher). In T9, Pharrell, who has also turned around for the contestant, agrees with Christina suggesting that the contestant can do *all that* (a general stretcher) with either himself or coach Christina. Pharrell also uses another general stretcher, *thing*, in the same turn, which is used to maintain the momentum of the conversation. From this point on, however, one can observe an increase in competition between Pharrell and Christina.

Pharrell, towards the end of T9, claims he is also a producer and not just a vocalist. In T12, Pharrell goes as far as to claim that, although Christina can also produce records, the *thing* (a general stretcher) that he *would* (a possibility stretcher) love to do is 'be a part of this point going forward' in the contestant's life. Pharrell also confirms that the contestant would still be a *very* (a scalar stretcher) fortunate artist if he was on Christina's team as she is 'an amazing coach', a compliment which Christina reciprocates in the next turn, T13. Christina boasts about her achievements by saying that she has *pretty much* (a scalar stretcher) grown up on stage. This claim forces Pharrell, in T14 and T16, to claim that he has also coached such influential singers as Justin and Britney. In an attempt to belittle Pharrell's claims, Blake, in T18 and T20, enquires about the identity of these singers. With the aim of further highlighting her credibility and experience, Christina relates, in T21, how she has worked with both Justin and Britney *before* (an approximate stretcher) Pharrell had encountered them on the Mickey Mouse Club. The competition between the coaches continues in T25, where Pharrell metaphorically likens himself to a greenhouse and Christina to just a growing plant, causing her to retort, in T26, by saying that she is like a tree that can grow and break out of the greenhouse because she is *so* big (a scalar stretcher).

Excerpt 5 (13/1/9): Five speakers over 17 speaking turns. Three coaches have turned around for the contestant, Brandon.

> T1 Miley: I want to say the reason my name is not lit up is I always want to make sure that I'm valuable to whoever I have on my team. And I didn't know how I could help make you any better, and I also really like watching Blake and Adam fight, so you guys go for it!
> [the audience cheers and applauds]
> T2 Adam: It is a lost art to sing a song like that with subtlety and nuance and with soul. There is **something** old school about how you deliver a vocal. Look Ray is Ray; Ray is the best ever, so it's **really** tough to sing that song because we all think of him, but fortunately for your case I **really** didn't think of him the whole time, it was you!
> T3 Blake: Man I hear some Willy Nelson in there.
> T4 Adam: [to Blake] Bro, you have lost your mind. [audience laughter]
> T5 Jennifer: I hear Donny Hathaway. Do you listen to Donny Hathaway?
> T6 Brandon: He is one of my favourites!
> T7 Jennifer: I don't know if they've got the photo of when I won last season, as I don't think you won your last season, and I don't think you

want your last season. I'm sorry Miley I don't think you won your first season, but J Hudson did! All the way in the UK! [audience applause] Firstly I want to say that style of music doesn't **really** have a platform today and I want to help give it a platform.

T8 Adam: I can't argue with her, she's Jennifer Hudson. I'm not going to be in that fight, but there is a fight I can win. I've been doing this show, the *American Voice*! [audience laughter]

T9 Jennifer: I can take you overseas baby! [audience laughter]

T10 Adam: She's right, if you want to win the UK Voice, go over there; she'll take you. And you **probably could** win. But this is a different **thing**, and I also want to …

T11 Jennifer: [starts singing] *So many places!*

T12 Adam: OK!!

T13 Jennifer: Including the UK.

T14 Adam: I can't do that!

T15 Jennifer: That sound that special, you see how passionate I am about it. Does he [looks at Adam] look passionate to you? [audience laughter]

T16 Adam: I am **real** passionate about it, dude, I chose you first. Don't you want leadership?! They fell like dominoes after I turned around. It **seems** to me that I am the clear choice here!

T17 Blake: Can I just say one last **thing** because **I think** this needs to be pointed out? [points to himself encouraging the contestant to pick him] Come on man! [audience laughter]

In T1, Miley, the only coach who has not turned around for this contestant, explains her reason for this: she was unsure whether she could help the contestant. This is clearly an attempt to encourage Brandon and inform that there was nothing wrong with his performance. In T2, Adam tries to appeal to Brandon by saying that there is *something* (a general stretcher) *old school* about the way in which he delivered the song and that, despite the fact that it is *really* (a scalar stretcher) difficult to sing Ray's original song, the contestant has managed to do it. Adam claims that during the contestant's performance, he *really* (a scalar stretcher) did not think about Ray's version of the song, only the contestant's rendition. In a further attempt to increase his own credibility, Adam, in T4, also tells Blake that he has lost his mind for claiming that he has heard some Willy Nelson in the performance. In T5, Jennifer maintains that she has heard some Donny Hathaway in the performance, to which the contestant confirms that he is one of his favourite singers. Jennifer, in T7, boasts about her coaching achievements by reminding everyone that she won *The Voice* competition the previous year. She also states that the style of music which interests the contestant doesn't *really* (a scalar stretcher) have a current platform and that she wants to be the coach to give it one.

Having heard about Jennifer's success in the UK version of *The Voice*, Adam rather sarcastically suggests that the current competition is the *American Voice*, and therefore he is able to help the contestant more than Jennifer, in T8. Adam continues, in T10, by saying that if the contestant goes to the UK, he *probably could* (possibility stretchers) win, but given the fact that the *American Voice* is a different *thing* (a general stretcher), Adam would be a better choice. At this point, Jennifer begins singing *So many places* in an attempt to undermine Adam's position, whose focus appears to be solely on the *American Voice*. In T15, Jennifer also questions whether Adam has a genuine passion for the contestant, to which Adam, in T16, retorts by saying that he is *real* (a scalar stretcher) passionate and that he *seems* (an epistemic stretcher) to be the clear choice for the contestant. In T17, Blake also uses *thing* (a general stretcher) and *I think* (an epistemic stretcher) to compete with the other coaches to win over the contestant.

Excerpt 6 (15/6/7): Four speakers over seven speaking turns. Four coaches have turned around for the contestant, Funsho.

> T1 Adam: Bruno is impossible, he's one of the greatest singers and, and that higher part of your voice shows me that you **literally** have it all, and it's amazing to hear a vocalist that is **so** complete. I knew that there was going to be **multiple** chair turns, and it is scary to turn first because you're like I don't want to show my hand **so** fast, but I laid and they followed!
>
> T2 Kelly: Oh my gosh! No way! We were dancing; we were having a good time; we were listening.
>
> T3 Jennifer: That's right!
>
> T4 Kelly: What it reminded me of, it's like that Boyz II Men's 'Motownphilly'. I thought it was amazing the fact you did have the

capability of coming out here and doing **such** a well-known song, but you made it your own and I thought that was **really** hard to do. So I **would** love you on my team. **I think** that you **would** make a great addition …

T5 Jennifer: Hi I'm Jennifer and I **would like** to be your coach **one day**; do you dance too?

T6 Funsho: I can bust **a move or two**.

T7 Kelly: That was humble, you **really** dance!

In this excerpt, all the coaches have turned around for Funsho and the competition between them is intense. In T1, Adam commends the contestant on being able to sing Bruno Mars's song so successfully. He claims that the contestant *literally* (a scalar stretcher) has it all and that, as a singer, he is *so* (a scalar stretcher) complete. Furthermore, he claims that he knew that *multiple* (a quantifying stretcher) coaches would turn around for this contestant. Adam also prides himself for being the first person to turn around for Funsho, in an attempt to encourage him to join his team. Adam also declares that he did not want to show his hand *so* (a scalar stretcher) fast and that, as soon as he did, the other coaches followed him. The use of the booster *so* not only conveys the idea that the contestant's performance was too good to resist turning around for, but also discredits the other coaches for lacking initiative.

Having heard this, Kelly and Jennifer, in T2 and T3, retort by saying that they did not turn around as quickly as Adam simply because they were enjoying the song and Funsho's performance. In T4, Kelly also commends the contestant for singing *such* (a scalar stretcher) a famous song and on making it his own, something which, according to her, is *really* (a scalar stretcher) difficult to do. Kelly also says that she *thinks* (an epistemic stretcher) the contestant *would* (a possibility stretcher) be a great addition to her team. In T5, Jennifer states that she *would like* (a possibility stretcher) to be Funsho's coach *one day* (a general stretcher). The use of the general stretcher is an attempt to remain humble while, at the same time, encouraging the contestant to choose her as his coach. In T6, the contestant replies that he can bust *a move or two* (a vague quantifier). Having heard this, in an attempt to win his favour, Kelly tells the contestant that he is just being humble and that he can *really* (a scalar stretcher) dance.

In this section, evidence obtained from this study highlights that EL was used by the interactants either to support each other's arguments, or to compete with each other when battling over the contestant in question. This demonstrates the versatility of EL (Zhang, 2015).

6.3　Manifestation of Elasticity

The elasticity of language is manifested in its fluidity, stretchability and strategy (Zhang, 2015). One manifestation of elasticity is where an elastic item cannot be clearly identified as belonging to one of the four lexical categories, or it can simultaneously perform more than one pragmatic function, as discussed in Sect. 3.3. This section focuses on the issue of the multifunctionality of EL in both Chinese and English.

6.3.1　Manifestation of Elasticity in the Chinese Data

The discussion of the following examples aims to show how the elasticity of language is manifested in the Chinese data, in terms of the phenomena of fluidity and multifunctionality.

Excerpt 7 (6/5/10): Four speakers over five speaking turns. Two of the four coaches have turned around for the contestant, Xiao.

T1 Chen: Ta **youdian** rang wo xiang dao **bijiao** jiejin Whitney Houston, huozhe shi Toni Braxton **nazhong**, nü heiren de **nazhong**, hai **man** ziru de. (她**有点**让我想到**比较**接近 Whitney Houston, 或者是 Toni Braxton **那种**, 女黑人的**那种**, 还**蛮**自如的。 She reminds me **a little bit** of Whitney Houston or Toni Braxton **type**, to **some** degree, female African American singer **type**, **quite** natural.)

T2 Liu: Ta you **yixie** zhangwo de jiqiao shi Soul he Gospel **naxie** … (她有**一些**掌握的技巧是 Soul 和 Gospel **那些** … She has **some** skills to master Soul and Gospel and **those kinds** …)

T3 Chen: Dui, Soul de dongxi. (对, Soul 的东西。 Yes, soul's stuff.)

T4 Zhou: Zhege dui women laishuo shi laoge le ba? Na ni yinggai shi **ting** nianqing de, zen me hui xuan yige zhege gequ? (这个对我们来说是老歌了吧？ 那你应该是**挺**年轻的， 怎么会选一个这个歌曲？

This is an old song for us, right? You should be **quite** young, why did you choose this song?)

T5 Xiao: Wo shi yiwei jiulinghou nüsheng, danshi **tebie** xihuan you shi-jian chendian de dong xi. (我是一位九零后女生, 但是**特别**喜欢有时间沉淀的东西。I am a 90s girl, but I **really** like things that have history.)

This is one of the final auditions and, due to the limited number of positions left in each team, the competition between the coaches is intense. Coaches Chen and Na have turned around for contestant Xiao, a bar singer, who finally chose Chen to be her coach. A number of elastic items can be seen in the exchange, as highlighted above. In T1, coach Chen praises Xiao, by saying that the contestant reminded him of Whitney Houston, Toni Braxton and other *types* ('nazhong', a general stretcher) of female African American singers. The reason behind using this type of general extender could be that it is either impossible to list all such singers, or it is not important to provide a comprehensive list.

The focus here is the interpretation of *youdian* ('somewhat' or 'a little bit') in Chen's comments. In T1, he says that 'She *somewhat* reminds me of Whitney Houston' or 'She reminds me *a little bit* of Whitney Houston'. *Somewhat* is a scalar stretcher and *a little bit* is an approximate stretcher. In the former, it is a moderate degree that is relevant, and in the latter case, it is a moderate quantity that is relevant (Zhang, 2016). There is apparently no clear distinction here, demonstrating an overlap between the two categories. Both possible stretchers serve a just-right elastic function to provide information about Chen's comments on the performance.

Excerpt 8 (3/2/1): Five speakers over six speaking turns. Three of the four coaches have turned around for the contestant, Qin.

T1 Qi: **Wo juede** jiu shi liangge zi "guoyin", yinwei ting ni changge, wan-quan meiyou bao liu … (**我觉得**就是两个字"过瘾", 因为听你唱歌, 完全没有保留 … **I think** just two words "absolutely enjoyed it", because listening to you singing, there is no reservation…)

T2 Na: Qishi **wo neng ganjue** dao ta yao xuan shui. (其实**我**能**感觉**到她要选谁。**I** can actually **feel** who she is going to choose.)

T3 Wang: Bu, ye **buyiding**. (不，也**不一定**。No, **not necessarily**.)

…… …

T4 Yang: Xiaolin a, wo xiang gen ni shuo **liangju**. Wo juede ni zhan zai zhe ge tai shang, qishi ni yijing zhidao ni nenggou chang cheng zheyang. (晓林啊，我想跟你说**两句**。我觉得你站在这个台上，其实你已经知道你能够唱成这样。Xiao Lin, I want to say **a few words**. I think you stand on this stage, you actually already knew that you can sing like this.)

T5 Qin: Qishi wo ye bu zhidao, wo **hen** jinzhang na shihou. (其实我也不知道，我**很**紧张那时候。Actually, I didn't know. I was **very** nervous at that time.)

T6 Yang: Ni xuan le wo, wo manman de hui rang ni zhidao de. [all laugh] Wo gaosu ni, ni shenshang zhezhong dongxi, qiangda shi qiangda, danshi **wo juede** ni yao **geng** tigao dehua, ni yao zuo **yidiandian** jianfa. Lai wo zhe, wo hui rang ni **geng** wanmei. (你选了我，我慢慢地会让你知道的。我告诉你，你身上这种东西，强大是强大，但是**我觉得**你要**更**提高的话，你要做**一点点**减法。来我这，我会让你**更**完美。You choose me, I will let you know gradually. Let me tell you, while you are strong, **I think** if you want to be **more** powerful, you need to do **a little** reduction. Come to me, I'll make you **even more** perfect.)

Coach Na has not turned around for contestant Qin, and therefore she is sufficiently relaxed to hazard a guess as to who Qin will choose, in T2. Coach Wang has turned around for Qin, so he is being more prudent, and therefore, in T3, he says *not necessarily* ('buyiding'). Wang's statement can serve more than one function here. If he has indeed no idea what coach will be chosen, then this will serve a just-right elastic function, that is, to simply describe what he is thinking. If, on the other hand, Wang has some idea who might be chosen, then this serves a self-protection elastic function that is less certain in tone and shields him from the possibility of later being wrong. A combination of both functions could well be applicable in this case.

Coach Yang thinks, in T4, that Qin already knows how good she is on stage. In T5, Qin says she does not know, as she was *very* ('hen') nervous at that time. She uses either a just-right elastic or an intensifying elastic strategy here. In the former, Qin does not know how well she might perform that day, and therefore her statement simply provides the right amount of information. In the latter, she uses an intensifier in the utterance to increase the intensity of her tone.

Excerpt 9 (4/3/2): Two speakers over two speaking turns. All four coaches have turned around for the contestant, Zhang.

> T1 Zhou: Ni lai wo zheli keyi wan **henduo** dongxi. (你来我这里可以玩**很多**东西。You come to me and we'll have **a lot of** fun.)
>
> T2 Yu: **Haoxiang** wo ye keyi. [laughs and applauds] Ni zuo ge xuanze **ba**. (**好像**我也可以。你做个选择**吧**。It **seems** I can do that too. **Please** make a choice.)

Coach Zhou persuades Zhang to join his team by playing the *having lots of fun* card, in T1. Not to be outdone, in T2, coach Yu says it *seems* ('haoxiang') he can also offer the same thing to Zhang, and politely ('ba' is a softener) asks him to make a choice. Yu's utterance serves two possible functions here: mitigating and/or self-protection elastic. In the former, Yu is being modest and highlights the fact in a less authoritative tone. In the latter, he does not want to definitively state the fact just in case the others do not share his view and, if this is the case, the veiled statement would protect him from being mocked. It is also possible that Yu uses the EL here for both mitigating and self-protection purposes.

Excerpt 10 (3/2/8): Three speakers over seven speaking turns. Three of the four coaches have turned around for the duo, contestants Robynn and Kendy.

> T1 Yang: Neng gei women yanshi **yixia** ma? (能给我们演示**一下**吗? Can you **please** give us a demonstration?)
>
> T2 Robynn: Wo hui B-Box **yidiandian**. (我会B-Box**一点点**。I can do B-Box **a little bit**.)
>
> T3 Yang: Lai **yixia**. (来**一下**。**Please** do it.)
>
> T4 Robynn: [performing B-Box]
>
> T5 Na: Bucuo a! (不错啊! Great!)
>
> T6 Yang: Hao a! (好啊! Good!)
>
> T7 Robynn: Jiu **zheme** duo eryi. (就**这么**多而已。I only got **this** much.)

In T1, coach Yang asks contestant Robynn to give a demonstration, to which she replies, in T2, that she can do *a little bit* ('yidiandian') of B-Box. *A little bit* can be an approximate stretcher (quantity) and/or a scalar stretcher (degree). Robynn's utterance can serve a just-right elastic function if she is referring to her actual ability, and/or a self-protection elastic function if she can do more than *a little bit*, but still says this to protect herself from the situation where she performs badly. Regarding the second strategy, her caution is unfounded as the coaches are very impressed with her demonstration. In T7, Robynn maintains that that is all she can do, and again she is using either a just-right strategy if that is indeed her real limitation and/or using it to show modesty, in which case it serves a mitigating elastic function.

The analysis of Excerpts 7–10 shows that the classification of lexical category and pragmatic function is not definitive, and there can be some fluidity between the categories. The data demonstrate that EL can simultaneously serve more than one function. This fluidity and multifunctionality is representative of the elastic language used in the Chinese data.

6.3.2 Manifestation of Elasticity in the English Data

The discussion of the following examples aims to demonstrate how the elasticity of language is manifested in the English data, in terms of the phenomena of fluidity and multifunctionality.

Excerpt 11 (14/1/3): Three speakers over five speaking turns. Adam and Alicia have turned around for the contestant, Rayshun.

> T1 Adam: … there were certain **things** that **could** have been **a little bit** better.
> T2 Rayshun: Yay! I agree!
> T3 Adam: That's what I'm about, helping **somebody**, **really** tap into the next **thing**. That's going to make them even better, let's just do it right now!
> T4 Alicia: He wouldn't be able to go right now if I hadn't turned around as well!
> T5 Adam: Sadly for me, there is you! [audience laughter]

Having commended the contestant's singing ability and performance, Adam continues by saying, in T1, that there were certain *things* (a general stretcher) that *could* (a possibility stretcher) have been *a little bit* (a scalar stretcher) better. The general stretcher *things* serves two functions: it provides information relevant to the context (just-right elastic) and also gives the speaker an opportunity to avoid being too specific in detail (evasive elastic). The possibility stretcher *could* enables the speaker to vaguely highlight the possibility of potential improvement without necessarily specifying how. The use of the softener *a little bit* also serves two functions: it enables the speaker to tone down the force of the utterance and, at the same time, saves the speaker's *face* from the possibility of being challenged. Capitalising on the points he has mentioned in T1, Adam encourages the contestant, in T3, to choose him to be his coach by saying that he is only concerned with helping *somebody* (a general stretcher) to be *really* (a scalar stretcher) the next *thing* (a general stretcher). The first use of general stretcher not only helps the speaker to maintain the momentum of the conversation, but also allows him to refer to all potential contestants, including the current contestant, without explicitly mentioning them. The use of the booster *really* not only increases the tone of the utterance, but also creates a sense of in-group solidarity and rapport. The final use of general stretcher allows the speaker to maintain the momentum of the conversation without clarifying what the next *thing* actually is. Therefore, all the above items serve multiple functions in the data.

Excerpt 12 (13/9/8): Two speakers over three speaking turns. Two coaches have turned around for the contestant, Whitney.

T1 Miley: I'm **really** proud to say I'm the first one in Voice history to have an all-female team and I **would** love to keep that going! [the audience cheers]

T2 Whitney: That's dope!

T3 Miley: I want to celebrate females in this industry because **I think sometimes** we can get lost.

Miley, one of the two coaches who have turned around for the contestant, is telling her that she is *really* (a scalar stretcher) proud to have an all-female team, in an attempt to persuade her to join her team. The booster not only increases the tone of the utterance, but also employs positive politeness strategies and rapport building mechanisms to appeal to a contestant who, as a female, is supposed to relate well to this proposal. Miley also states that she *would* (a possibility stretcher) love to do this again. This possibility stretcher could be used to indicate the likelihood of her having an all-female team in the future without necessarily over-committing herself to this proposition, in case this proves impossible, thus saving her face from being challenged and/or refuted.

Excerpt 13 (15/1/6): Three speakers over four speaking turns. Three coaches have turned around for the contestant, Radha.

> T1 Adam: First of all, that beginning threw me back **so** far into my chair that I didn't know if I was going to be able to get back up again,
> T2 Kelly: Yay!
> T3 Adam: And then I pressed because I'm not an idiot! [audience laughter] But then I got scared and I'm like who am I going to block? Gonna block Kelly? Or am I going to go with Jennifer? It was **so** hard to figure out who to block, I know you love them both.
> T4 Jennifer: Well, we will never know!

Praising the contestant on her impressive performance, Adam says, in T1, that the way she sang threw him *so* (a scalar stretcher) far back into his chair. The use of the booster *so* increases the tone of the utterance, while at the same time creates a sense of friendship and solidarity with both the contestant and the audience. In T2, Kelly, who has also turned around, agrees with Adam. In T3, Adam confirms how *so* difficult it was for him to decide upon which coach to block. The booster *so* not only increases the tone of the utterance, but also saves the speaker's face by highlighting that both Kelly and Jennifer are remarkable coaches, and the fact that he decided to block one of them has nothing to do with their singing and/or coaching abilities.

Excerpt 14 (11/5/10): Two speakers over two speaking turns. Two coaches have turned around for the contestant, Kylie.

T1 Blake: The only reason it took me **so** long to push my button is because we're down to the wire here. I speak from experience. Alicia can't do that because she's new here, but I wanted you to know that **somebody** that's been through it can be a rock for you through this **thing** and I can't wait to get in there and start working with you, because I've been waiting on you, waiting on you, Kylie.

T2 Kylie: Thank you so much!

Both Blake and Alicia have turned around for this contestant. In T1, Blake is explaining why it took him *so* long to push the button. The booster *so* enables the speaker to confess and highlight why it took him longer than expected to turn around, while at the same time enabling him to implicitly convey the idea that the contestant, due to her impressive singing ability, deserved Blake to turn around sooner. Blake also uses the general stretchers *somebody* and *thing* which allow him to refer to himself and the competition, respectively, in a general way.

6.4   Concluding Remarks

The findings discussed in this chapter confirm that there are similarities between the Chinese and English use of EL. For example, of the four lexical elastic items, both languages used scalar stretchers most frequently and followed the same ranking: scalar stretcher (most frequent), epistemic stretcher, general stretcher and approximate stretcher (least frequent). In terms of the impact of contextual influences, such as the level of competitiveness manifested by the number of coaches that turned around, similar trends also emerged in the Chinese and English data. For example, the two-coach-turned scenario is the most frequently observed in both languages, namely the majority of contestants were successful in getting at least two coaches to turn around for them. Furthermore, the frequency of occurrence of the three and four-coach-turned cases are also similar in the two languages.

In all coach-turned situations, both the Chinese and English data demonstrated that less approximate stretchers were used compared to other lexical categories. An overall correlation exists between the frequency of general stretchers and the number of coaches that turned around: the higher the level of the competition, that is the more coaches that turned around, the more general stretchers were used. Both languages used intensifiers in a similar fashion, showing no significant differences across the five situations. Furthermore, both languages used a much greater number of boosters than downtoners which suggests that persuasion, supposedly achieved through the use of boosters, was the most sought-after function in the discourse.

In the Chinese data, as more coaches turned around, there was a corresponding decrease in the proportion of softeners and epistemic stretchers that were used. One possible reason for this finding would be that as more coaches turned around, the competition between them increased and, as a consequence, the coaches felt the need to adopt a stronger tone and be more confident. A similar pattern is found in the English data in that the proportion of softeners and epistemic stretchers becomes either less frequent, or remains unchanged, as the number of turned coaches increases.

There is some variation between the Chinese and English data. For example, in the English language case, there were twice as many occasions where no coaches turned around, possibly suggesting that the Chinese coaches were less strict than their English-speaking counterparts. In addition, the Chinese coaches used approximately 12% more intensifiers which indicates that the Chinese preferred a stronger tone of speech.

Relatively speaking, there is some degree of consistency within the Chinese data in that the Chinese coaches routinely used EL across all the five possible scenarios (i.e. the number of coaches that turned around), but this is not quite the same for the English-speaking situation. The influence of the level of competition does not appear to make much difference to the Chinese coaches: for example, they used a similar number of approximators regardless of whether zero coaches or all four coaches turned around.

The data also show that EL can facilitate collaboration as well as competition between the interactants. Moreover, some interesting phenomena also emerged. In the English data set, for example, Excerpt 53 (*kind of* creepy versus *real* creepy), two opposing stretchers were used in the same speaking turn: they perform the function of cancelling/complementing each other. Amongst others, the elasticity of language was manifested through the multifunctionality of the EL that was used in this study.

References

Aijmer, K. (1984). 'Sort of' and 'kind of' in English conversation. *Studia Linguistica, 38,* 118–128.

Aijmer, K. (2002). *English discourse particles: Evidence from a corpus.* Amsterdam: John Benjamins.

Brown, P., & Levinson, S. C. (1987). *Politeness: Some universals in language usage.* Cambridge: Cambridge University Press.

Carter, R. (2003). The grammar of talk: Spoken English, grammar and the classroom. In *New perspectives on English in the classroom* (pp. 5–13). London: Qualifications and Curriculum Authority.

Channell, J. (1994). *Vague language.* Oxford: Oxford University Press.

Cheng, W. (2007). The use of vague language across spoken genres in an intercultural Hong Kong corpus. In J. Cutting (Ed.), *Vague language explored* (pp. 161–181). Basingstoke: Palgrave Macmillan.

Holmes, J. (1993). New Zealand women are good to talk to: An analysis of politeness strategies in interaction. *Journal of Pragmatics, 20*(2), 91–116.

Lakoff, G. (1973). Hedges: A study in meaning criteria and the logic of fuzzy concepts. *Journal of Philosophical Logic, 2*(4), 458–508.

Suzuki, T. (2008). *A corpus-based study of the speech act of "comforting": Naturalness and appropriateness for English language teaching.* Paper presented at the 13th PAAL Conference, University of Hawaii, Manoa, USA.

Zhang, G. (2015). *Elastic language: How and why we stretch our words.* Cambridge: Cambridge University Press.

Zhang, G. (2016). How elastic *a little* can be and how much *a little* can do in Chinese. *Chinese Language and Discourse, 7*(1), 1–22.

7

Elastic Language and Impact Factors

In this chapter, the relationship between EL and the factors that have an impact on its use is discussed. The pattern of EL use that was observed in the Chinese and English data can be influenced by a number of underpinning factors based on culture and social relationships.

7.1 Directness and Indirectness

There are two types of speech act: direct and indirect (Searle, 1975). Imagine this scenario: a teacher walks into a classroom and says, 'It is stuffy here'. The students may interpret this either in its literal sense as a statement (a direct speech act), or in its non-literal sense as a request (an indirect speech act) (Asher & Lascarides, 2001; Clark, 1979; Morgan, 1977). In certain contexts, we can "communicate a message which is informative, truthful, relevant and succinct" or communicate the same message in a more indirect way; and choosing an indirect message, politeness seems to be a plausible reason (Terkourafi, 2011, p. 2861).

In this study, direct and indirect speech acts are manifested by how the contestants conveyed their messages regarding their choice of coach.

© The Author(s) 2019
G. Zhang and V. Parvaresh, *Elastic Language in Persuasion and Comforting*,
https://doi.org/10.1007/978-3-030-28460-2_7

At the end of each blind audition, those contestants who had more than one coach turning around for them, needed to make a choice as only one coach could be selected. This was accomplished by either direct or indirect means: the former involved immediately calling out the name of the chosen coach, and in the latter case the contestant first paved the way and prepared the audience for his/her final announcement. The strategies that were adopted in the indirect approach included expressing appreciation for the other coaches who had turned around but were not being chosen, praising their (musical) achievements or telling jokes to minimise the unpleasantness associated with having to reject them. The following example from the Chinese data demonstrates how an indirect ending unfolded.

Excerpt 1 (1/2/2): Five speakers over 18 speaking turns. All four coaches have turned around for the contestant, Wang.

> T1 Wang: Xianzai shi rang wo xuanze shi ba? (现在是让我选择是吧? Now it is time for me to choose, right?)
> T2 Yang/Liu: Dui. (对。Yes.)
> T3 Wang: **Zheme** kuai? (**这么**快? **So** fast?)
> T4 Yu: A? (啊? Ah?)
> T5 Liu: Na xia ge yue juede ye xing. (那下个月觉得也行。Well, perhaps that's also OK for you to do it next month.) [laugh together]
> T6 Wang: Qishi wo zhenshi mei xiang dao, qishi wo jintian xinli shi you yige da fangxiang de. Yang Kun laoshi, wo yi zhi du **tebie** xihuan ni. (其实我真是没想到，其实我今天心里是有一个大方向的。杨坤老师, 我一直都**特别**喜欢你。Actually, I didn't expect this, in fact I have had a general direction in mind today. Teacher Yang Kun, I have been **particularly** fond of you.)
> T7 Yang: Bie shuo **naxie** gongwei hua. (别说**那些**恭维话。Don't give me **those** smooth talks.)
> T8 Wang: Danshi wo kan dao Na jie, wo shizai shi **youdian** ren bu zhu. Na jie, wo **hao** xihuan ni. (但是我看到那姐, 我实在是**有点**忍不住。那姐, 我**好**喜欢你。But I **somewhat** can't help it when seeing Sister Na. I like you **so much**, Sister Na.)
> T9 Na: Xiexie! (谢谢! Thank you!)
> T10 Wang: Wo **tebie** xiang gen ni zou, dan shi... (我**特别**想跟你走, 但是。。。I **really** want to go with you, but ...)

T11 Yu: 'Danshi' chulai le, 'danshi' chulai le. ('但是'出来了, '但是'出来了。Here is the 'but', here is the 'but'.)

T12 Na: Shenme shihou shuo 'dan shi' le, wo mei ting jian. (什么时候说'但是'了, 我没听见。When she said 'but', I didn't hear it.)

T13 Wang: Halin... eh. (哈林。。。Halin, eh.)

T14 Yu/Na: Wanle, wanle! (完了! 完了! It's over! Finished!)

T15 Wang: Wo shi **zhende** **tebie** **tebie** xiang gen Liu Huan laoshi zou. (我是**真的特别特别**想跟刘欢老师走。I **truly** **really** **really** want to go with Teacher Liu Huan.)

T16 Yu: Ni kan ta guo bu guo fen! Sige ren de mingzi ta jiang le yilun! (你看她过不过分! 四个人的名字她讲了一轮! Look, she has gone too far! She mentioned all four names!)

T17 Liu: Nage, **wo ganjue** ni de yisi shi yao gen yuedui na tongzhi zou. (那个, **我感觉**你的意思是要跟乐队那同志走。Well, **I feel** that you want to go with the comrade in the band.)

[all laugh] [long pause]

T18 Wang: Wo xuan, wo haishi xuan Halin. (我选, 我还是选哈林。I choose, I still choose Halin.)

The above excerpt highlights that, before the contestant Wang announced Halin as her choice of coach, she spoke to every single coach who had turned around for her, trying very hard to praise them all, thereby reducing the disappointment that her final choice might cause the other three coaches who were not selected. This example is representative of an indirect ending in the Chinese data. This type of communication conveys mitigation and politeness through the use of EL.

Table 7.1 shows that there were a total of 211 auditions where contestants were required to choose between coaches, with two coach cases being the most frequent and four coach cases the least frequent. Of the 211 cases where contestants had to decide between coaches, two-thirds of them took a direct approach, while only one-third took an indirect approach, indicating that most contestants preferred a direct approach over an indirect one.

While all three coach-turned scenarios preferred a direct approach over an indirect one, Table 7.1 demonstrates that, in the Chinese context, the two and four-coach-turned situations are very similar in the split between direct and indirect approaches. The three-coach-turned situation was 10% less direct and 10% more indirect than the other two types, but in terms of the difference between the three cases, it is not statistically significant according to the results presented in Table 7.1. This means that the contestants, whether they had two, three or four coaches turning around for them, behaved in a similar manner when choosing a direct or an indirect approach to make their final choice.

Table 7.2 shows that, in the English data, there were a total of 210 cases where more than one coach turned around for each contestant. Of these, the number of occasions when two coaches turned around outnumber the total of the other two situations, and all four coaches turning around is the least frequent scenario. Of the 210 cases, approximately 58% employed a direct approach with the remaining 42% of cases employing an indirect approach, which indicates that the majority of contestants preferred a direct approach over an indirect one.

Table 7.1 Impact of the number of coaches that turned around in the Chinese data

	Direct	Indirect	Total
2 turned	59 (70.2%)	25 (29.8%)	84
3 turned	43 (60.6%)	28 (39.4%)	71
4 turned	39 (69.6%)	17 (30.4%)	56
Total	141 (66.8%)	70 (33.2%)	211[a]
Chi-squared ($p<0.01$)	χ^2 [d.f.2, $n=211$] $=1.898$, $p=0.38712796$ (insignificant)		

[a]211 refers to the number of auditions where at least two coaches turned around for the contestant and represent situations in which the contestants need to choose between coaches by adopting either a direct or an indirect approach

Table 7.2 Impact of the number of coaches that turned around in the English data

	Direct	Indirect	Total
2 turned	73 (64.0%)	41 (36.0%)	114
3 turned	28 (51.9%)	26 (48.1%)	54
4 turned	20 (47.6%)	22 (52.4%)	42
Total	121 (57.6%)	89 (42.4%)	210
Chi-squared ($p<0.001$)	χ^2 [d.f.2, $n=210$] $=4.377$, $p=0.11208475$ (insignificant)		

Table 7.2 also shows a negative correlation in the English data: as the number of coaches that turned around increases, the number of direct approaches that are adopted decreases. In other words, in the two-coach-turned case, approximately two-thirds of contestants employed a direct approach. In the three-coach-turned case, the percentage of contestants choosing direct and indirect approaches were approximately the same. And finally, in the four-coach-turned case, slightly more contestants favoured an indirect approach. This differs from the observations made in the Chinese data in that, in the Chinese context, a direct approach was preferred in all three scenarios where more than one coach turned around.

Despite the variations uncovered, when it came to a contestant choosing a direct or an indirect approach, in terms of the difference between the three turning cases, it is not statistically significant according to the results given in Table 7.2.

7.2   Gender Factor

Do men stretch language less than women? This question was raised by Channell (1994) more than two decades ago. However, we should not lose sight of the fact that the relationship between languages and gender in general, and EL use and gender, is far from conclusive. Channell (1994) argues that vagueness is "stereotypically associated" more with women than with men, "whether or not they actually use more vague expressions" (p. 193). In this respect, Cutting (2007) finds that in mixed-sex dialogues "females use double the density of VL that males do" (p. 228). However, in a recent study, Parvaresh (2018) reveals that the density and use of vague expressions is very closely tied to the mode of communication and that, on occasions, men could be found to use a much denser proportion of vague language. Zhang (2015), based on institutional data, also finds that men actually use more hedges and are less direct, which is not consistent with the common perception that men are more straight-talking and assertive than women (Cutting, 2007, p. 228). Murphy (2010) reports that the vague booster *very* occurs "less frequently in the male data" (p. 132), a finding which is not supported in Parvaresh (2018) who instead finds more instances of boosters in male data. In this section, the gendered use of language in terms of the direct/indirect approach adopted is discussed, based on the evidence of how the contestants expressed their choice of coach.

In the Chinese data, out of a total of 316 contestants, 169 (53.5%) were male and 147 (46.5%) were female. In Table 7.3, of the relevant cases (at least two coaches turned around) which involved 211 contestants, on average a direct approach was adopted in two-thirds of cases, with an indirect approach accounting for only one-third. This trend more or less applies to all three categories: male, female and mixed gender groups. The gender difference between the three is statistically insignificant. All the evidence points to the conclusion that, while there are some differences between the three gender groups, in the Chinese context under investigation there is no statistically significant variance in terms of the preference for a direct or an indirect approach.

In the English data, out of a total of 298 contestants, 156 (52.3%) were male and 142 (47.7%) were female. As Table 7.4 shows, a total of 210 contestants were successful in getting more than one coach to turn around, and of these 112 (53.3%) were male and 98 (46.6%) were female. On average, both male and female contestants adopted a direct approach slightly more frequently than an indirect approach. However, the difference between the two genders was not found to be statistically significant. This result is in keeping with the Chinese findings, namely that there was no gender impact in both languages in terms of the preference for a direct/indirect approach.

Table 7.3 Gender factor in the Chinese data

Gender/approach	Direct	Indirect	Total
Male contestant $N=107$	73 (68.2%)	34 (31.8%)	107
Female contestant $N=101$	66 (65.3%)	35 (34.7%)	101
Chi-squared (M/F) ($p<0.01$)	χ^2 [d.f.1, $n=208$]=0.194, $p=0.6596081$ (insignificant)		
Mixed $N=3$	2 (66.7%)	1 (33.3%)	3
Total	141 (66.8%)	70 (33.2%)	211
Chi-squared (M/F/mixed) ($p<0.01$)	χ^2 [d.f.2, $n=211$]=0.194, $p=0.90755601$ (insignificant)		

Table 7.4 Gender factor in the English data

Gender/approach	Direct	Indirect	Total
Male contestant $N=112$	67 (59.8%)	45 (40.2%)	112
Female contestant $N=98$	54 (55.1%)	44 (44.9%)	98
Chi-squared ($p<0.01$)	χ^2 [d.f.1, $n=210$] $=0.477$, $p=0.48978434$ (insignificant)		
Total	121 (57.6%)	89 (42.4%)	210

7.3   Cultural Factor

There is a close interaction between cultural changes, uncertainty and the use of language in a community (Pierson, 1992). Zhu's (1999, 2005) studies, based on the data of written business communication among Chinese, Australians and New Zealanders, finds that the Chinese emphasise *guanxi* (connections) and relationship building, and they prefer an 'emotional approach' over a 'logical approach'. Kirkpatrick (1991) identifies indirectness in Chinese language and attributes it to a preference for an inductive approach, as opposed to a Western deductive approach. He finds that, in request letters, the Chinese tended to leave the main message of the request to the end of the letter, rather than placing it at the beginning, and this appears to be 'not to the point' to Westerners. Hall (1976) proposes a division of high and low-context cultures. The former, including China, tend to communicate with covert information. The latter, including America, do so with overt information. Overt information with clarity of expression does not require as much shared context as covert information, and both sides may consider the opposite group's expressions to be inappropriate.

The Chinese tend to talk about 'process' rather than 'things', and Chinese language is verb-rich as opposed to English which is noun-rich. Consequently, the vagueness of categories may not be as salient in Chinese as in English (Link, 2013). This study investigates whether veiled language occurs in the Chinese data, and if so, in what forms and for what purposes. Language games are, of course, not unique to

Chinese, but they are expected to be present in other languages as well. Therefore, the findings that are based on the Chinese data are expected to have some relevance to language studies in general.

Cultural factors include a number of aspects. In this section, we look into the potential differences between Mainland Chinese and overseas Chinese in terms of EL use. The Mainland Chinese include those people who grew up and were educated in China; the overseas Chinese include Chinese Canadian, Chinese Malaysian, Chinese Singaporean, Chinese American, Chinese Brazilian and Chinese Australian. The contestants within these two groups have a different cultural exposure, and so, would they use EL differently? This question can be answered by using the evidence provided in Table 7.5 which is based on the direct/indirect approaches adopted when choosing a coach.

Table 7.5 shows that both groups preferred a direct approach over an indirect one, particularly in the overseas Chinese group. This indicates that the overseas Chinese spoke more directly: four in five cases were direct approaches, with only one in five being indirect. In the case of the Mainland Chinese, they also preferred a direct approach, but to a lesser degree than the overseas Chinese, with a direct approach accounting for approximately two-thirds of the total. However, while some differences exist between the two groups, it is not statistically significant, as shown in Table 7.5.

Another culturally related factor is political correctness, which could play a role in EL use across both the Chinese majority (known as Han) and Chinese minority groups. These two groups of contestants might have different cultural backgrounds, and this fact could motivate the coaches to be particularly careful when they are talking to the minority group in order to avoid making discriminatory remarks.

Table 7.5 Mainland Chinese versus overseas Chinese

	Direct	Indirect	Total
Overseas Chinese $N=21$	17 (81.0%)	4 (19.0%)	21
Chinese $N=190$	124 (65.3%)	66 (34.7%)	190
Total	141 (66.8%)	70 (33.2%)	211
Chi-squared ($p<0.01$)	χ^2 [d.f.1, $n=211]=2.1$, $p=0.14729914$ (insignificant)		

When addressing minority contestants, the coaches would tend to be more polite and careful with their remarks to avoid causing any offence to what might be perceived as being a disadvantaged group. This non-Han group includes overseas Chinese (e.g. Chinese American, Chinese Australian and Chinese Malaysian), minorities in China (e.g. Hani minority) and suchlike. The data in Table 7.6 and Fig. 7.1 show some slight differences between the Han and non-Han groups, for example, in the case of the Han group, 2% more epistemic stretchers and 1% less general stretchers were used than in the non-Han group. Both groups exhibit the same trend: (from the most to the least frequent) intensifiers, epistemic stretchers, general stretchers, softeners and approximate stretchers. The difference between the Han and non-Han groups is not statistically significant, as shown in Table 7.6.

Table 7.6 Comparison between Han and non-Han groups

	AQ	GE	Intensifier	Softener	EP	Total
Han	476	898	3591	677	1182	6824
	(7.0%)	(13.2%)	(52.6%)	(9.9%)	(17.3%)	
Non-Han	216	422	1556	292	450	2936
	(7.4%)	(14.4%)	(53.0%)	(9.9%)	(15.3%)	
Chi-squared ($p<0.01$)	χ^2 [d.f.4, $n=9760$] $= 7.596$, $p=0.10754985$ (insignificant)					

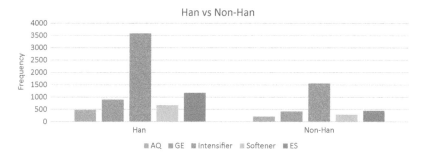

Fig. 7.1 Comparison between Han and non-Han groups

7.4   Age Factor

Age, as a social factor, has been linked to the use of language (Murphy, 2010). However, there is a lack of literature in this area, particularly on the relationship between age and the use of EL or vague language. This section attempts to investigate the possible impact of age on the use of EL, for example in teenage auditions, the interactants (coaches and contestants) might use more softeners than in adult auditions.

The comparison in Table 7.7 aims to see whether the language used in teenage discourse is different from that in adult discourse. The results show the same trend across the two groups. The frequency ranking (from most to least frequent) is as follows: intensifiers, epistemic stretchers, general stretchers, softeners and approximate stretchers. There are some slight differences between the two groups, for example the language used in teenage auditions contained approximately 2% less general stretchers but approximately 3% more epistemic stretchers. This suggests that speakers in the teenage discourse were slightly less general but were more uncertain for some reason. However, the difference between the two groups is not statistically significant, as shown in Table 7.7.

As Table 7.8 and Fig. 7.2 show, there is a consistent trend across the two groups, namely both groups in the English data have the same frequency ranking (from most to least frequent): intensifiers, epistemic stretchers, general stretchers, approximator/quantifiers and softeners. In

Table 7.7   Adult versus teenage contestants in the Chinese data

	AQ	GE	Intensifier	Softener	EP	Total
Teenager[a]	18 (6.4%)	32 (11.4%)	147 (52.5%)	27 (9.6%)	56 (20.0%)	280
Adult[b]	674 (7.1%)	1288 (13.6%)	5000 (52.7%)	942 (9.9%)	1576 (16.6%)	9480
Total	692	1320	5147	969	1632	9760
Chi-squared ($p<0.01$)	χ^2 [d.f.4, $n=9760$] $=2.994$, $p=0.55882999$ (insignificant)					

[a]16 and 17 years old
[b]18 and above

Table 7.8 Adult versus teenage contestants in the English data

	AQ	GE	Intensifier	Softener	EP	Total
Teenager[a]	76 (8.4%)	168 (18.6%)	400 (44.2%)	58 (6.4%)	202 (22.3%)	904
Adult[b]	302 (9.1%)	686 (20.6%)	1246 (37.4%)	260 (7.8%)	840 (25.2%)	3334
Total	378	854	1646	318	1042	4238
Chi-squared ($p < 0.01$)	χ^2 [d.f.4, $n = 4238$] $= 14.554$, $p = 0.00572153$ (significant)					

[a]16 and 17 years old
[b]18 and above

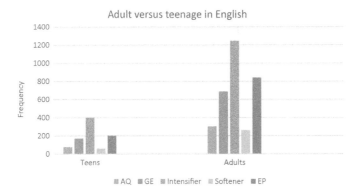

Fig. 7.2 Adult versus teenage contestants in the English data

adult discourse, coaches and contestants used more softeners, epistemic stretchers and general stretchers, but fewer intensifiers. This indicates that in teenage discourse, the interactants used a stronger speech tone than in adult discourse because more intensifiers, and less softeners, epistemic and general stretchers were used. This result is slightly unexpected if one assumes that, in teenage discourse, coaches would have had the tendency to use more softeners when talking to teenagers. There is a definite difference between teenage and adult discourses, and this has been found to be statistically significant, as shown in Table 7.8.

7.5   Concluding Remarks

This chapter has discussed the impact of relevant factors, including gender, cultural and age-related influences on the use of EL. By mentioning 'relevant' factors here highlights the fact that there are other factors which could influence the outcome of the competition. For example, it appears that most winners in the Chinese competition sang romantic and popular love songs, rather than rock 'n' roll songs. This type of factor does not relate to language use and thus is not relevant to this study.

The findings show that while there were some differences between the groups, almost all the differences have not been statistically substantiated. The only exception is the impact of age in the English data, where the use of EL did differ between teenage and adult groups. This suggests that the use of EL in the data was largely consistent among the different groups, across the different discourses.

References

Asher, N., & Lascarides, A. (2001). Indirect speech acts. *Synthese, 128*(1–2), 183–228.

Channell, J. (1994). *Vague language.* Oxford: Oxford University Press.

Clark, H. H. (1979). Responding to indirect speech acts. *Cognitive Psychology, 11*(4), 430–477.

Cutting, J. (2007). Doing more stuff—Where's it going? Exploring vague language further. In J. Cutting (Ed.), *Vague language explored* (pp. 223–243). Basingstoke: Palgrave Macmillan.

Hall, E. T. (1976). *Beyond culture.* New York: Anchor Books.

Kirkpatrick, A. (1991). Information sequencing in Mandarin in letters of request. *Anthropological Linguistics, 33*(2), 183–203.

Link, P. (2013). *Anatomy of Chinese: Rhythm, metaphor, politics.* Cumberland, RI: Harvard University Press.

Morgan, J. L. (1977). *Two types of convention in indirect speech acts* (Center for the Study of Reading Technical Report 52). University of Illinois.

Murphy, B. (2010). *Corpus and sociolinguistics: Investigating age and gender in female talk.* Amsterdam: John Benjamins.

Parvaresh, V. (2018). 'We are going to do a lot of things for college tuition': Vague language in the 2016 US presidential debates. *Corpus Pragmatics, 2*(2), 167–192.

Pierson, H. D. (1992). Communication issues during a period of radical transition: The case of Hong Kong. *Communication Quarterly, 40*(4), 381–390.

Searle, J. R. (1975). Indirect speech acts. In P. Cole & J. L. Morgan (Eds.), *Syntax and semantics. Volume 3: Speech acts* (pp. 59–82). Cambridge, MA: Academic Press.

Terkourafi, M. (2011). The puzzle of indirect speech. *Journal of Pragmatics, 43*(11), 2861–2865.

Zhang, G. (2015). *Elastic language: How and why we stretch our words.* Cambridge: Cambridge University Press.

Zhu, Y. X. (1999). *Business communication in China.* Commack: Nova Science Publishers.

Zhu, Y. X. (2005). *Written communication across cultures.* Amsterdam: John Benjamins.

8

Conclusions

This study has explored the pragma-linguistic use of EL (language stretching in particular) by Chinese and American English speakers in a TV reality show discourse, which is lacking in the existing literature on vague language studies. The theoretic framework of this study adopts the elasticity theory (Zhang, 2015), which informs the analysis and discussion of how and why EL was used. The analysis is primarily a qualitative one, coupled with a quantitative discussion (e.g. frequency). The findings contribute to the field of vague/elastic language use from a cross-language perspective on the speech acts of persuasion and comforting by using some novel resources. The conclusions provide far-reaching insights into the pragmatic use of language.

8.1   Conclusions

EL is defined in this study as a language with fluidity. This section provides answers to the three research questions that were raised at the beginning of this book: the lexical patterns of language stretching that

© The Author(s) 2019
G. Zhang and V. Parvaresh, *Elastic Language in Persuasion and Comforting*,
https://doi.org/10.1007/978-3-030-28460-2_8

were revealed; the pragmatic functions; the similarities and differences between Chinese and English speakers; and how sociocultural factors impact on language stretching from a cross-cultural perspective.

8.1.1 Research Question 1: How and Why Is EL Used in Persuasion and Comforting?

Persuasion and comforting are both speech acts but they focus on different aspects: persuasion is a directive speech act and comforting is an expressive speech act (Asher & Lascarides, 2001). Naturally, in the data, some expressions (e.g. *extremely*) tended to be used for persuasion, while others (e.g. *perhaps*) for comforting.

The first research question was explored at two levels: the lexical level ('how' question) and the discoursal level ('why' question). The 'how' question was investigated through the ways in which elastic expressions were used in the data. Four categories of elastic expressions were investigated in this study: approximate stretcher, general stretcher, scalar (intensifier or softener) stretcher and epistemic stretcher. The data show that the interactants tended to stretch words to deal with situations ranging from sensitive to competitive ones, to mitigate criticisms, for requests or suggestions, or to deflect slip-ups. The most frequent category of elastic expression was found to be that of scalar words (intensifiers in particular), with the least frequent being approximate words. This would appear to suggest that participants were more interested in strengthening or softening their speech tones than simply exchanging information. This pattern also serves the two primary speech acts in this study: persuasion (e.g. *extremely*) and comforting (*kind of*). Of particular interest in this study was how the four functions of approximation, generalisation, mitigation and stance marking were manifested in the data.

The 'why' question was answered through revealing the pragmatic functions of the EL used in the data. Generally speaking, in this study EL performed both collaborative and competitive functions between the interactants. The study revealed that EL was used to serve at least the following six functions: conveying just-right information, building rapport among participants, mitigating speech tones, intensifying speech tones, for self-protection and performing evasive moves. This study discussed both collaborative and competitive language stretching; EL played an important role in both discourses. The findings support the claim that the two seemingly opposing features can complement each other (Zhang, 2015).

These six categories overlapped in some cases, for example, as seen in the interconnection between self-protection and evasiveness. This is in keeping with the fluidity principle of EL. Moreover, there appeared to be a cancellation phenomenon in the data under investigation: two opposing stretchers occurred in one speech turn, with the latter cancelling the former's utterance (e.g. 'It's *kind of* okay, no actually it is *definitely* okay'). This demonstrates a change of mind on the part of the speaker, with the stretched utterance being accepted on the basis of the stretchability of EL.

Zhang (2015) claims that some correlation exists between elastic lexical items and the pragmatic functions they tend to perform. For example, softeners tend to perform a mitigating elastic function. While conventional use was evident in this study, there were a number of cases where other types of unconventional elastic items were used, for example intensifiers may also serve a mitigating function. A comforting act could be performed not only by the use of hedges (typically *kind of, a bit*), but also by using intensifiers (e.g. *very, extremely* exemplified in Excerpt 38, in the English data). The same feature was observed in the Chinese data, where in mitigating an unpleasant situation, such as the contestant failing the audition, both hedges and intensifiers were able to perform the same role from a different angle (exemplified in Excerpts 31 and 34).

The above finding supports the claim that there is no exclusive category to serve the functions of persuasion and comforting. These speech acts are a skill and an art (Hyland, 2005a, 2005b), and to master them the speaker needs to make use of whatever effective means they can to carry out their communicative goals.

8.1.2   Research Question 2: What Are the Similarities and Differences Between Chinese and English?

Comparing the results of the Chinese and English use of EL, almost all aspects of the two languages displayed similar trends, including the use of EL at lexical and pragmatic function levels. This indicates that there is a consistent trend when Chinese and English speakers use EL in the context of TV reality shows. For example, Chinese and English speakers all preferred to use scalar stretchers more frequently than the other three lexical categories, and the same lexical ranking was evident in the two languages: scalar stretcher (most frequent), epistemic stretcher, general stretcher and approximate stretcher (least frequent).

Similar patterns also occurred in the two languages in terms of the impact of the level of competitiveness (e.g. how many coaches competed for the same contestant). For all five situations (from zero to four coaches in competition with each other), both Chinese and English used less approximate stretchers compared with other lexical categories. There is an overall correlation between the frequency of general stretchers used and the number of coaches competing with each other: the higher the level of the competition between the coaches, the more general stretchers were used. In the case of intensifiers, none of the two languages showed much difference across the five different situations. Both groups used many more boosters than downtoners, suggesting that persuasion in TV discourse is performed primarily by the use of boosters. Fewer softeners were used in the Chinese discourse which suggests that a stronger speech tone existed and perhaps also a more demanding competition. English also used less softeners and epistemic stretchers, or remained unchanged, as the number of coaches turning around increased. This would infer that these two categories are not influenced by the level of competition between the coaches.

There are some differences between Chinese and English in the data. More Chinese coaches turned around than their English-speaking counterparts, with the latter having twice as many zero-coach-turned cases than the Chinese, perhaps suggesting that the Chinese had a more lenient attitude. The Chinese coaches also appeared to adopt a stronger tone of speech because they used approximately 12% more intensifiers than in the English context. This finding indicates a negative correlation: a stronger tone carries a softer attitude. In other words, a mitigated tone does not necessarily bring a lenient attitude. Furthermore, the Chinese data present a relatively consistent trend over the five coach turning situations (0–4 coaches turned), which is not the case in the English data. This would indicate that the Chinese were more insensitive towards the level of competition when they used EL in the TV show discourse.

8.1.3 Research Question 3: How Do Sociocultural Factors Impact on Language Stretching?

The results pertaining to this research question are reasonably consistent across the Chinese and English data. Differences in the impact of gender, culture and age on the use of EL are primarily statistically insignificant. Both languages follow similar patterns in all three sociocultural impacts, although some minor discrepancies do exist, for example, the impact of age on English data, where the use of EL differed between teenagers and adults. This suggests that, in the English data, when coaches and contestants interacted they exhibited different linguistic behaviours in their use of EL.

An important issue is the shared versus the cultural-specific features of language stretching. This study seems to suggest that universality exists more than specificity in Chinese and English speech. This finding is based on the analyses of the social, cultural and linguistic factors that influence how the participants in the different cultural groups behaved.

This study provides empirical evidence that EL is an effective tool for achieving communicative goals, but can act as a double-edged sword by functioning collaboratively as well as competitively. For example, this study investigated the phenomenon of evasiveness in Chinese and English: how overstretching language (e.g. using 'weasel words') both shapes, and is shaped by, different cultural framings. The significance of this is to reveal the 'dark' side of language stretching, to present a full and realistic picture of how it operates in communication.

The contribution of this study is to advance the knowledge of language stretching, including how English and Chinese speakers encoded their EL in reality television discourse, how language stretching interacts with, for example, sociocultural factors, the different types of stretching and redressing devices, cross-language variations and the correlations between the speakers' language stretching patterns and their sociocultural orientations and norms.

The outcomes also contribute to the conceptual and empirical enrichment of the field of the pragmatics of language. It benefits the study of language and cross-cultural communication in general, and the insights and resources inform strategies when bridging different cultures, language pedagogy and professional training. The findings are valuable for giving language stretching the recognition that it deserves.

8.2   Implications and Future Research

The implication of this study is that while the elasticity of language is not contextually resolvable, it is usually not troublesome in communication, as interactants can negotiate a mutually 'workable' solution to keep interactions running smoothly. The speech acts of persuasion and comforting in language are non-discrete, nonlinear, fluid and simultaneously multifunctional. The findings here challenge all-or-none theories in linguistics and promote refreshing insights into EL stretching in cross-cultural communication.

This study is one of the few attempts to explore how Chinese and English speakers use EL and how communication games are played out in different cultures. The evidence-based findings help speakers from different cultures to understand each other better and to interact more effectively, thereby reducing miscommunication.

In the TV reality show discourse that was under investigation in this study, the speech acts of persuasion and comforting are of prime importance. Further investigation into these speech acts in other discourses would provide a comparison with this study. Language stretching has been studied in different discourses: institutional discourse (Zhang, 2015), academic discourse (Ruzaitė, 2007) and political speech (Parvaresh, 2018). On the basis of four different discourse types, Cheng (2007) claims that everyday conversations employ different forms of vague language than public discourse; on average, vague expressions are used more frequently in everyday conversations than in public speeches.

The data pertaining to the TV shows in this study is from the arena of public discourse, so it is important to determine how different it might be to types of non-public discourse. Another area for future research is the relationship between the use of EL and relevant social factors. For example, the relationship between the use of EL and a person's level of education may need further research. EL can be an indicator of a person's level of education as a correlation exists between the reduced use of EL by less educated speakers (Beeching, 2016). On the contrary, Cutting (2012) suggests that some people believe that the use of vague language would indicate a less educated person. These inconsistencies require further clarification, and therefore further research is needed to determine whether the use of EL is related to the speaker's educational level, particularly across different languages and cultures.

References

Asher, N., & Lascarides, A. (2001). Indirect speech acts. *Synthese, 128*(1–2), 183–228.

Beeching, K. (2016). *Pragmatic markers in British English: Meaning in social interaction*. Cambridge, UK: Cambridge University Press.

Cheng, W. (2007). The use of vague language across spoken genres in an intercultural Hong Kong corpus. In J. Cutting (Ed.), *Vague language explored* (pp. 161–181). Basingstoke: Palgrave Macmillan.

Cutting, J. (2012). Vague language in conference abstracts. *Journal of English for Academic Purposes, 11*(4), 283–293.

Hyland, K. (2005a). Stance and engagement: A model of interaction in academic discourse. *Discourse Studies, 7*(2), 173–192.

Hyland, K. (2005b). *Metadiscourse: Exploring interaction in writing*. London: Continuum.

Parvaresh, V. (2018). 'We are going to do a lot of things for college tuition': Vague language in the 2016 US presidential debates. *Corpus Pragmatics, 2*(2), 167–192.

Ruzaitė, J. (2007). *Vague language in educational settings: Quantifiers and approximators in British and American English*. Frankfurt am Main: Peter Lang.

Zhang, G. (2015). *Elastic language: How and why we stretch our words*. Cambridge: Cambridge University Press.

References

Adolphs, S., Atkins, S., & Harvey, K. (2007). Caught between professional requirements and interpersonal needs: Vague language in healthcare contexts. In J. Cutting (Ed.), *Vague language explored* (pp. 62–78). Basingstoke: Palgrave Macmillan.

Aijmer, K. (1984). 'Sort of' and 'kind of' in English conversation. *Studia Linguistica, 38,* 118–128.

Aijmer, K. (2002). *English discourse particles: Evidence from a corpus.* Amsterdam: John Benjamins.

Aijmer, K. (2013). *Understanding pragmatic markers.* Edinburgh, UK: Edinburgh University Press.

Allan, K. (1986). *Linguistic meaning* (Vols. 1 & 2). London: Routledge & Kegan Paul.

Alston, W. P. (1964). *Philosophy of language.* Englewood Cliffs, NJ: Prentice-Hall.

Andersen, G. (2010). A contrastive approach to vague nouns. In G. Kaltenboeck, W. Mihatsch, & S. Schneiders (Eds.), *New approaches to hedging* (pp. 35–49). London: Emerald.

Asher, N., & Lascarides, A. (2001). Indirect speech acts. *Synthese, 128*(1–2), 183–228.

Atkinson, J. M., & Heritage, J. (Eds.). (1984). *Structures of social action: Studies in conversation analysis.* Cambridge: Cambridge University Press.

Austin, J. L. (1956). A plea for excuses: The presidential address. *Proceedings of the Aristotelian Society, 57,* 1–30.

Austin, J. L. (1962/1975). *How to do things with words.* Cambridge, MA: Harvard University Press.

Bach, K., & Harnish, R. M. (1979). *Communication and speech acts.* Cambridge, MA: Harvard University Press.

Beeching, K. (2016). *Pragmatic markers in British English: Meaning in social interaction.* Cambridge, UK: Cambridge University Press.

Bell, A. (1991). *The language of news media: Language in society.* Oxford: Blackwell.

Bello, R., & Edwards, R. (2005). Interpretations of messages: The influence of various forms of equivocation, face concerns, and sex differences. *Journal of Language and Social Psychology, 24*(2), 160–181.

Berndt, R. S., & Caramazza, A. (1978). The development of vague modifiers in the language of pre-school children. *Journal of Child Language, 5*(2), 279–294.

Biber, D., Johansson, S., Leech, G., Conrad, S., & Finegan, E. (2010). *Longman grammar of spoken and written English* (8th ed.). London: Longman.

Bloom, P. (2017). *Against empathy: The case for rational compassion.* London: Penguin Random House.

Boakye, N. G. (2007). *Aspects of vague language use: Formal and informal contexts.* Unpublished M.A. thesis, University of South Africa.

Bradac, J. J., Mulac, A., & Thompson, S. A. (1995). Men's and women's use of intensifiers and hedges in problem-solving interaction: Molar and molecular analyses. *Research on Language and Social Interaction, 28*(2), 93–116.

Brown, P., & Levinson, S. C. (1987). *Politeness: Some universals in language usage.* Cambridge: Cambridge University Press.

Burleson, B. R. (1985). The production of comforting messages: Social-cognitive foundations. *Journal of Language and Social Psychology, 4*(3–4), 253–273.

Cambridge Online Dictionary. (2019). Available at https://dictionary.cambridge.org/dictionary/english/slingshot. Last accessed 15 Apr 2019.

Carter, R. (2003). The grammar of talk: Spoken English, grammar and the classroom. In *New perspectives on English in the classroom* (pp. 5–13). London: Qualifications and Curriculum Authority.

Carter, R., & McCarthy, M. (1997). *Exploring spoken English.* Cambridge: Cambridge University Press.

Carter, R., & McCarthy, M. (2006). *Cambridge grammar of English.* Cambridge: Cambridge University Press.

Channell, J. (1994). *Vague language.* Oxford: Oxford University Press.

Chen, W. Z., & Wu, S. X. (2002). *Fanchou yu Mohu Yuyi Yanjiu* (in Chinese) [A study on category and semantic fuzziness]. Fujian, China: Fujian People's Publishing House.

Cheng, W. (2007). The use of vague language across spoken genres in an intercultural Hong Kong corpus. In J. Cutting (Ed.), *Vague language explored* (pp. 161–181). Basingstoke: Palgrave Macmillan.

Cheng, W., & Tsui, A. B. M. (2009). 'Ahh ((laugh)) well there is no comparison between the two I think': How do Hong Kong Chinese and native speakers of English disagree with each other? *Journal of Pragmatics, 41*(11), 2365–2380.

Cheng, W., & Warren, M. (2001). The use of vague language in intercultural conversations in Hong Kong. *English World-Wide, 22*(1), 81–104.

Cheng, W., & Warren, M. (2003). Indirectness, inexplicitness and vagueness made clearer. *Pragmatics, 13*, 381–400.

Cheshire, J. (2007). Discourse variation, grammaticalisation and stuff like that. *Journal of Sociolinguistics, 11*(2), 155–193.

Clark, H. H. (1979). Responding to indirect speech acts. *Cognitive Psychology, 11*(4), 430–477.

Cohen, L. J. (1997). Ordinary language philosophy. In P. V. Lamarque (Ed.), *Concise encyclopedia of philosophy of language* (pp. 35–37). Oxford: Elsevier.

Cook, G. (2007). 'This we have done': The vagueness of poetry and public relations. In J. Cutting (Ed.), *Vague language explored* (pp. 21–39). Basingstoke: Palgrave Macmillan.

Cotterill, J. (2007). 'I think he was kind of shouting or something': Uses and abuses of vagueness in the British courtroom. In J. Cutting (Ed.), *Vague language explored* (pp. 97–114). Basingstoke: Palgrave Macmillan.

Creswell, J. W. (2008). *Educational research: Planning, conducting, and evaluating quantitative and qualitative research* (3rd ed.). Upper Saddle River, NJ: Prentice Hall.

Creswell, J. W. (2009). *Research design: Qualitative, quantitative, and mixed methods approaches* (3rd ed.). Los Angeles: Sage.

Creswell, J. W., & Plano Clark, V. L. (2007). *Designing and conducting mixed methods research*. Thousand Oaks: Sage.

Crystal, D., & Davy, D. (1975). *Advanced conversational English*. London: Longman Publishing Group.

Cutting, J. (2007a). Introduction to 'vague language explored'. In J. Cutting (Ed.), *Vague language explored* (pp. 3–20). Basingstoke: Palgrave Macmillan.

Cutting, J. (Ed.). (2007b). *Vague language explored*. Basingstoke: Palgrave Macmillan.

Cutting, J. (2007c). Doing more stuff—Where's it going? Exploring vague language further. In J. Cutting (Ed.), *Vague language explored* (pp. 223–243). Basingstoke: Palgrave Macmillan.

Cutting, J. (2012). Vague language in conference abstracts. *Journal of English for Academic Purposes, 11*(4), 283–293.

Cutting, J. (2015). *Dingsbums und so*: Beliefs about German vague language. *Journal of Pragmatics, 85,* 108–121.

Dafouz-Milne, E. (2008). The pragmatic role of textual and interpersonal metadiscourse markers in the construction and attainment of persuasion: A cross-linguistic study of newspaper discourse. *Journal of Pragmatics, 40*(1), 95–113.

Dörnyei, Z. (2007). *Research methods in applied linguistics.* Oxford: Oxford University Press.

Drave, N. (2002). Vaguely speaking: A corpus approach to vague language in intercultural conversations. In P. Peters, P. Collins, & A. Smith (Eds.), *Language and computers: New frontiers of corpus research.* Papers from the Twenty-First International Conference of English Language Research and Computerized Corpora (pp. 25–40). The Netherlands: Rodopi.

Drew, P., & Heritage, J. (1992). Analyzing talk at work: An introduction. In P. Drew & J. Heritage (Eds.), *Talk at work* (pp. 3–65). Cambridge: Cambridge University Press.

Eelen, G. (2001). *A critique of politeness theory.* London: Routledge.

Eisenberg, E. M. (1984). Ambiguity as strategy in organizational communication. *Communication Monographs, 51,* 227–242.

Evison, J., McCarthy, M., & O'Keeffe, A. (2007). 'Looking out for love and all the rest of it': Vague category markers as shared social space. In J. Cutting (Ed.), *Vague language explored* (pp. 138–157). Basingstoke: Palgrave Macmillan.

Fernández, J. (2013). A corpus-based study of vague language use by learners of Spanish in a study abroad context. *Social and Cultural Aspects of Language Learning in Study Abroad, 37,* 299.

Fernández, J. (2015). General extender use in spoken Peninsular Spanish: Metapragmatic awareness and pedagogical implications. *Journal of Spanish Language Teaching, 2*(1), 1–17.

Fetzer, A. (2010). Hedges in context: Form and function of *sort of* and *kind of.* In G. Kaltenbock, W. Mihatsch, & S. Schneider (Eds.), *New approaches to hedging* (pp. 49–71). Bingley: Emerald.

Fraser, B. (1996). Pragmatic markers. *Pragmatics, 6*(2), 167–190.

Gassner, D. (2012). Vague language that is rarely vague^p: A case study of "thing" in L1 and L2 discourse. *International Review of Pragmatics, 4*(1), 3–28.

Glinert, L. (2010). Apologizing to China: Elastic apologies and the meta-discourse of American diplomats. *Intercultural Pragmatics, 7*(1), 47–74.

Goffman, E. (1981). *Forms of talk.* Philadelphia: University of Pennsylvania Press.

Goffman, I. (1967). *Interaction ritual: Essays on face-to-face interaction.* Garden City, NY: Anchor Books.

Grice, P. (1975). Logic and conversation. In P. Cole & J. Morgan (Eds.), *Syntax and semantics. Volume 3: Speech acts* (pp. 41–58). New York: Academic Press.

Hall, E. T. (1976). *Beyond culture.* New York: Anchor Books.

Holmes, J. (1988). Doubt and uncertainty in ESL textbooks. *Applied Linguistics, 9*(1), 21–44.

Holmes, J. (1990). Hedges and boosters in women's and men's speech. *Language & Communication, 10*(3), 185–205.

Holmes, J. (1993). New Zealand women are good to talk to: An analysis of politeness strategies in interaction. *Journal of Pragmatics, 20*(2), 91–116.

Holmes, J. (1995). *Women, men and politeness.* London: Longman.

Hu, G., & Cao, F. (2011). Hedging and boosting in abstracts of applied linguistics articles: A comparative study of English- and Chinese-medium journals. *Journal of Pragmatics, 43,* 2795–2809.

Hyland, K. (1998a). *Hedging in scientific research articles.* Amsterdam: John Benjamins.

Hyland, K. (1998b). Persuasion and context: The pragmatics of academic metadiscourse. *Journal of Pragmatics, 30*(4), 437–455.

Hyland, K. (2000). Hedges, boosters and lexical invisibility: Noticing modifiers in academic texts. *Language Awareness, 9*(4), 179–197.

Hyland, K. (2005a). Stance and engagement: A model of interaction in academic discourse. *Discourse Studies, 7*(2), 173–192.

Hyland, K. (2005b). *Metadiscourse: Exploring interaction in writing.* London: Continuum.

Janney, R. (2002). Cotext as context: Vague answers in court. *Language & Communication, 22,* 457–475.

Jick, T. D. (1979). Mixing qualitative and quantitative methods: Triangulation in action. *Administrative Science Quarterly, 24,* 602–611.

Jucker, A. H., Smith, S. W., & Ludge, T. (2003). Interactive aspects of vagueness in conversation. *Journal of Pragmatics, 35,* 1737–1769.

Kaltenböck, G., Mihatsch, W., & Schneider, S. (Eds.). (2010). *New approaches to hedging.* Bingley, UK: Emerald.

Kendon, A. (2004). *Gesture: Visible action as utterance.* Cambridge: Cambridge University Press.

Kirkpatrick, A. (1991). Information sequencing in Mandarin in letters of request. *Anthropological Linguistics, 33*(2), 183–203.

Koester, A. (2007). "About twelve thousand or so": Vagueness in North American and UK offices. In J. Cutting (Ed.), *Vague language explored* (pp. 40–61). Basingstoke: Palgrave Macmillan.

Koester, A. (2010). *Workplace discourse.* London: A & C Black.

Labov, W. (1972). *Sociolinguistic patterns.* Philadelphia, PA: University of Pennsylvania Press.

Lakoff, G. (1973). Hedges: A study in meaning criteria and the logic of fuzzy concepts. *Journal of Philosophical Logic, 2*(4), 458–508.

Lakoff, R. (1982). Persuasive discourse and ordinary conversation, with examples from advertising. In D. Tannen (Ed.), *Analyzing discourse: Text and talk* (pp. 25–42). Washington, DC: Georgetown University Press.

Lauwereyns, S. (2002). Hedges in Japanese conversation: The influence of age, sex, and formality. *Language Variation and Change, 14,* 239–259.

Leech, G. (1983). *Principles of pragmatics.* London: Longman.

Levinson, S. C. (1983). *Pragmatics.* Cambridge: Cambridge University Press.

Li, S. (2017). A corpus-based study of vague language in legislative texts: Strategic use of vague terms. *English for Specific Purposes, 45,* 98–109.

Lin, C. L. (2010). Discourse analysis and the teaching of translation. In V. Pellatt, K. Griffiths, & S. Wu (Eds.), *Teaching and testing interpreting and translating* (pp. 27–49). Bern: Peter Lang AG.

Link, P. (2013). *Anatomy of Chinese: Rhythm, metaphor, politics.* Cumberland, RI: Harvard University Press.

Lorenzo-Dus, N., & Blitvich, Pilar. (2013). *Real talk: Reality television and discourse analysis in action.* London: Palgrave Macmillan.

Malyuga, E., & McCarthy, M. (2018). English and Russian vague category markers in business discourse: Linguistic identity aspects. *Journal of Pragmatics, 135,* 39–52.

Mauranen, A. (2004). 'They're a little bit different': Observations on hedges in academic talk. In K. Aijmer & A. Stenström (Eds.), *Discourse patterns in spoken and written corpora* (pp. 173–198). Amsterdam: John Benjamins.

Metsä-Ketelä, M. (2016). Pragmatic vagueness: Exploring general extenders in English as a lingua franca. *Intercultural Pragmatics, 13*(3), 325–351.

Mey, J. L. (2001). *Pragmatics: An introduction.* London: Blackwell.

Mihatsch, W. (2010). The diachrony of rounders and adaptors: Approximation and unidirectional change. In G. Kaltenböck, W. Mihatsch, & S. Schneider (Eds.), *New approaches to hedging* (pp. 93–122). Bingley, UK: Emerald.

Miskovic-Lukovic, M. (2009). *Is there a chance that I might kinda sort of take you out to dinner?* The role of the pragmatic particles *kind of* and *sort of* in utterance interpretation. *Journal of Pragmatics, 41*(3), 602–625.

Morgan, J. L. (1977). *Two types of convention in indirect speech acts* (Center for the Study of Reading Technical Report 52). University of Illinois.

Moxey, L., & Sanford, A. (1993). *Communicating quantities: A psychological perspective.* Hove, UK: Lawrence Erlbaum.

Mulder, J., Williams, C. P., & Moore, E. (2019). Sort of in Australian English: The elasticity of a pragmatic marker [Special issue]. *Journal of Asian Pacific Communication, 29*(1), 9–32.

Mumford, S. (2009). An analysis of spoken grammar: The case for production. *ELT Journal, 63*(2), 137–144.

Munné, F. (2013). The fuzzy complexity of language. In A. Massip-Bonet & A. Bastardas-Boada (Eds.), *Complexity perspectives on language, communication and society* (pp. 175–196). Heidelberg: Springer.

Murphy, B. (2010). *Corpus and sociolinguistics: Investigating age and gender in female talk.* Amsterdam: John Benjamins.

Myers, G. (1994). *Words in ads.* London: Edward Arnold.

Nicolls, M. (2015). *Empathy: Giving comfort.* Retrieved from https://www.wellbeing.com.au/mind-spirit/mind/empathy-giving-comfort.html.

O'Keeffe, A. (2003). 'Like the wise virgins and all that jazz': Using a corpus to examine vague language and shared knowledge. In U. Connor & T. Upton (Eds.), *Applied corpus linguistics: A multidimensional perspective* (pp. 1–20). Amsterdam: Rodopi.

Overstreet, M. (1999). *Whales, candlelight, and stuff like that: General extenders in English discourse.* Oxford: Oxford University Press.

Overstreet, M. (2005). And stuff und so: Investigating pragmatic expressions in English and German. *Journal of Pragmatics, 37*(11), 1845–1864.

Parvaresh, V. (2015). Vague language that is vague^p in both L1 and L2: A comment on Gassner (2012). *International Review of Pragmatics, 7*(1), 129–143.

Parvaresh, V. (2017). Panegyrists, vagueness and the pragmeme. In V. Parvaresh & A. Capone (Eds.), *The pragmeme of accommodation: The case of interaction around the event of death* (pp. 61–81). Cham, Switzerland: Springer.

Parvaresh, V. (2018). 'We are going to do a lot of things for college tuition': Vague language in the 2016 US presidential debates. *Corpus Pragmatics, 2*(2), 167–192.

Parvaresh, V. (2019). Moral impoliteness. *Journal of Language Aggression and Conflict, 7*(1), 77–102.

Parvaresh, V., & Ahmadian, M. J. (2016). The impact of task structure on the use of vague expressions by EFL learners. *The Language Learning Journal, 44*(4), 436–450.

Parvaresh, V., & Eslami Rasekh, A. (2009). Speech act disagreement among young women in Iran. *CLCWeb: Comparative Literature and Culture, 11*(4), 11.

Parvaresh, V., Tavangar, M., Rasekh, A. E., & Izadi, D. (2012). About his friend, how good she is, and this and that: General extenders in native Persian and non-native English discourse. *Journal of Pragmatics, 44*(3), 261–279.

Parvaresh, V., & Tayebi, T. (2014). Vaguely speaking in Persian. *Discourse Processes, 51*(7), 565–600.

Parvaresh, V., & Tayebi, T. (2018). Impoliteness, aggression and the moral order. *Journal of Pragmatics, 132*, 91–107.

Parvaresh, V., & Zhang, G. (Eds.). (2019). Vagueness and elasticity of 'sort of' in TV discussion discourse in the Asian Pacific [Special issue]. *Journal of Asian Pacific Communication, 29*(1), 1–132.

Peirce, C. S. (1902). Vagueness. In M. Baldwin (Ed.), *Dictionary of philosophy and psychology II* (p. 748). London: Macmillan.

Pierson, H. D. (1992). Communication issues during a period of radical transition: The case of Hong Kong. *Communication Quarterly, 40*(4), 381–390.

Pocheptsov, O. G. (1992). Mind your mind: Or some ways of distorting facts while telling the truth. *ETC: A Review of General Semantics, 49*(4), 398–404.

Pomerantz, A. (2005). Using participants' video stimulated comments to complement analyses of interactional practices. In H. T. Molder & J. Potter (Eds.), *Conversation and cognition* (pp. 93–113). Cambridge: Cambridge University Press.

Powell, M. (1985). Purposive vagueness: An evaluative dimension of vague quantifying expressions. *Journal of Linguistics, 21*, 31–50.

Prince, E. F., Frader, J., & Bosk, C. (1982). On hedging in physician-physician discourse. In R. J. Di Pietro (Ed.), *Linguistics and the professions* (pp. 83–97). Norwood, NJ: Ablex.

Psathas, G. (1995). *Conversation analysis: The study of talk in interaction.* Thousand Oaks, CA: Sage.

Reah, D. (1998). *The language of newspapers.* London: Routledge.

Rowland, T. (2007). 'Well maybe not exactly, but it's around fifty basically?': Vague language in mathematics classrooms. In J. Cutting (Ed.), *Vague language explored* (pp. 79–96). Basingstoke: Palgrave Macmillan.

Ruzaitė, J. (2007). *Vague language in educational settings: Quantifiers and approximators in British and American English.* Frankfurt am Main: Peter Lang.

Ryoo, H. K. (2005). Achieving friendly interactions: A study of service encounters between Korean shopkeepers and African-American customers. *Discourse and Society, 16*(1), 79–105.

Sabet, P. G. (2013). *Interaction through vague language: L1 and L2 perspectives.* Unpublished Doctoral dissertation, Curtin University.

Sabet, P., & Zhang, G. (2015). *Communicating through vague language: A comparative study of L1 and L2 speakers.* London: Palgrave Macmillan.

Schönefeld, D. (Ed.). (2011). *Converging evidence: Methodological and theoretical issues for linguistic research.* Amsterdam: John Benjamins.

Scollon, R., & Scollon, S. W. (1995). *Intercultural communication.* Oxford: Blackwell.

Searle, J. (1965). What is a speech act? In M. Black (Ed.), *Philosophy in America* (pp. 1–16). London: Allen & Unwin.

Searle, J. R. (1975a). *A taxonomy of illocutionary acts.* Minneapolis: University of Minnesota Press.

Searle, J. R. (1975b). Indirect speech acts. In P. Cole & J. L. Morgan (Eds.), *Syntax and semantics. Volume 3: Speech acts* (pp. 59–82). Cambridge, MA: Academic Press.

Sears, D. O., & Kosterman, R. (1994). Mass media and political persuasion. In S. Shavitt & T. Brock (Eds.), *Persuasion: Psychological insights and perspectives* (pp. 251–278). Boston: Allyn and Bacon.

Shirato, J., & Stapleton, P. (2007). Comparing English vocabulary in a spoken learner corpus with a native speaker corpus: Pedagogical implications arising from an empirical study in Japan. *Language Teaching Research, 11*(4), 393–412.

Shuy, R. W. (2014). *The language of murder cases.* Oxford: Oxford University Press.

Sinclair, J. M. (1991). *Corpus concordance collocation.* Oxford: Oxford University Press.

Sobrino, A. (2015). Inquiry about the origin and abundance of vague language: An issue for the future. In R. Seising, E. Trillas, & J. Kacprzyk (Eds.), *Towards the future of fuzzy logic* (pp. 117–136). Cham, Switzerland: Springer.

Speer, S. A. (2002). 'Natural' and 'contrived' data: A sustainable distinction? *Discourse Studies, 4,* 511–525.

Spencer-Oatey, H. (Ed.). (2004). *Culturally speaking: Managing rapport through talk across cultures.* London: A&C Black.

Sperber, D., & Wilson, D. (1986/1995). *Relevance: Communication and cognition*. Oxford: Blackwell.

Stubbs, M. (1986). A matter of prolonged field work: Notes towards a modal grammar of English. *Applied Linguistics, 7,* 1–25.

Stubbe, M., & Holmes, J. (1995). You know, eh and other 'exasperating expressions': An analysis of social and stylistic variation in the use of pragmatic devices in a sample of New Zealand English. *Language and Communication, 15*(1), 63–88.

Suzuki, T. (2008). *A corpus-based study of the speech act of "comforting": Naturalness and appropriateness for English language teaching.* Paper presented at the 13th PAAL Conference, University of Hawaii, Manoa, USA.

Tagliamonte, S. A., & Denis, D. (2010). The stuff of change: General extenders in Toronto, Canada. *Journal of English Linguistics, 38*(4), 335–368.

Tannen, D. (1984). *Conversational style: Analyzing talk among friends.* Norwood, NJ: Ablex.

Tausczik, Y. R., & Pennebaker, J. W. (2010). The psychological meaning of words: LIWC and computerized text analysis methods. *Journal of Language and Social Psychology, 29*(1), 24–54.

Tayebi, T. (2018). *Impoliteness in Persian: A cultural linguistics perspective.* Unpublished Ph.D. thesis, Monash University, Australia.

Terkourafi, M. (2001). *Politeness in Cypriot Greek: A frame-based approach.* Unpublished Ph.D. thesis, University of Cambridge, UK.

Terkourafi, M. (2011). The puzzle of indirect speech. *Journal of Pragmatics, 43*(11), 2861–2865.

Terraschke, A., & Holmes, J. (2007). 'Und Tralala': Vagueness and general extenders in German and New Zealand English. In J. Cutting (Ed.), *Vague language explored* (pp. 198–220). Basingstoke: Palgrave Macmillan.

Thaler, V. (2012). Mitigation as modification of illocutionary force. *Journal of Pragmatics, 44*(6–7), 907–919.

The Voice (U.S. TV series). (2019). Adapted from https://en.wikipedia.org/wiki/The_Voice_(U.S._TV_series). Last accessed 15 Apr 2019.

Thornborrow, J., & Morris, D. (2004). Gossip as strategy: The management of talk about others on reality TV show 'Big Brother'. *Journal of Sociolinguistics, 8*(2), 246–271.

Tolson, A. (2006). *Media talk: Spoken discourse on TV and radio.* Edinburgh: Edinburgh University Press.

Trappes-Lomax, H. (2007). Vague language as a means of self-protective avoidance: Tension management in conference talks. In J. Cutting (Ed.), *Vague language explored* (pp. 117–137). Basingstoke: Palgrave Macmillan.

Vallauri Lombardi, E. (2016). Implicits as evolved persuaders. In K. Allan, A. Capone, & I. Kecskes (Eds.), *Pragmemes and theories of language use* (pp. 724–748). Cham, Switzerland: Springer.

van Deemter, K. (2012). *Not exactly: In praise of vagueness.* Oxford, UK: Oxford University Press.

van Dijk, T. (1988). *News as discourse.* Hillsdale, NJ: Lawrence Erlbaum.

Verschueren, J. (1999). *Understanding pragmatics.* New York: Oxford University Press.

Walsh, S., O'Keeffe, A., & McCarthy, M. (2008). '…post-colonialism, multilingualism, structuralism, feminism, post-modernism and so on and so forth': A comparative analysis of vague category markers in academic discourse. In A. Adel & R. Reppen (Eds.), *Corpora and discourse: The challenges of different settings* (pp. 9–29). Amsterdam: John Benjamins.

Watts, R. J. (2003). *Politeness.* Cambridge: Cambridge University Press.

Wierzbicka, A. (2003). *Cross-cultural pragmatics: The semantics of interaction* (2nd ed.). Berlin: Mouton de Gruyte.

Williamson, T. (1996). *Vagueness.* London: Routledge.

Wu, T. P. (1999). *Mohu Yuyanxue* (in Chinese) [Fuzzy linguistics]. Shanghai: Shanghai Foreign Language Education Press.

Zhang, G. (2011). Elasticity of vague language. *Intercultural Pragmatics, 8,* 571–599.

Zhang, G. (2013). The impact of touchy topics on vague language use. *Journal of Asian Pacific Communication, 23,* 87–118.

Zhang, G. (2014). The elasticity of I think: Stretching its pragmatic functions. *Intercultural Pragmatics, 11*(2), 225–257.

Zhang, G. (2015). *Elastic language: How and why we stretch our words.* Cambridge: Cambridge University Press.

Zhang, G. (2016). How elastic *a little* can be and how much *a little* can do in Chinese. *Chinese Language and Discourse, 7*(1), 1–22.

Zhang, G. (2019). The pragmatic use of 'sort of' in TV forums: A Chinese perspective. *Journal of Asian Pacific Communication, 29*(1), 62–85.

Zhang, G., & Sabet, P. G. (2016). Elastic 'I think': Stretching over L1 and L2. *Applied Linguistics, 37*(3), 334–353.

Zhao, X., & Zhang, G. (2012). *Negotiating with vague language: A Chinese perspective.* Beijing: China Social Sciences Press.

Zhu, Y. X. (1999). *Business communication in China.* Commack: Nova Science Publishers.

Zhu, Y. X. (2005). *Written communication across cultures.* Amsterdam: John Benjamins.

Index